FEEDING WOMEN OF THE TALMUD, FEEDING OURSELVES

FEEDING WOMEN OF THE TALMUD, FEEDING OURSELVES

Uplifting the voices of Talmudic Heroines and honoring them with simple, vegan recipes

by **Kenden Alfond**

Talmud content editor: Tiki Krakowski

Cover and book design: Rachel Mendelson

JEWISH FOOD HERO

*Nourishing your mind,
body, and spirit*

ISBN Paperback: 978-1684427000
Hardcover: 978-1684427017

Turner Publishing Company
Nashville, Tennessee
www.turnerpublishing.com

Library of Congress Cataloging-in-Publication Data

Names: Alfond, Kenden, author.
Title: Feeding women of the Talmud, feeding ourselves : uplifting the voices of Talmudic heroines, and honoring them with simple, vegan recipes / by Kenden Alfond.
Description: [Nashville, Tennessee] : [Turner Publishing Company], [2022] | Series: Jewish food hero | Includes bibliographical references and index.
Identifiers: LCCN 2021046007 (print) | LCCN 2021046008 (ebook) | ISBN 9781684427000 (paperback) | ISBN 9781684427017 (hardcover) | ISBN 9781684427024(ebook)
Subjects: LCSH: Jewish cooking. | Vegan cooking. | Women in rabbinical literature. | Food--Religious aspects--Judaism.
Classification: LCC TX724 .A444 2022 (print) | LCC TX724 (ebook) | DDC 641.5/676--dc23/eng/20211028
LC record available at https://lccn.loc.gov/2021046007
LC ebook record available at https://lccn.loc.gov/2021046008

Created by Kenden Alfond
Cover & book design by Rachel Mendelson
Talmud content editor: Tiki Krakowski

Printed in the United States of America

To the women in my family:

my grandmothers, Bibby and Ellen;

my mother, Joan;

and my daughter, Yaël

TABLE OF CONTENTS

Introduction..1

Agrat bat Mahalat................................7
Tej – Ethiopian honey wine................11

Bat Abba Surah................................13
No-bake vegan millionaire squares................17

Bathsheba................................19
Rich chocolate and red wine mini cakes................23

Beloreya................................25
Fresh tangy cabbage and radish spread......29

Bruriah................................32
Seven herbs and species focaccia................35

The Carpenter's Wife................................37
Fesenjoon: tangy eggplant and walnut stew
................................40

A Certain Divorced Woman................42
Mother's joy infusion................45

Cleopatra................................48
Caramelized leek barley with white bean
   smash, spinach, asparagus, and beet
   potion................................51

Daughter of Nakdimon ben Gurion........55
Lemon, saffron, and barley risotto................58

The Daughter of Rabbi Hanina ben
   Dosa................................60
Quick pickled quince................63

The Daughter of the Emperor................65
Red wine mushroom soup, served in baked
   squash................................69

Donag................................72
Kvass: fermented rye bread and raisin
   beverage................................75

Em................................77
Grandmother's borscht................80

Hannah, the wife of rabbi Mani................83
Sephardic-style chilled cucumber soup......87

Hanina's Daughter-in-Law................89
Miscarriage recovery tea................92

Haruta................................94
Beet, pomegranate, and parsley salad........97

The Hated Daughter-in-Law................100
Curried nettle vegan sausage rolls................102

Homa..104
Fiery fudgy brownies...........................108

Hova..110
Bourbon cinnamon pecan pie............114

Ifra Hurmiz...................................116
Dandelion-pumpkin seed pesto.........119

Ikku..121
Ellen's four-bean salad with dry mustard
    vinaigrette....................................124

Imma Shalom.................................126
Vegan chocolate babka........................131

Immarta bat Talei.........................133
Calm your nervous system tonic.........137

Jonah's Wife.................................139
Vegan yakitori.....................................142

Kimchit..144
Spiced acorn squash breakfast bake....149

Likhlukhit......................................151
Zoharit skin, hair, and gut support......155

Lilith...157
Millet coriander croquettes with pumpkin
    truffle cream sauce........................161

The maiden who prays constantly...164
Vegan nutty chocolate chip cookies....167

Mar Shmuel's daughters...............170
Apple sage muffins..............................174

Mar Ukva's wife...........................176
White bean kale stew with matzo balls.....179

Marta bat Beitus...........................181
Turkish Sand Cookies.........................185

Matron healer from Tiberias.........187
Medicinal elderberry syrup.................191

Matun..193
Roasted Garlic Soup...........................196

Michal bat Kushi...........................198
Gluten-free amaretto cake..................201

Miriam bat Bilgah.........................204
Wild red rice roasted vegetable platter
    with pomegranate molasses and
    fresh herbs....................................207

Miriam of Tarmod.........................209
Charoset rugelach...............................212

The mother from Tzippori.............214
Magnesium-boosting smoothie...........217

The mother of Mar Bar Ravina.....219
Slow-cooked caramelized oranges......221

Nefata...223
Red wine braised mushroom and barley
    stuffed cabbage holishkes..............225

The potential bride and the hairdresser....228
Creamy celeriac purée with frizzled leeks....231

The prostitute from a city overseas....233
Sweet beet loaf cake....236

Queen Helena of Adiabene....238
Grape and lemon squares....243

Rabbi Akiva's daughter....245
Saffron couscous with beluga lentils and
pomegranate....248

Rabbi Elazar ben Azaryah's wife....250
Corn latkes with mango salsa....253

Rabbi Hama bar Bisa's wife....257
Vegan lullabye bread....260

Rabbi Yehuda Hanasi's maidservant....262
Purslane, pomegranate, and tofu
bourekas....267

Rabbi Yohanan's sister / Reish Lakish's
wife....269
Fermented lemon spread....273

Rabbi Ze'eira's wife....276
Mustard, miso, and maple dressing....280

Rachel, the wife of Rabbi Akiva....282
Smoky eggplant salad with herbs,
tahini, and pomegranate....285

Rav Adda bar Mattana's wife....288
Aguají (green plantains soup)....291

Rav Hisda's daughter....293
Roasted sweet potatoes with tamarind
and crispy shallots....299

Rav Rehumi's wife....303
Salty peanut spaghetti squash....306

Rav's wife....308
Jachnun – Yemenite sweet slow-cooked
buttery pastry rolls....113

Rav Yosef's wife....313
Sweet potato and golden beet cholent....317

Ravina's mother....319
Creamy coconut, red lentil, and
apple soup....322

Serach bat Asher....324
Nut and beet stuffed dates and prunes....328

Shlomtzion / Salome Alexandra....330
Black-eyed pea soup....335

The sotah woman....337
Black and white cookies....341

The two Miriams....344
Mini fire-roasted stuffed peppers....349

Two spirits speaking with each other....351
Vegan carrot cake....355

Tzafenat bat Peniel....358
Medicinal magnesium jello....362

TABLE OF CONTENTS

The wife of Abba Hilkiya 364
Almond-carob bread pudding 368

The wife of Rabbi Hanina ben Dosa 370
Abundant water challah rolls 373

The Woman from Drokart 375
Kahk biscuits 377

Woman who asks about taking challah 380
Vegan challah clouds 384

The woman with mistaken articulation 387
Creamy vegan noodle kugel 389

Yalta 391
Babylonian sour 395

Yehudit 398
Nourishing womb tonic 402

Yirmatia and her mother 404
Golden turmeric lemon cake 407

Acknowledgments 410

Contributor Index 411

Talmud Index 414

INTRODUCTION

This project allows contemporary Jewish women to retell and glean meaning from the stories of 69 women in the Talmud and honor them with vegan or plant-based recipes.

Adding a woman's point of view to these female Talmudic stories, which were recorded and edited by men, is a bright and encouraging testament to our generation of women engaging in Jewish learning.

The cookbook formula offers Jewish text and recipes together to produce true "food for thought."

These community cookbook/studybook projects are collective efforts, involving diverse women from all around the world. *Feeding Women in the Talmud, Feeding Ourselves* is the co-creation of 129 Jewish women: 69 rabbis, rabbinical students, Jewish teachers, and emerging thought leaders contributed to the Talmudic narratives and 60 female professional chefs and passionate homecooks contributed to the recipes.

The recipes in this book are all vegan and/or plant-based, except in the cases when honey is used. Some will become weekly favorites, while others are meant for special events and holidays. This book seeks to add more Jewish female stories and delicious vegan and plant-based foods to our tables, so we can connect to Judaism and healthy food at the same time.

ABOUT THE TALMUD[1]

Talmud means "study" in Hebrew. It is a fundamental Jewish text, a record of Jewish oral law and the commentaries expounding on these laws.

Rabbinic Jewish texts discuss two Torahs (teachings) – the Written Torah made up of the Five Books of Moses, Prophets, and Writings, and the Oral Torah, which consisted of a related dynamic and ever-evolving tradition. The Talmud reflects one of the earliest attempts to codify and preserve the Oral Torah so that it would not be lost in times of persecution. The Talmud consists of two parts:

---

1. Thanks to Rabbinat Debbie Zimmerman and Tiki Krakowski for refining this section "About the Talmud."

- **The Mishnah** was compiled approximately in the year 200 CE in the Land of Israel. It is a collection of oral laws and practices recorded in Hebrew to preserve the wisdom and tradition of Rabbinic Judaism in that time.
- **The Gemara** is a written record of the oral discussions, rabbinical analysis, and commentary on the Mishnah, as well as the teachings of the rabbis in the centuries following the destruction of the Second Temple.

There are two Talmuds developed in two different geographic locations. The Jerusalem, or Palestinian, Talmud (aka Talmud Yerushalmi) was produced by Jewish scholars in Northern Israel and completed sometime around 350–400 CE. The Babylonian Talmud (aka Talmud Balvi) was produced by Jewish scholars living in Babylonia and was compiled in Late Antiquity (between the 3rd–6th centuries CE). The text continued to evolve for another 200 years.

HOW THIS COOKBOOK IS ORGANIZED:

This cookbook is organized around female stories in the Talmud, presented alphabetically.

Each chapter is devoted to one female character in the Talmud and has the following sections:

- Story: a concise "true to the text" recounting of the female character's story in the Talmud.
- Context: This section seeks to enhance the stories by exploring their context: providing historical, social, literary, and/or liturgical context for the story; describing what falls before and/or after the particular story in the Talmud and exploring how the context and position of the story reveals more about its meaning.
- Aggadah: a modern commentary or fictional story, uplifting the subject's voice without attempting to neutralize her imperfections, flaws, or struggles.
- Prompts: meaningful questions arising from the story, meant to inspire further reflection for readers today.
- Food offering: one vegan or plant-based recipe, each inspired by or honoring the female Talmudic character.

HOW TO USE THIS COOKBOOK

As a traditional cookbook

Dip in and out at your leisure; be inspired by new recipes coupled with intellectual and spiritual stimulation to deepen the experience.

As a learning experience

Go at your own pace, work through the book learning about the female biblical characters, and enjoy plant-based recipes that might have nourished them.

As a meaningful collective experience

Create a group learning and eating experience by using this book like a book club text. Invite your friends to read a specific female narrative and then cook the recipes together. Think about other recipes that might nourish each biblical character. Use the prompts for reflection as discussion topics to get beyond the small talk that can sometimes dominate our social gatherings.

CHARITY

All of the contributors, including me, volunteered their time and intellectual energy to create this book. As such, all of Jewish Food Hero's proceeds from the sale of this book will be donated to a Jewish nonprofit every year.

A FINAL NOTE

Each woman in these stories is a world of her own. Reading about these women might bring up a wide range of emotions and feelings: from happy and delighted, curious and surprised, sad and despairing, to angry and disgusted. Some of the situations faced by the women in the Talmud might feel jarring and removed from our modern experience and sensibilities, while others may feel frustratingly familiar when they pivot on chronic and enduring themes.

The Talmud was written during the first century CE, when specific laws, values, and norms about gender and sexuality reflected a reality in which women and men were viewed as separate classes of people.[2] On the one hand, the rabbis, like all men and women of their time, were living in a patriarchal society: women were subordinate, and had respective social status and legal rights. Some of these sorrowful stories illustrate the impact of this legal and social reality on women and womanhood at this time. On the other hand, some of these stories show women with individual agency and social influence as they engage in aspects of their public and private lives, including in Torah learning and the Halachic process.

It is important to avoid the temptation to read these female stories as simplistic historical proof of either end of a spectrum of attitudes held by the rabbis about women.[3]

The essence of this project is to connect with and search for meaning in these female stories in the Talmud, as a means to uplift the voices and perspectives of women, from both the Talmud and our community.

May these stories from the Talmud and vegan and plant-based recipes nourish your body, mind, and spirit. I'm so glad you're here.

To your health and inspiration,

Kenden

2. Baskin, Judith, *Women in Rabbinic Literature*, My Jewish Learning, retrieved from: https://www.myjewishlearning.com/article/women-in-rabbinic-literature.
3. Hauptman, Judith, "Rereading the Rabbis: A Woman's Voice."

STORY

Agrat is a female demon in the Talmud.

She is introduced when Rabbi Yossi, the son of Rabbi Yehuda, tells Rabbi Yehuda Ha'Nasi not to go out alone at night. The source for this warning is a *baraita*[1] – a rabbinic teaching from between 0–200 CE – which says, "do not go out alone on Tuesday or Friday nights, because 'Agrat, daughter of Mahalat' and her 180,000 angels of destruction stalk the earth that night!"

The *baraita* continues, saying that Agrat, the daughter of Mahalat, used to stalk the earth with her angels of destruction every day of the week. But one time, she came across Rabbi Hanina ben Dosa, and said, "Rabbi Hanina! I came here to put you in danger. But the Heavens spoke and said 'Beware of Hanina and his Torah!', so I cannot." Hanina then said, "If the Heavens think me important, then I command you: Never travel through an inhabited place again!" Agrat bat Mahalat pleaded and said, "Please give me just a little space!" And so Rabbi Hanina left her a little space, and allowed her to stalk the earth, but only on Tuesday and Friday nights.

Agrat bat Mahalat later came upon Rabbi Abaye and said the same thing: "Abaye! If the Heavens hadn't spoken to say, 'Beware of Abaye and his Torah!', I would have put you in danger." And so Abaye retorted in the exact same way as his colleague: "If I am important in the Heavens, then I decree that you shall not pass through any inhabited place!" This time, Agrat did not ask for leniency. However, the Gemara asks, "If Abaye commanded her not to come through inhabited places, then why does she still do so?!" The Sages explain that Agrat and her demons are only found on paths *near* inhabited places, because their horses flee along those paths, and they simply come to lead them back home.

After this, Agrat bat Mahalat is never heard from as a character in the Talmud again. She's only mentioned once more – in a spell to ward off witchcraft, elsewhere in Tractate Pesachim.[2]

---

1. See below, Talmud b. Pesachim 112b.
2. Talmud.b.Pesachim.111a.

PASSAGES

Talmud.b.Pesachim.112b

CONTEXT

This story is an example of demonology – or the attempt to explain the world through the existence of demons. In the Jewish tradition, like others, there are demons everywhere and in every aspect of life: bathrooms, kitchens, travel, different times of day, public health, childbirth, etc. This is one story among many that tries to explain why bad things happen to people when they are out at night, and to try and provide a way for people to keep themselves secure in this unknown: by claiming that if only you just avoid walking on certain days (Tuesdays and Fridays), you will be safe.

The conflation of women with demons is ancient, and arises from the same place where demons come from – the unknown. The unknown has power that can produce fear and a desire for control – and in a male world this is true both for demons and women. An earlier *sugya* in the same tractate includes Agrat's name in a list of demons to ward off witchcraft. In the context of these *sugyas*, the character "Queen of Demons" is introduced to play the part of the unknowable and fearsome "other," and explain the unexplainable misfortunes that befall a person in the dark.

AGGADAH

As soon as she reached the gates of Heaven, Agrat bat Mahalat began to plot revenge. Unprovokedly, the last moments of her serene and studious life were spent under attack from a man, who slew her on the short road between her lover Asya's home and her own home.[3]

Shocked at the unjust theft of her remaining years, she initially hoped to haunt and torture the man who abused her so cruelly. But, upon meeting many women who had suffered similar fates at the hands of men, they soon formulated a much sweeter revenge.

Agrat bat Mahalat gathered this group of women – bubbling over 180,000 strong – and flew them down to Earth as the sun began to set. They came down to where Agrat had died,

---

3. Asya is another female demon listed in an incantation to ward off witchcraft, in Talmud.b.Pesachim.111a.

and, fanning out across the planet, intervened to save every woman they found in duress. More specifically, though, they were making unsafe for *men* what was always unsafe for *them*. Daggers in the hands of attackers would switch directions mid-swipe, to slash those who wielded them. Feet would shrink in stirrups and snakes would strike at heels.[4] From the innocuous to the deadly, word soon spread among the men of the world that it was unsafe to travel at night.

Agrat bat Mahalat and her 180,000 demons, however, did not inflict their vengeance on anyone who was not a man. And so, women suddenly found themselves protected and free on roads devoid of danger from men.

And oh, was this the *sweetest* revenge.

Women, leaving their husbands, brothers, and fathers at home, would find each other in the dead of night. Without fear of violation or attack, women were free: some would sing, some would dance, some would experience sapphic pleasure and others platonic love, some would gather, and some would sip a *mashkeh*.[5] Covens could hone their witchcraft; healers could trade their skills; and women could *live* with abandon – their shrieks of pleasure and joy mistaken for the cackles of demons.

Over time, these evenings of liberation were boxed down by a countervailing patriarchy, from *every night*, to Tuesday and Friday eves. But Agrat and her women would cede no more. In vengeance for her death, the Queen of Demons reclaimed these nights on the road back for those who needed them most.

---

4. Referencing "shrinking feet" and snakes as witchcraft a traveler should beware of, mentioned on the same page of the Talmud as above, ibid.

5. A Mishnaic category for drinks other than water, commonly connoting alcoholic beverages.

PROMPTS

- Who owns the street in the nighttime? Who gets to feel safe in the dark, outside?
- What is the magic that's possible in an "inhabited" place, vs. an uninhabited one? What types of encounters do we expect in those locales?
- What is the strength in numbers? How can we be a "horde of angels" to those we love in their times of danger?

Binya Kóatz *(she/they) is a frum transfemme Ashkenazi/Sefardi Jewess from Queens, currently living on Ohlone Land in the Bay Area.*

TEJ — ETHIOPIAN HONEY WINE

Perhaps Agrat bat Mahalat and her 180,000 demons and all the women who joined them enjoyed Tej – Ethiopian Honey Wine – together.

Tej is a fermented honey wine and is one of the oldest alcoholic beverages produced. It is often home processed and consists of three main ingredients: honey, water, and shiny-leaf buckthorn, commonly referred to as gesho.

I created this recipe by combining the best parts of my mother's and sister's respective Tej recipes. The taste is sweet, similar to a dessert white wine with an even more subtle alcohol taste. The alcohol content can take people by surprise, so enjoy in moderation.

Prep Time: 1 hour
Fermentation Time: 4 days + 7 days + 22 days
Yield: 40×12 oz (250ml) bottles
(14+ liters in total)

Tools:

- Cheesecloth
- Kitchen scale
- Small soup pot
- Wide-mouthed glass vessel(s) with lid(s) (with total capacity of 15 liters)
- Wooden spoon

Ingredients:

- 8.8 lbs (4kg) honeycomb
- 15 liters drinking water
- 3.3 lbs (1.5kg) shiny-leaf buckthorn, coarsely ground
- 150g fresh ginger, finely grated or chopped
- 200g fresh turmeric root, finely grated or chopped

Instructions:

1. Ensure the wide-mouthed glass vessel is extremely clean: wash with boiling water or on the hottest cycle of a dishwasher.

2. Pour the honeycomb into the clean glass vessel and add the water.

3. Stir until the liquid is a uniform golden amber color.

4. Cover loosely and leave at room temperature for 4 days.

5. After 4 days, place the shiny buckthorn in a small soup pot with a small amount of water. Warm the mixture over a very low heat for 20 minutes – simmer; absolutely *do not boil.* Turn off the heat and allow the shiny buckthorn to steep and chill for 30 minutes, or until room temperature.

6. Meanwhile, grate the ginger and turmeric with a tiny bit of water in a food processor, or finely chop.

7. Add the grated ginger and turmeric to the cooled gesho mixture.

8. Fold the ginger, turmeric, and cold gesho mixture into the honey and water mixture.

9. Loosely cover with a lid, and allow to ferment at room temperature for a week.

10. After seven days, strain the mixture through a cheesecloth to remove the pieces of gesho, ginger, and turmeric.

11. Wash the glass vessel and place the strained Tej back into it, making sure to leave a few inches at the top of the jar empty. Cover again with a lid – this time airtight.

12. Leave to ferment for 22 days at room temperature. *Do not open!*

13. Strain the Tej a second time.

14. Transfer into smaller bottles and refrigerate until serving.

15. Please note that a few bottles might not hold on to their fermentation fizziness correctly, and these can be discarded.

Fanta Prada *is an Ethiopian-Israeli restaurateur, model, lawyer, and entrepreneur. She co-owns Balinjero, where she introduces visitors to the joy of Ethiopian culture through food.*

STORY

Bat (the daughter of) Abba Surah was born into an extremely affluent family. Yet this fact did not guarantee she would remain wealthy her whole life. In Talmudic times, when a woman left her father's home, she entered into her husband's, accepting his financial circumstances as her own. Though a *ketubah*, a legal marriage contract, dictates that a man must provide a basic standard of living for his wife, it does not guarantee the same level of financial comfort she may have enjoyed prior to her marriage. She becomes financially tied to her husband, without individual ownership of possessions. Any money she earns or inherits belongs to her husband.

However, upon Bat Abba Surah's marriage to the Sage Rav Papa, her father and her groom made a special arrangement. This marriage contract stipulated that Bat Abba Surah retained her own possessions and independently managed her expenses. Bat Abba Surah became the precedent in rabbinic thought for a financially independent woman.

The Talmud mentions Bat Abba Surah one other time, when we learn that she compares the pain of vaginal intercourse to "the feeling of hard bread on the gums."

PASSAGES

Talmud.b.Sanhedrin.14b, Talmud.b.Ketubot.39b, and *Talmud.b.Ketubot.52b–53a + Rashi*

CONTEXT

According to a discussion in Tractate Sanhedrin, Bat Abba Surah's financial independence enabled her to serve on the same court as her husband for the purposes of evaluating tithed produce. Since their finances were not intertwined, they were counted as distinct individuals – a unique situation for a woman at that time.

In the midst of a debate over the fine charged to a rapist for the pain caused to his female victim in Tractate Ketubot, three male rabbis attempted to imagine the experience of rape. The discourse then jumps to discuss the pain "every woman" feels the first time they have

vaginal intercourse. Each Rabbi recounts a metaphor they originally heard from a woman in their family. Rav Pappa reports his wife's metaphor last: "it is like the feeling of hard bread on the gums."

AGGADAH

Bat Abba Surah's first name is lost to history. In the Talmud, she is only named in reference to her father. Her reputation and anomalous status were connected to her inherited wealth. This inherited wealth enabled her father to secure her unique marriage contract, keeping her distinct from her husband. Her family's wealth gave her a different role than most women within the patriarchal system at the time, but she nevertheless remained within that system.

Hearing Rav Pappa's report about his wife's visceral metaphor for the loss of virginity may be jarring for the modern reader. One feels as if they are eavesdropping on "guy talk," a men's discussion of women in which women are imagined and objectified. Women's voices are strikingly absent in a conversation that has everything to do with women's experience.

It is also striking that their conversation associatively jumps so easily between forceful rape and consensual sex. Perhaps modern readers can relate to this still persistent idea that rape and sexual harassment remain under the umbrella of sex, rather than what they actually are: pure violence.

Unable to relate to the female physical experience, the all-male academy draws on personal testimony from their female family members. One wonders how this information was acquired. Did they ask their wives and mothers to share personal sexual experiences for the expressed purpose of Torah study? Or were these intimate details shared privately, whispered under the covers in confidence, only to be announced in the study hall and recorded for generations? On the one hand, this snippet of text can feel voyeuristic. On the other, it can come as a great relief to women, who long to see their stories told in the Talmud.

PROMPTS

- What are the merits and challenges associated with being a financially independent woman?

- Who are the financially independent women you know? How do you feel about their (or your!) circumstance and the decisions which led to it? How do you think finances should be shared between spouses, if at all?

- How should people treat information about their partner's sexual experiences? In what circumstances, if any, is it appropriate to share intimate details with others?

Ora Weinbach *studies at Yale Divinity School and is a Wexner Graduate Fellow. She serves as the Community Educator at The Jewish Center in NYC.*

NO-BAKE VEGAN MILLIONAIRE SQUARES

This recipe is a variation on "Millionaire's Shortbread." I think the recipe is perfect for Bat Abba Surah because of its name.

This recipe is yummy and fun to make. It has a vegan almond flour "shortbread" layer, a date and nut butter "caramel" layer, and a chocolate top.

Prep Time: 20 minutes
Cook Time: 0
Yield: 12–15 square pieces, depending on the size

Tools:

- Bread loaf pan (8½″×4½″×2½″)
- Food processor
- Kitchen scale
- Large mixing bowl
- Measuring cups and spoons
- Metal soup spoon
- Sharp knife
- Spatula

Ingredients:

For the vegan shortbread:

- 2 cups (200g) almond flour (or use 75% almond flour and 25% rolled oats)
- ¼ cup (54g) coconut oil
- 1 tbsp maple syrup
- ½ tsp salt

For the caramel layer:

- ½ cup (120g) natural almond butter or peanut butter
- 1 cup (180g) pitted dates
- 2 dried figs
- 1 tsp vanilla extract
- 3 tsp fresh lemon juice, divided

For the chocolate layer:

- 10.6 oz or more (100g–150g) 54%–72% vegan chocolate
- 1 tsp coconut oil

Instructions:

Line the bread pan with parchment paper so it is easy to lift the No-Bake Vegan Millionaire Squares out of the bread pan and cut them on a cutting board.

Make the shortbread:

1. Place all shortbread ingredients in a food processor and blitz until a paste forms (3 to 5 minutes).
2. Using your hands, press the paste into the bottom of a lined baking pan and smooth evenly with a metal spoon.
3. Place in the refrigerator to chill for a minimum of one hour.

For the caramel layer:

1. Pulse all caramel ingredients in a food processor until a paste forms (5 minutes).
2. Using your hands, press the paste on top of the shortbread layer. Add a little bit of fresh lemon juice and smooth evenly with the back of a metal spoon.
3. Place in the refrigerator for a minimum of one hour.

Make the chocolate layer:

1. Melt chocolate and coconut oil over low heat or in a microwave until smooth.
2. Pour over the caramel layer, tilting the bread pan back and forth so it spreads evenly.
3. Place in the refrigerator overnight or for 24 hours. This allows the millionaire squares to set and cut more easily.
4. Lift the millionaires out of the bread pan, peel away the parchment paper, and using a sharp knife, cut the millionaires into squares.

Yaël Alfond-Vincent *is a Franco-American living in Paris. She will be celebrating her Bat Mitzvah in 2023.*

BATHSHEBA / בתשבע

STORY

Bathsheba was a wife of King David and the mother of King Solomon. She is mentioned in the Hebrew Bible and in rabbinic literature.

The Talmud discusses her primarily in the context of whether or not King David is to blame for their illicit relationship. David desired Bathsheba – at that time wife of Uriah the Hittite – and made her pregnant with Solomon. King David then orchestrated the death of Bathsheba's husband and married her himself.

However, one Talmudic source[1] discusses Bathsheba not as a conquest or wife, but as a mother. The rabbis explore the relationship between King Solomon and his mother by expanding a tale about King Lemuel and his mother in the Book of Proverbs (31:1–4).[2]

In the Book of Proverbs, the mother of King Lemuel castigates him for his overuse of wine. Invoking the fact that she birthed him, she admonishes him, saying that kings who get inebriated forget the law and infringe on the rights of the poor.[3]

The rabbis say that the above story from the Proverbs teaches us that Bathsheba sees King Solomon engaged in excessive drinking and takes action to change his behavior.[4] She ties him to a pole and delivers a speech designed to turn him away from his foolish course to follow a path of righteousness.

Bathsheba uses three arguments to convince Solomon to change his ways. First, she argues that society perceives King David as a God-fearing father, and thus any character flaws in

---

1. Talmud.b.Sanhedrin.70b.

2. The rabbis often identify lesser known biblical characters with more central characters. In this case, the rabbis assume that Lemuel is another name for Solomon.

3. Proverbs 31:1–4.

4. In other rabbinic sources (e.g., Midrash.Leviticus.Rabbah.12.5), Solomon has stayed up late drinking with his new wife, an Egyptian princess, on the eve of the Temple dedication. Seeing that the priests need the key to the Temple, which is safely lodged under the king's pillow, his mother wakes him up and strikes him with her shoe before reciting a speech about the negative effects of women and wine. This context is lacking in the Talmud.

their son will be attributed to her, the mother. Second, she describes a harem culture in which King David's concubines did not have sexual relations with him after they conceived. She had to go to extra lengths to "push herself in" to have relations with the king while pregnant, in the belief that doing so would strengthen the fetus. Finally, she tells Solomon that while the other mothers in the king's court vowed that their sons would be ready for kingship, she wanted more for her son. She wanted her son to lead through Torah and prophecy. She tells Solomon that he is letting her down by failing to be the model leader that she had prepared him to be.

The rabbis imagine that King Solomon's mother does convince him. He responds that he has been foolish, less of a man even than Noah and Adam, who were not exactly paragons of virtue.[5]

PASSAGES[6]

Talmud b. Sanhedrin 70b

CONTEXT

At the beginning of a chapter about the topic of rebellious children, there is a lengthy discussion about the effects of wine. The story about King Solomon and his mother falls at the end of this discussion and combines the themes of rebellion and alcohol consumption.

While King Solomon's behavior does not fit into rabbinic legal definitions of childhood rebellion, by placing the tale here the rabbis imply that debauchery reflects poorly on one's parents and is therefore a form of rebellion. Bathsheba also stresses that poor behavior on

---

5.   Talmud b. Sanhedrin 70b: אמר ר' יצחק מניין שחזר שלמה והודה לאמו דכתיב (משלי ל, ב) כי בער אנכי מאיש ולא בינת אדם לי כי
בער אנכי מאיש מנח דכתיב (בראשית ט, כ) ויחל נח איש האדמה ולא בינת אדם לי זה אדם הראשון:
Rabbi Yitzhak says: From where can it be learned **that Solomon repented and admitted to his mother** that she was justified in her rebukes? **As it is written: "For I am more foolish than a man, and have not the understanding of a man"** (Proverbs 30:2). This should be understood as follows: **"For I am more foolish than a man [ish]";** that is, I am more foolish than Noah, who sinned with wine and is called "a man," **as it is written: "And Noah began to be a farmer** [ish ha'adama]" (Genesis 9:20). **"And have not the understanding of a man** [adam]"; **this** is a reference to **Adam the first** man, who also sinned with wine, in accordance with the opinion of Rabbi Meir, who says that the Tree of Knowledge was a grapevine.

6.   Bathsheba appears in the Bible in II Samuel 11–12, and in 1 Kings 1–2. The Talmud speaks of her relationship with David on Talmud b.Sanhedrin.107a. *Talmud.b.Sanhedrin.70b.*

the part of a child may be more harmful to a mother than to a father because of societal perceptions.

AGGADAH

One of the most emotionally challenging parts of parenting is that we cannot control our children. As we raise young children, this fact is inconvenient. We want them to eat certain foods, go to sleep at a certain time, and learn some basic life skills – but we have no actual control over whether or not they do. When our children emerge into adulthood, this challenge becomes existential. What if our child adopts values that feel alien or abhorrent to us? What if they make choices that are harmful to their health and wellbeing? We come face-to-face with how much our identity is tied up with our children's conduct. It feels like if they are good, we have done good. If they do ill in society, then we have failed.

Before Solomon's birth, Bathsheba is disempowered. Desired by a king who uses treachery to deprive her of her husband, she has no control of her fate. Motherhood has crystalized a thread of power for her. From the moment of pregnancy, she behaves with determined perseverance. Confronted by a son who has turned to alcohol, she now fears that her maternal labor was for naught. As modern readers, we chafe at and disagree with Bathsheba's use of physical force but we empathize with the sense of desperation that led her there.

Bathsheba is ultimately successful in convincing her wayward son to repent. She uses her personal, maternal power to turn the most powerful man in the land from a path of apathetic drunkenness to a path of righteousness. She achieves her ultimate goal of applying all her resources to bring her son to a better version of himself: for her own benefit, for his benefit, and for the benefit of Israel. Her story reminds us that the parent-child relationship continues into adulthood and that even the most powerful of kings still has a mother.

PROMPTS

- The rabbis stress that a child's debauchery reflects poorly on their parents. Solomon's mother fears she, rather than his father, will be blamed for his bad behavior. Does society hold parents responsible for their children's behavior, even when they are adults? Are mothers and fathers praised or blamed disproportionately for their parenting?

- Reflect on a time that you used "tough love" with a person you were in a position of responsibility or authority for. Reflect on a time when you were on the receiving end of tough love tactics. What are your main conclusions from these experiences?
- Solomon's mother wishes her son would give up wine. She implies that a lifestyle of alcoholism makes him less respectable as a king and clouds his judgment. What are the pros and cons of consumption for you personally – whether drugs or alcohol, or other substances including caffeine and sugar?
- Solomon's mother expresses the wish that her son be "vigorous and fair-skinned." Today we read this as prejudice on the basis of skin color. How can adults relate to children in ways that dismantle entrenched colorism and racism?

Rabbi Miriam-Simma Walfish is faculty at the Hadar Institute. She revels in the process of learning Torah with and from her students.

RICH CHOCOLATE AND RED WINE MINI CAKES

Bathsheba's story made me think about the connections between Judaism, alcohol, and parenthood. It has always struck me that Jewish parents give their children alcohol during religious rituals, and at the same time drunkenness is strongly discouraged. I wanted to offer a recipe that mirrored this, with a small amount of alcohol in a recipe adults and kids will love.

These rich chocolate and red wine mini cakes are moist, decadent, and with a delicate berry flavor from the red wine and strawberry swirl frosting. They are vegan, oil-free, and lower in sugar than traditional chocolate cakes. We're also using spelt flour as a whole-grain option.

Prep Time: 30 minutes
Cook Time: 20 minutes
Yield: 6 mini cakes

Tools:

- Baking spray
- Blender
- Measuring cups and spoons
- Medium glass bowl
- Large mixing bowl
- Piping bag (optional)
- Small oven-safe ramekins
- Whisk

Ingredients:

For the cake:

- ½ cup (120ml) unsweetened applesauce
- 1 cup (240ml) red wine
- ½ cup (100g) sugar
- 1 tsp vanilla extract
- 1½ cups (180g) spelt flour
- 5 tbsp (35g) unsweetened cocoa powder
- 1 tsp baking soda
- A pinch of salt

For the frosting:

- 1 cup (140g) raw cashews
- 3 tbsp (45ml) maple syrup
- 1 tbsp (15ml) fresh lemon juice
- 3 tbsp (45ml) water
- 1½ tbsp (30g) strawberry jam (or a small handful of fresh strawberries)

Instructions:

1. Place cashews in a medium bowl and cover with boiling water. Allow to soak for 20–30 minutes.
2. Preheat the oven to 350° F (175° C).
3. To make the cake, in a large mixing bowl, combine unsweetened applesauce, red wine, sugar, and vanilla extract. Whisk until combined.
4. Add flour, cocoa, baking soda, and a pinch of salt to the bowl and gently whisk until all the ingredients are combined. Don't overmix.
5. Spray 6 ramekins with baking spray and evenly divide the batter among the ramekins.
6. Place in the oven to bake until set and slightly puffed, around 16–20 minutes. Test by inserting a toothpick in the middle – it should come out clean with only a few moist crumbs and no liquid batter.
7. While the cakes are baking, add the drained soaked cashews, maple syrup, lemon juice, and water to a high-speed blender and blend until completely smooth and creamy, at least 3–4 minutes. You may need to stop and scrape the sides of the blender to ensure everything is blending nicely.
8. If using fresh strawberries, add to the blend and blend until smooth. If using jam, transfer the cashew frosting to a small bowl and swirl in the jam.
9. Remove the baked cakes from the oven and allow to cool completely before topping with the strawberry cashew frosting.

From the Jewish Food Hero Kitchen

BELOREYA / בלוריא

STORY

Beloreya,[1] whose name is always followed by the moniker הגיורת, *hagiyoret,* "the female convert," is mentioned twice in the Babylonian Talmud.[2]

In the first story[3] we find Beloreya, the female convert, grappling with two lines of Torah that seem to portray conflicting views about the nature of God. One verse portrays God as "the awesome God, who shows no favor."[4] Yet the other, drawn from a line of the priestly benediction, offers that God shall "bestow His favor upon you and grant you peace."[5] Beloreya shares her puzzlement with Rabban Gamliel II, who is the Nasi (president) of the Sanhedrin, one of the most prominent Torah scholars of her day.

Then, Rabbi Yose HaKohen joins the conversation and suggests that the verses do not contradict each other. Rather, they just describe different circumstances regarding repentance. The first text, he argues, refers to contexts where one person has sinned against another person. In that case God does not offer forgiveness until the person who was hurt forgives the offender. However, the second text refers to contexts where a person has sinned against God, in which case God will show the person forgiveness.

In the second instance[6] we learn that during Beloreya's conversion, her slaves preempted her by immersing in the mikvah before she did. Through their conversion, the slaves were given the authority to free themselves. As such, the freedom of the slaves became a matter of rabbinic debate, as the rabbis wrestled with what the slaves' status would have been if Beloreya had immersed in the mikvah first and the slaves had followed suit.

1. Alternative spelling *B'Luria,* Valeria.
2. Babylonian Talmud, Rosh Hashanah 17b, Talmud b. Yevamot 46a.
3. Babylonian Talmud, Rosh Hashanah 17b.
4. Deuteronomy 10:17 (JPS Hebrew-English Tanakh).
5. Numbers 6:26 (JPS Hebrew-English Tanakh).
6. Babylonian Talmud, *Yevamot* 46a.

PASSAGES

Talmud b. Rosh Hashanah 17b

CONTEXT

In the Hebrew Bible, references to *"ger"* allude to the stranger in the non-citizen sense. It isn't until later that the rabbis differentiate between *ger toshav* (resident alien) and *ger tzedek* (righteous convert). In both cases, the word *"ger"* others the person in question. A search of the word הגיורת, the female convert, yields that Beloreya is the only woman assigned with that identity.

There is, however, a famous *"giyoret"* in the Tanach: Ruth. We are told about Ruth, a Moabite woman who was left widowed from her marriage to Machlon, an Israelite. And when her mother-in-law Naomi urges Ruth to return to Moab, Ruth famously replies: "Do not urge me to leave you, to turn back and not follow you. For wherever you go, I will go; wherever you lodge, I will lodge; your people shall be my people, and your God my God" (Ruth 1:16), affirming her place among the Israelites. Rabbinic texts accept this utterance as a legitimate form of conversion. The text reaffirms Ruth's rightful place among the Israelites by naming her son among the ten generations between Judah and David (Ruth 4:17–22).

AGGADAH

Converting to Judaism has always been a life-changing decision. Today, Jews by choice are met with myriad responses. In some circles, they are welcomed by a rabbi to undergo a conversion process. Their learning process may take place in group and/or one-on-one settings. They may also be provided with a set of Jewish texts and books to familiarize themselves with Jewish practice, ideology and theology, as well as a timeline during which time they can anticipate going before the *beit din* to formalize their conversion. In other circles, they are shunned and dissuaded from converting three times. If the person returns a fourth time, they are accepted into the conversion process.[7] In those more strict circles, the learning style is more informal and the person seeking to convert is often not given a set timeline by which to expect to complete the process. In all cases, the learning styles and approaches for people seeking to convert are subjective and dependent on the sponsoring rabbi.

---

7. Ruth Rabbah 2:16 to Ruth 1:8–12.

Once a person has successfully converted, they may be asked to verify time and again the legitimacy of their conversion. However, Jewish texts prohibit reminding, taunting, or discriminating against a person who has undergone conversion, whether on a one-on-one basis or within a communal setting.[8]

A Jew by choice, Beloreya's name is always followed by the moniker הגיורת, "the female convert." What was the intention behind coupling her name with this reminder? What was the impact on her then and now? Was the word meant to increase her merit, or to keep her within a peripheral category?

And what of Beloreya's name, which does not appear in other commonly read texts? One possibility is that it could allude to "Luria" as her geographic origin. Beloreya's name is also very similar to another Talmudic figure, "Beruriah," and so adding the moniker "*Hagiyoret*" to Beloreya's name could have been a way to differentiate between the two women. Although there is nothing else written about Beloreya outside of these two instances, within these examples we find the story of a woman whose conversion and Jewish learning outlived her. She is canonized as a woman of status, means, and influence amongst the Rabbis.

What about our personal behavior toward those who choose to convert to Judaism today? Are we using the label "convert"? Each experience of conversion to Judaism is unique and courageous. We might reach for terms that highlight that a person has made the choice to join the Jewish community. In searching for words to describe other people and their unique existence and characteristics, we may use words that carry meaning beyond that which we intend. On some level, it is irrelevant whether our own personal intention is to imbue the word "convert" with a special positive meaning, or a negative one. In either case, when we label someone a "convert" we simultaneously designate them within a category which is distinct from simply being "a Jewish person."

---

8. Exodus 22:20; Talmud b. Bava Metzia 59b:13 and Mishnah Bava Metzia 4:10.

PROMPTS

- Is there a difference between someone being referred to as a convert, and someone referring to themself this way?
- Beloreya was able to engage closely with the sitting president of the Sanhedrin. Today, do potential converts have enough access to rabbis and Jewish scholars?
- Does our community do a good enough job to include, give equal access to, and encourage all marginalized Jewish people to participate in learning opportunities?

Daphne Lazar Price *is the Executive Director of the Jewish Orthodox Feminist Alliance and an adjunct professor of Jewish law at Georgetown University Law Center.*

FRESH TANGY CABBAGE AND RADISH SPREAD

A few things can be gleaned from Beloreya's situation in life. One, based on the fact she had servants, I assume she was wealthy. Two, having lost those servants, she likely struggled with the proper maintenance of her household.

I was inspired by the book Dream Interpretation: From Classical Jewish Sources,*9 which attributes auspicious significance to appearances of cabbage and radish in dreams:*

> *Cabbage is a good sign and wealth will come to you (R. Hai Gaon)* [10]

> *Radish is a sign your circumstances will improve, and a good life will be yours (Rashi)* [11]

I created a new napa cabbage and daikon radish spread, to help spread the essence of success to Beloreya's life.

When I made this spread, I served it with avocado, bean sprouts, and tempeh sautéed in soy sauce, all on top of a flatbread.

Prep Time: 15 minutes
Cook Time: 5 minutes
Yield: 6–8 servings

Tools:

- Blender or food processor
- Bowl
- Cutting board
- Knife

Ingredients:

- 1 daikon radish, chopped to large chunks
- 5 napa cabbage leaves
- ⅓ cup olive oil (more or less)
- A handful of fresh cilantro
- 1 head of garlic (about 12 cloves), peeled
- Juice of 2 lemons (4–6 tbsp)
- Salt to taste, optional

---

9. Almoi, Solomon Ben Jacob Almoli and Elman, Yaakov (1988). *Dream Interpretation: From Classical Jewish Sources*, KTAV Publishing House.
10. Ibid, p. 78.
11. Ibid, p. 78.

Instructions:

1. Wash all the vegetables.

2. Chop the daikon radish, napa cabbage, and cilantro into rough chunks so they fit in the blender.

3. Peel all cloves in the head of garlic and add to the blender.

4. Squeeze the juice of 2 lemons into the blender.

5. Blend the mixture. Then, add olive oil slowly while continuously blending, until the mixture is smooth in appearance.

6. Season to taste and serve as a condiment for sandwiches, wraps, or as a simple dip.

Maayan Zik, an Orthodox Jewish Jamaican-American, is a social activist who has co-founded organizations such as Ker a Velt and Kamochah.

STORY

Bruriah[1] is the most legendary female scholar of the Talmud. She is believed to have lived during the second century CE, to have been the daughter of the great Sage Rabbi Hanna-niah ben Teradion, and to have married Rabbi Meir. She is mentioned several times in the Babylonian Talmud and in later writings as well. Since there are so many references to her, some people have suggested that Bruriah is actually a composite of multiple women.

Whether Bruriah was one woman or many, she is represented through the common thread of deep Torah knowledge. Bruriah is depicted to be an impressive scholar equal to, and sometimes even above and beyond, the male scholars she encounters. Rabbinic sources portray her challenging her father on halachic law and correcting her husband's under-standing of Torah.

While the Talmud focuses on Bruriah through the masculine pursuits of scholarship, later sources describe her solely as a wife and mother. The Midrash on the Book of Proverbs depicts Bruriah as a supportive wife to Rabbi Meir, a true woman of valor, when she hides the death of her sons on Shabbat from her husband until she can truly comfort him. A Talmudic commentary written by the medieval French rabbi Rashi, by contrast, introduces a tragic conclusion to Bruriah's life that seems out of character with previously recorded images of an erudite scholar and a virtuous wife and mother. Rashi writes that since Bruriah had mocked the Sages' notion that women were light-minded, Rabbi Meir sends one of his students to seduce her. But while the Talmud includes similar stories of male scholars, including Rabbi Meir, who face temptation by beautiful women but are saved or stopped from transgression, Bruriah succumbs to the student's advances. Moreover, when she learns that her husband has set her up, Bruriah strangles herself to death, and Rabbi Meir flees in disgrace from what he has done.

PASSAGES

Talmud b. Eruvin 53b[2]

---

1. The spellings Beruriah and Berurya are also commonly used.
2. See also, Pesachim 62b, Berakhot 10a, and Avodah Zarah 18b.

CONTEXT

The Talmud describes Bruriah's deep wisdom in relation to men: her knowledge is compared to men's. She is depicted as outwitting or criticizing men. To a contemporary reader, Bruriah appears to be virtuous and wise at some moments and petty and mocking at others. In the context of the times, however, Bruriah is simply acting like the male Rabbis of her day. Bruriah is a woman who transgresses the boundaries of male learning, but in acting like a man, she ensures that the gendering of knowledge as male remains intact.

Bruriah serves as a symbol of female Torah knowledge in the Talmud. She appears multiple times throughout the Talmud, in stories that describe her erudition rather than her so-called female virtues. By only describing Bruriah through her intellect, and as more knowledgeable than men, the Rabbis of the Talmud suggest that while female learning was accepted, it was considered to be quite exceptional.

AGGADAH

Bruriah can inspire women and gender non-conforming people to break into masculine and male-dominated spaces, but she also serves as a reminder of how women who break boundaries are represented and remembered.

Bruriah transgresses gender boundaries without defying Jewish tradition. In fact, her mastery of Jewish thought enables her to challenge social norms. She is an expert in halachic law and at times demonstrates an understanding of the complexities of Torah that exceed her husband's comprehension. Bruriah uses her knowledge to challenge other men as well. Thus, Bruriah demonstrates that Torah knowledge has no gender and that such wisdom empowers women to do spectacular things. But while Torah may not discriminate, society does, and Bruriah encounters stumbling blocks as she faces societal misperceptions and assumptions that learning and leadership are gendered male.

To become the Talmudic symbol of female Torah knowledge, Bruriah must prove that she is better than men. She masters more wisdom than men and develops a cleverer tongue than men. As Bruriah competes with men she transgresses the male-female gender divide and projects her body and voice into masculine space. She kicks a male student in the *beit midrash* and chastises his study habits. She criticizes a man for talking to a woman, by speaking to him. While men depicted in the Talmud may be physically and verbally

aggressive with other men, when Bruriah mimics their actions, readers accuse her of being snarky or condescending. Thus, the legacy of Bruriah's story reveals the dangers of women who imitate men, especially when they challenge gender stereotypes.

It is noteworthy that the rabbis decided to preserve Bruriah's stories of remarkable Torah knowledge in the Talmud, but unfortunately we can only understand her through the masculine lens of male writers. What if we could encounter Bruriah in her own words; what would she tell us? Perhaps we would learn that Bruriah first studied with her father and later with her husband, or maybe we would discover that she learned alongside her sister or even with other women. Perhaps Bruriah would bring us into a female space for learning, a women's *beit midrash* where she would poke a girl studying Torah and tease her for not reading out loud. Or what if Bruriah led us into a house of learning for all genders, where knowledge had no boundaries, and where Torah was accessible and equal to all? If we listen carefully for Bruriah's story through her own lost words, we can begin to imagine that such an inclusive place is possible.

PROMPTS

- Can you think of any masculine or male-dominated spaces (religious or secular) today?
- What do women or gender non-conforming people need to do to enter into and be successful in those kinds of spaces?
- What are some of the ways in which contemporary society depicts successful women and girls?
- What can we do to make spaces accessible to everyone? Can we reform existing spaces, or do we need to create new ones?

Dr. Elizabeth LaCouture is the director of the Gender Studies Program at the University of Hong Kong, where she researches Chinese women's history.

SEVEN HERBS AND SPECIES FOCACCIA

Bruriah was a strong and intelligent woman whose gifts were not aptly celebrated. Imagine her today, adorned with medals, degrees, and certificates. This bread is decorated to honor her.

This sourdough-based focaccia is made with some of the ingredients from the seven species of Israel.

- *The acidity of the bread is reminiscent of Bruriah's struggle and the obstacles she faced in making unpleasant decisions.*
- *Candied tomatoes are a reminder that, even if simple suffices, we can always go further.*
- *The sweet dates mark the sweetness of her victories against those who did not believe in her.*
- *The parsley is a reminder of the tears she shed during the attacks on her and the deaths of her sons.*
- *Olives and za'atar complete this dish like pearls on the bread whose "worth is far beyond that of rubies."*[3]

Prep Time: 6 hours
Cook Time: 20 minutes
Yield: 4–6 servings

Tools:

- Chopping board
- Large mixing bowl
- Rectangular baking dish 13″×9″×2″
- Paring knife

Ingredients:

- 115g sourdough starter
- 2½ cups (300g) unbleached all-purpose flour
- ¾ + ⅛ cup (210g) lukewarm water
- ¼ tbsp (5g) salt
- 7 tbsp extra virgin olive oil, divided
- 1 chive (green and white parts)
- 1 cup candied cherry tomatoes
- 3 branches parsley (stems attached)
- 3 branches cilantro (stems attached)
- 5 fresh cherry tomatoes (cut in half)
- 5 green olives
- 5 red olives
- 5 black olives
- 3 dates (cut in half)
- 1 tbsp za'atar

---

3. Proverbs 31:10.

Instructions:

1. Set aside some of the herbs and spices to garnish the bread before baking.
2. Mix sourdough started, flour, lukewarm water, salt and 4 tbsp oil for about 15 minutes in a stand mixer over medium speed or knead the dough by hand for 25 minutes.
3. Set aside and leave to rise for about 2 hours covered.
4. Oil a baking dish with 2 tablespoons extra virgin olive oil and put the dough inside.
5. Let it rise for about 3 hours uncovered.
6. Preheat oven to 350° F (180° C).
7. Lightly oil the top of the focaccia with 2 tablespoons extra virgin olive oil.
8. With lightly oiled hands, use your fingers to poke holes in the surface of the focaccia.
9. Decorate[4] the top of the focaccia with the remaining herbs and spices.
10. Bake for about 20 minutes.
11. Lightly brush the top with 1 tablespoon extra virgin olive oil once baked.

Hélène Jawhara Piñer is a PhD in history and an American Sephardi Federation Fellow. She is a Sephardic chef, author, and teaches in European universities.

---

4. On Tu B'Shevat, you could shape the dough like a decorated tree.

THE CARPENTER'S WIFE / אשת דנגרי

STORY

In the fifth chapter of Tractate Gittin, the rabbis share a reversal-of-fortune tale featuring three characters: a wife, a carpenter, and an apprentice.

The story unfolds like this:

The carpenter has an apprentice who sets his eyes on his master's wife. There comes a time when the carpenter needs to borrow money, so the apprentice offers a loan, and suggests he send his wife to collect it. The carpenter sends his wife, but his wife does not return.

After three days, the apprentice returns to the carpenter. The carpenter asks the apprentice where his wife is. The apprentice claims that he sent her home immediately, but had heard that she had been abused and raped on her way back home. The carpenter asks the apprentice what he should do, and the apprentice instructs him to divorce her. The carpenter hedges, saying that his wife has a large *ketubah* and he does not have the financial means to pay the marriage contract. The apprentice offers him another loan to fund the divorce. The carpenter accepts the advice and the loan, leaves the apprentice, and divorces his wife.

The apprentice then marries the carpenter's ex-wife. Later, when the carpenter's debt is due and he cannot repay it, the apprentice suggests that he come and work off his debt instead. The apprentice and his wife sit and eat and drink, while the carpenter serves them. All the while the carpenter cries, his tears falling into their cups.

PASSAGES

Talmud b. Gittin 58a

CONTEXT

The rabbis of the Talmud blame the destruction of the Second Temple on acts of baseless hatred. *Sinat chinam*, baseless hatred, and its opposite, *ahavat chinam*, baseless love, are enduring themes of the Jewish holiday of Tisha B'Av.

Tractate Gittin focuses on the ways in which divorce is performed. The story about this triad is a divorce story as well as the last of the catastrophic tales told in Gittin to further

illustrate the concept of *sinat chinam*, baseless hatred. The most well known of these tales is the story of Kamtza and Bar Kamtza[1], in which Bar Kamtza mistakenly receives an invitation meant for Kamtza, and arrives at a wealthy man's party. Knowing that his friend considered Bar Kamtza an enemy, the wealthy man – despite not even knowing him – forces Bar Kamtza to leave the feast. The rabbis who were present at the feast sit by, their passivity giving sanction to the humiliation of Bar Kamtza by their host.

Bar Kamtza's humiliation transforms into vengeful rage. He tells the authorities a falsehood about the Jewish community, and hurts an innocent animal to make it unfit for sacrifice in order to entrap the rabbis. The rabbis suffer from analysis paralysis, prioritizing appearances (i.e., the ritual sacrifice) over taking preemptive and reparative action. The conflict escalates from its petty beginning between two strangers and ultimately leads to a war between the Jews and the Romans.

AGGADAH

The Carpenter's Wife story unfolds in private workspaces and in the bedroom. Baseless hatred spills out of a defined male master-apprentice relationship, ensnaring the wife who was apparently perceived as nothing more than a vacant pawn to be passed between the two men. As readers, we are left to decide for ourselves if the wife had any agency.

The text states that the apprentice "set his eyes" on his master's wife. This impulse is presented as the motivational force for the apprentice's consequent trickery, manipulation, and lies, which permeate the tale and bolster the asymmetrical master-apprentice power dynamic.

The carpenter, for his part, seems to lack emotional and financial intelligence. He is oblivious to his apprentice's lust for his wife and fails to search for her when she goes missing for three days. When told that his wife may have been sexually assaulted, he responds with apathy, allowing his actions to be entirely dictated by the apprentice.

And what about the wife? Her passive journey from one man's wife to another leads us to see her as a victim, married first to a man who appears indifferent to her and then to a man who manipulated, potentially violated, and then spread violent rumors about her. She seems to be an empty recipient onto, and through which, baseless hatred is expressed.

---

1.   Talmud. B. Gittin 55b and 56a.

The last image of her being served food and drink alongside the apprentice while her former husband cries tears into her cup is jarring – it opens up the possibility that maybe she was not simply a victim. Might she have been aware of and involved in the plan, emboldening the apprentice and ending up right where she wanted to be at the story's end?

The Talmud is using the male characters' appalling treatment of this female character – their partner in the intimate relationship of marriage – and her passive acceptance to illustrate the moral depravity of people at this time. The tales of Kamtza and Bar Kamtza and the Carpenter's Wife show us six characters, each of whom acts out of baseless hatred toward another person. These acts of baseless hate, expressed in these stories through each character's actions or lack thereof, illustrate how moral rot had inundated all realms of society.

For the most part, these ancient stories show us men acting out of baseless hatred, but today we know that this is not a solely male domain. Regrettably, each of us can act on the baseless hatred we feel toward others, regardless of gender – even if those manifestations are in their own way gendered. As our community continues to reflect on *sinat chinam*, each person must see themselves in these tales in order to dismantle *sinat chinam*, baseless hatred, and cultivate *ahavat chinam*, baseless love.

PROMPTS

- Define baseless hatred. Define baseless love.
- Name and describe the baseless hatred displayed by each character in these Talmudic stories: the wealthy man, Bar Kamtza, the rabbis, the carpenter, the apprentice, the carpenter's wife.
- How are manifestations of baseless hate gendered?
- What are some concrete actions a person can take to increase expressions and actions of baseless love in their family and community?

Kenden Alfond

FESENJOON: TANGY EGGPLANT AND WALNUT STEW

The Story of the Carpenter's Wife is about the cruelty we can inflict upon one another. To me, Fesenjoon represents the opposite of cruelty, instead embodying warmth and devotion. This recipe, which I serve on Shabbat, is pure love. A little sweet and a little tart, this recipe is one of our favorite family meals.

Like many Persian recipes, this one is all about giving the ingredients plenty of time to come together so that the flavors can fuse into one glorious entity.

This tangy eggplant and walnut stew is best served with basmati rice and a cooling salad.

Prep Time: 40 minutes

Cook Time: 1 hour

Yield: 4 servings

Tools:

- Baking paper
- Baking tray
- Cutting board
- Kitchen scales
- Knife
- Large frying pan
- Large saucepan with lid
- Measuring cups and spoons
- Wooden spoons

Ingredients:

- 8 Lebanese eggplants (long and thin)
- 1 tbsp + 2 tbsp vegetable oil
- 2½ cups (270g) walnut halves
- ⅓ cup (100ml) pomegranate molasses
- 2 scant cups (450ml) + ½ cup (125ml) boiling water
- 1 large yellow onion, finely diced
- ¼ tsp turmeric powder
- 2–3 tbsp sugar
- Pinch of cinnamon
- Olive oil
- Kosher sea salt
- Black pepper

Instructions:

1. Preheat the oven to 350° F (180° C).

2. Cut the Lebanese eggplants in half lengthwise (if using larger eggplants, cut into 1.5-cm-thick slices). Optional: lay them cut side up, sprinkle with kosher sea salt, and leave to sweat for 30 minutes. Wipe away liquid and salt.

3. Brush olive oil all over the eggplants and place on a lined baking tray cut side up. Cook in the oven for approximately 30 minutes, until the tops are lightly golden and browned – it might take an additional 15 minutes. Set aside.

4. Meanwhile, grind the walnuts into tiny chunks. Add 1 tablespoon of vegetable oil to the frying pan and saute the ground walnuts over medium heat, stirring frequently, for 15 minutes.

5. Add pomegranate molasses and 2 cups (450ml) of boiling water to the walnuts. Mix well and lightly simmer for 15–20 minutes on low to medium heat, until the mixture thickens and you can see a layer of walnut oil on top.

6. Remove from heat and set aside.

7. Saute the chopped onions in 2 tbsp vegetable oil in a large saucepan over medium heat, stirring frequently, until slightly brown (do not burn).

8. Add ¼ teaspoon of turmeric, cinnamon, salt, and pepper to the onions and stir well.

9. Pour the pomegranate and walnut mixture into the saucepan and mix well. Add ½ cup of boiling water.

10. Bring the mixture to a boil, then lower the heat. Half cover and simmer for 30 minutes – 1 hour, until the Fesenjoon sauce has thickened to a creamy consistency. Check on the mixture intermittently and stir to prevent sticking to the bottom.

11. Add sugar to the Fesenjoon sauce in the last 15 minutes of cooking. Start by adding 1 tablespoon; mix well and taste. If you'd like it to be sweeter, add a tablespoon at a time, up to a total of 3 tablespoons.

12. Ladle the Fesenjoon onto a serving plate or bowl and top with the warmed roasted eggplants, and serve.

Penelope Winston, *a lover of methodical Persian cooking, is a mother of two young boys and lives with her husband in Sydney, Australia.*

STORY

One passage in the Babylonian Talmud, in Tractate Ketubot 60a, mentions a certain divorced woman who did not wish to nurse her son.

This nameless divorced woman comes before one of the leading authorities of her generation, Shmuel, to deal with this issue. The rabbis present the child before a lineup of women, presumably to influence the mother to change her mind; perhaps she will be moved by the fact that her child recognizes her. Instead of reaching for the nursling, she turns away from him. Rav Dimi bar Yosef insists that she "lift up" her eyes and embrace her child.

PASSAGES

Talmud b., Ketubot 60a

CONTEXT

In the third century CE in Babylonia, wet nurses were available to feed children whose mothers either could not produce adequate milk to feed them or chose not to for some other reason. This mother's ambivalence toward nursing a child who clearly was bonded to her is noteworthy. To the modern reader of this passage, it might indicate that something else is going on that the ancient rabbis either did not understand or chose not to include in this passage.

The story is related in the midst of discussions about how long a child should be allowed to nurse, at what age a baby might recognize its mother, and how. This is all relevant to the topic of *ketubot*, or marriage contracts, as the rabbis of the Talmud understand breastfeeding a child to be one of the duties that a woman owes her husband. This duty is complicated by the fact that the mother and father of the child in question are divorced; does the mother owe her ex-husband or her child this duty? Because children of divorced parents are understood to "belong" to their fathers after divorce, the complicated relationship between a divorced mother nursing an infant who ultimately belonged to their father's household is a point of discussion among halachic authorities.

AGGADAH

It took her hours to rise from her bed each morning. Her mind was thick and cloudy; taking care of even her most basic bodily functions required all of her effort. She could barely eat or drink. *I understand why he could no longer have me as his wife*, she thought to herself as she felt the many knots in her hair break the teeth of her ivory comb. *I am hardly a human being, much less a mother or a wife.* She yanked the comb through her hair again, knowing that today she had to present herself to Shmuel, at the *beit din* of Neharedea.

In his wisdom, as both a Rav and a physician, he would see why her diminished body would no longer feed her son. He would understand why it was just not possible. *My son,* she thought, screaming internally. *No longer my son.* With her *get*[1] in hand, she knew that her son would only ever remember his father, and probably his new mother, the woman her ex-husband planned to marry. Better for the baby to forget her now. Better she should be forgotten by everyone.

Standing before Shmuel, she wished she could disappear. To have her weakness, her pain, and her inability to continue this motherly obligation on display – there was no moment more difficult in her life up to this point. And then, to stand in this line! Are they truly bringing the child before her? *Oh please, let him pass, let him have forgotten,* she prayed; he was still so young. But the joy on his face as he saw her, as he reached for her. She turned away. She could not bear the pain. Let it be finished, the words of Rav Dimi bar Yosef echoing behind her as she fled, "lift up your eyes and take your son!" How cruel. The child was no longer her son, though she would forever be his mother.

---

1.   A Jewish religious document that legally enacts a divorce between a Jewish couple.

PROMPTS

- In what ways might expectations around breastfeeding cause damage to new mothers?
- How do modern understandings about postpartum depression affect our expectations of new mothers?
- What space can we make for ambivalent feelings about motherhood, and parenthood, at all ages and stages?
- What expectations do we have of parents of any gender while they are nurturing infants?

Danielle Kranjec *is currently Director of Campus Initiatives at the Shalom Hartman Institute of North America. She is the creator of the "Kranjec Test" for inclusivity.*

MOTHER'S JOY INFUSION

In the story we have just read, we do not know this woman's name, yet we can see that she is depressed and disconnected from her newborn child. Intense emotions and physical fatigue following childbirth are familiar to many women. Women need support after they give birth. One way to ease the transition into motherhood is to use healing herbs.

This blend of herbs is both calming and uplifting to the mind, body, and spirit. It opens the heart for connection, soothes nerves, eases anxiety, and helps create an inner sense of peace.

Enjoy 3 to 5 cups per day. Safe for daily use. Safe for pregnant and nursing women.

Prep Time: 5 minutes
Cook Time: 10 minutes
Yield: 32 oz quart jar (makes 4 cups)

Tools:

- Teapot with a strainer or 32 oz glass jar
- Fine sieve

Ingredients:

Herbs needed for Mother's Joy Infusion can be purchased individually.

Mother's Joy can be enjoyed in all stages and phases of life, morning or night, and is especially lovely for women to drink postpartum.

For the tea blend:

- 1 cup (30g) dried chamomile flowers
- 1 cup (15g) dried lemon balm leaves
- ½ cup (10g) dried rose buds
- ½ cup (10g) dried oat straw
- ¼ cup (5g) rosemary leaves
- ¼ cup (5g) lavender flowers

For the tea:

- 4 tbsp Mother's Joy tea blend
- 4 cups of hot water

Instructions:

1. Make the herbal tea blend and store in an airtight glass container.
2. Boil 4 cups of water.
3. Add 4 tablespoons of the herbal tea blend to the jar or teapot.
4. Pour hot water over the herbs.
5. Cover and let steep for 10 minutes.
6. Strain, sweeten to your desire, and enjoy.

 Shayna Judelman *is a community herbalist and founder of One Earth Herbs. Shayna runs an herbal apothecary from her home in the Judean hills.*

STORY

Cleopatra, an Egyptian queen, is featured several times throughout the Talmud.

In Tractate Sanhedrin, she engages in conversation with Rabbi Meir. Here, she raises a question on whether the dead will be resurrected with or without clothing, and is subsequently answered by Rabbi Meir. He says to her: If wheat, which is buried naked, meaning that the kernel is sown without the chaff, emerges with several garments of chaff, all the more so will the righteous, who are buried with their garments, arise with their garments.

In Tractate Niddah, the Gemara describes a medical experiment Cleopatra ran. In this experiment, she gave her convicted maidservants a medical beverage of sorts, as to ensure they were not already pregnant. She then had her maidservants engage in sexual intercourse to impregnate them prior to their planned execution. Following their deaths, she operated on them to examine how the embryos had developed. Her experiment is used as proof against Rabbi Yishmael's opinion regarding the development of the fetus.

PASSAGES[1]

Niddah 30b

CONTEXT

Cleopatra is a well-known cultural historical icon, but though there were several figures with this name throughout Egyptian history, it is likely to be Cleopatra VII who features in the Talmudic passages discussed here, since she is recorded as living closest in time to the Sages.

A notable aspect of the Sanhedrin narrative is that Cleopatra, a non-Jew, is engaging with Rabbi Meir on questions around Jewish ideas of life and death using Talmudic lines of reasoning.

---

1. See also, Talmud.b.Shabbat.3b–5a, Talmud.b.Sanhedrin.90b, Talmud.b.Niddah.30b.

In the Niddah section, the story about Cleopatra's experiments is presented as proof to counter a point made by Rabbi Yishmael. While Cleopatra is demonstrated to have some knowledge in both sections, the overall tone of the *sugyot* still places the authority in the hands of the rabbis.

AGGADAH

The stories of Cleopatra in the Babylonian Talmud focus on a situation many women are familiar with – having her knowledge doubted by the male authorities in her life. Focusing primarily on the story in Niddah, as it is more substantive, Cleopatra is initially positioned as an authority. But Rabbi Yishmael's response is to call her a fool.

What's really compelling here, though, is that the Gemara does not immediately take Rabbi Yishmael's side. It argues back to Rabbi Yishmael's objections by making points about Cleopatra's knowledge and the details of her experiments. One might anticipate the Gemara taking the side of its own (Rabbi Yishmael), but instead, it respects Cleopatra's political authority and her knowledge.

Despite this apparent acknowledgment of her skill and defense of her ideas, the Gemara still yields to Rabbi Yishmael in the end. This narrative can provide insight into the values of exploring other perspectives, persevering in the face of disrespect, and more.

In discussion of her scientific experiments, it is important to note the lack of ethics involved. Cleopatra is able to engage in these experiments due to her position of power, which makes it difficult for the women she experimented on to consent. It is difficult to claim that the Gemara rejected her experience solely on the basis of ethical violation, considering that widespread concepts of research ethics and consent are relatively modern.[2]

Cleopatra had everything running against the likelihood of the Talmud taking her seriously – notably her gender, and an outsider to the Jewish community – yet she has significant status and authority. The inclusion of the narrative, then, seems to be stressing that there is great value in hearing what people of other backgrounds have to say and fully giving their perspectives and knowledge respect.

---

2. https://www.unlv.edu/research/ORI-HSR/history-ethics.

PROMPTS

- How can we respect the opinions of people we are unfamiliar with, or who come from different backgrounds?
- In what ways can we push back on others' ideas, including potential ethical violations, while also respecting their knowledge?

Jordana Barnett *studies at Barnard College and the Jewish Theological Seminary. In her free time, she loves to read, bake, garden, crochet, and learn Talmud.*

CARAMELIZED LEEK BARLEY WITH WHITE BEAN SMASH, SPINACH, ASPARAGUS, AND BEET POTION

I was inspired by Cleopatra's scientific curiosity. Her experimentation prompted me to take an experimental approach to constructing this recipe. Each different component builds on the last, like a scientific research process, resulting in a finished dish made step by step.

Prep Time: 20 minutes
Cook Time: 55 minutes
Total Time: 1 hour, 15 minutes
Yield: 4 servings

Tools:

- Blender
- Chef's knife
- Cutting board
- Dutch oven, 5-quart
- Kitchen scale
- Measuring cups and spoons
- Mixing bowl
- Potato masher/fork
- Skillet/grill pan
- Spatula

Ingredients:

Caramelized leek barley:

- 3 medium to large leeks (300g) (white and light green parts, reserve dark green parts for another use), sliced lengthwise, rinsed well
- 2 tbsp (30ml) low-sodium tamari or soy sauce
- 3 cups (220g) shiitake mushrooms, diced
- 4 cloves (12g) garlic, minced
- 2 tsp (5g) smoked paprika
- 1 cup (220g) pearled barley
- 2.5 cups (590ml) vegetable broth
- 1 cup (235ml) filtered water, plus more as needed
- ½ tsp (2g) freshly ground black pepper, or to taste

White bean smash:

- 15 oz (425g; 1 can) white beans, cooked and drained
- 2 tsp (10g) rosemary, finely chopped
- ⅛ tsp (0.5g) salt
- ½ tsp (2g) black pepper

Grilled asparagus with spinach:

- 1 bunch asparagus (approximately 1 lb or 450g); substitute locally available vegetables if asparagus is not available
- 2 cups spinach (60g)

Beet potion:

- 1 medium beet (35g), cooked and cooled
- ¾ cup (120g) cashews
- ½ cup (119ml) filtered water
- 2 tbsp (30ml) apple cider vinegar
- Juice of half a lemon
- 3 garlic cloves (9g)
- ½ serrano pepper (optional)

Instructions:

Caramelized leek barley:

1. Slice leeks crosswise into 3-inch pieces, then lengthwise into thin matchsticks.
2. Add tamari to coat the bottom of the Dutch oven. Add leeks and cook, stirring frequently, until leeks are soft, about 10 minutes. If needed, add filtered water 1 tablespoon at a time to prevent leeks from sticking.
3. Add mushrooms, garlic, and smoked paprika. Continue to cook, stirring frequently, until mushrooms soften and leeks are golden brown and caramelized, about 5–10 minutes. Again, add a little water at a time to prevent sticking.
4. Add barley and stir to combine.
5. Add vegetable broth, water, and black pepper. Bring to a boil.
6. Cover, reduce heat, and simmer for 25–35 minutes until barley is tender and liquid is absorbed. Add water as needed to get to desired consistency.

White bean smash:

1. Rinse, drain, and mash the cooked beans.
2. Remove rosemary leaves from the stem and chop finely.
3. Add salt, pepper, and rosemary to the bean smash. Stir well to incorporate.

Grilled asparagus with spinach:

1. Rinse and clean asparagus and spinach.
2. Cut the tough ends off of the asparagus and discard. Then, cut the remaining asparagus into 3 sections per spear.
3. Add asparagus to a warm skillet. Cook for 5–10 minutes, turning a few times while cooking to ensure consistency and prevent burning. When asparagus is still bright green and tender, remove from the heat.
4. Slice the washed spinach into thin strips.

Beet potion:

1. Place all ingredients in a blender and blend until completely smooth (pre-soaking the cashews for 5–10 minutes in hot water helps to soften).
2. Scrape down the sides of the blender with a rubber spatula and blend again.
3. Add filtered water as necessary to get to desired consistency.
4. Use immediately, or store in a glass jar in the refrigerator for up to 3 days. The potion will thicken once chilled; thin it out with a little water if needed.

To serve:

1. Place 2 heaping tablespoons of barley on a plate for the base.
2. Add 1 tablespoon of white bean smash and spread on top of the barley.
3. Top beans with ¼ of the spinach strips and ¼ of the asparagus spears, aligned in the same direction.
4. Finish with a delicate swirl of beet potion on top for color and sweetness.
5. Serve remaining beet potion in a small pitcher or condiment dish for diners to add as they please.

Denise Petrulis *is a Los Angeles-based experienced nonprofit professional. She transforms everyday ingredients into flavorful, health-promoting meals.*

DAUGHTER OF NAKDIMON BEN GURION /
בתו של נקדימון בן גוריון

STORY

The daughter of Nakdimon ben Gurion was set to inherit a large amount of money. But after her male family members died, she became destitute.

Rabban Yohanan ben Zakkai and his students found the daughter of Nakdimon ben Gurion in a field. She was so poor that she was eating barley in a dung heap left for animals. Rabban Yohanan ben Zakkai remembered her inheritance, and asked how she came to be so poor. She shared a proverb: "Salt for money is lacking" (*haser*), meaning, money comes and goes. Rabban Yohanan ben Zakkai reinterpreted this to mean that kindness [*hesed*] is salt for money, meaning that money disappears if it's not used for acts of kindness. He then asked about her father-in-law's money. She explained that all the family money had been combined and all of it was now gone.

Nakdimon ben Gurion's daughter asked Rabban Yohanan ben Zakkai if he remembered signing her ketubah. He told his students yes, and remembered there was a lot of money promised to her. He then cried out that Israel is fortunate because, "when Israel performs the will of God, no one can rule over them; when Israel doesn't perform the will of God, God delivers them into the hand of a lowly nation." He added, "not only that, but even into the hand of the animals of a lowly nation," like the suffering daughter of Nakdimon ben Gurion, forced to eat the barley left for the animals. Nakdimon ben Gurion lost all his money because he failed to give enough to charity; now his daughter had to beg for charity after his death.

The story continues as the Gemara then points out that Nakdimon ben Gurion did give to charity – he gave woolen garments to the poor. The Gemara attempts to reconcile this example in two different ways. First, it's possible that he gave these garments to the poor "for his own honor." Maybe his motivation was to make himself appear charitable, or to show that this expense meant nothing to him because his wealth was so vast. Second, the Gemara suggests that because he had so much wealth, he should have been giving far more than these garments. Whatever the reason, the Sages believed the daughter of Nakdimon ben Gurion was punished for her male family members' lack of charitable giving, despite the inheritance set aside for her.

PASSAGES

Talmud b. Ketubot 66b

CONTEXT

Before the destruction of the Temple, Nakdimon ben Gurion was one of the wealthiest residents of Jerusalem. It's possible that his wealth – and his daughter's – was lost in the destruction of the Temple. Rabban Yochanan was the rabbinic leader who stepped up after the destruction of the Temple. When he sees Nakdimon ben Gurion's daughter, he laments her destitution as yet another repercussion of the Temple's destruction.

This story also appears in a *tosefta*, which is far more critical of Nakdimon ben Gurion's daughter. In the Talmud, it seems the rabbis might be accusing her of losing her money, but it isn't clear. In the *tosefta*, the rabbis refuse to give her money and she curses them. The rabbis say that she will end up foraging in horse manure for food.

Either way, the text is designed to show how far the daughter of the wealthiest man in Jerusalem has fallen in the wake of the Temple's destruction – from having money for perfume to smelling of dung. The story is also a warning to give according to your means, and to give with the right intentions, or risk endangering the lives of your dependents in the future.

AGGADAH

Did they leave her where they found her, in the dung heap, eating barley left for animals? Nakdimon ben Gurion's daughter was destitute. When she asked the Rabbi who signed her *ketubah* for help, he asked where the money went. Was it an accusation, or was he just surprised? Either way, did he then help her?

She responded with a proverb: "Salt for money is lacking" (*haser*), meaning, money comes and goes. Instead of helping her, Rabban Yohanan ben Zakkai continued to focus on his own question: How did this happen?

Perhaps trying to appeal to their shared connection, she asked, "My teacher, do you remember when you signed on my marriage contract?" A plea: "Do you remember? Can you help me?" The story says that he turned to his students instead, and recalled her large dowry. Weeping, he continued, "How fortunate are you, Israel, for when Israel performs the will of the Omnipresent, no nation or tongue can rule over them; and when Israel does not perform the will of the Omnipresent, He delivers them into the hand of a lowly nation. Not only are they delivered into the hand of a lowly nation, but even into the hand of the animals of a lowly nation," referring to the animals whose food Nakdimon's daughter was forced to scavenge.

Did God punish Nakdimon's daughter because her male family members failed to give charitably? Does it matter? She asked for help, and Rabban Yohanan ben Zakkai justified her suffering with theology. It was a teachable moment – but the text does not mention if he helped her.

In their commentary, the Sages considered Rabban Yohanan ben Zakkai's argument that her male family members were uncharitable. Looking at examples of Nakdimon's giving, they imagined that he didn't give enough, considering his wealth, or that he gave for the wrong reasons.

Questions about philanthropic motivations are fascinating, and Jewish laws about *tzedakah* are important. But after the Sages discussed these issues, there's no mention of Nakdimon ben Gurion's daughter. They didn't tell us what happened to her, so we'll never know.

PROMPTS

- Sometimes it's helpful to consider the systemic reasons behind an individual's poverty, and sometimes it's more important to support that person outright. In this situation, the Sages decided to focus on the "why." What do you think about that choice?
- How do you respond when someone asks for help? What factors influence your response?
- How do you decide who and how to help?
- What does it mean to give charitably for the right reasons? What does it mean to give for the wrong reasons?

Heather Paul *is a Hillel educator, a writer, ritual artist, rabbinical student, and camp enthusiast.*

LEMON, SAFFRON, AND BARLEY RISOTTO

I chose to honor the Daughter of Nakdimon ben Gurion's riches-to-rags story by creating a nourishing barley dish.

I chose to make this risotto with barley (instead of rice) and saffron as the key ingredients, chosen especially to contrast one another. They are opposite ends of the spectrum: one is a humble grain and the other is more expensive than gold.

Cooked slowly, and with lots of great stock, risotto is one of the most comforting dishes. The comforting and satiating dish has subtle saffron and earthy turmeric flavors that are cut through by the brightness of lemon.

Prep Time: 15 minutes
Cook Time: 1 hour
Yield: 2 servings

Tools:

- Cutting board
- Knife
- Lemon zester
- Measuring cups and spoons
- Saucepan
- Stirring spoon

Ingredients:

- 1 onion, finely diced
- 1 tbsp olive oil
- A few sprigs of thyme
- 1½ tsp saffron
- 1 tsp turmeric
- 1 cup (190g) pearl barley
- Zest of one lemon
- Juice of half a lemon
  (or more to taste)
- 7 cups vegetable stock
  (homemade or store-bought)
- 1 tbsp extra virgin olive oil
- Salt and pepper to taste

Optional garnishes:

- Thyme leaves
- Gold leaf

Instructions:

1. Finely dice the onion and gently fry in the olive oil on medium heat.
2. Add the thyme and some salt and keep stirring until the onions are soft and golden in color.
3. Meanwhile, heat the stock to boiling, then remove from the heat. Add the saffron and let infuse for a few minutes, until the color starts to seep into the liquid.
4. Add the turmeric to the onion mix and keep stirring, not letting the onions catch on the bottom of the pan.
5. Add the dry barley and coat in the onion and thyme mix. Stir until the barley starts to toast, adding a little more olive oil if necessary.
6. Add a ladle of the hot stock to the barley mixture. Stir until the liquid is absorbed by the grain.
7. Continue adding stock ladle by ladle until you run out of stock or until the grain is about ¾ cooked – it should be firm and a little chewy. The liquid will have thickened from the starch in the barley and the risotto will have a relaxed and soupy consistency.
8. Add the lemon zest.
9. Once the barley is cooked completely, turn off the heat and remove the thyme stalks.
10. Season to taste with salt, pepper, a generous squeeze of lemon, and a drizzle of extra virgin olive oil. Cover with a lid and leave to relax for 5 minutes before stirring.
11. Serve, adding garnish with herbs and/or gold leaf for extra decadence.

Joanna Nissim lives in London and spends as much time as possible in Israel. Joanna is a passionate cook with a focus on Iraqi-Indian food.

THE DAUGHTER OF RABBI HANINA
BEN DOSA / ברתיה דרבי חנינא בן דוסא

STORY

One Shabbat eve, Rabbi Hanina ben Dosa saw his daughter looking quite melancholy. He approached her and asked, "My daughter, why are you so sad?" Pointing at the candlesticks, which usually contained enough oil to burn for the entire Shabbat, she replied, "I made a mistake, and instead of oil, I poured vinegar into the candlesticks. Now we won't have light for the entirety of the Shabbat." Rabbi Hanina ben Dosa smiled and said, "Is anything too great for God?" And with his words, a miracle occurred and the candlesticks burned from sundown to nightfall. The family was able to light the *Havdalah* candle, which ends the Shabbat, with the light from the still-burning Shabbat candles.

PASSAGES

Talmud b. Taanit 25a

CONTEXT

One of the few outright stated prohibitions on the Shabbat is kindling a fire.[1] For this reason, marking the beginning or end of Shabbat with fire is so important.

Lighting the Shabbat candles is considered one of three mitzvot set aside for women.[2]

Nowhere in the Talmud does it explicitly say what may be burned for the Shabbat candles. At the time of the Talmud, the primary material for lighting was oil.

Rabbi Hanina ben Dosa was quite poor. That his daughter used vinegar instead of oil could have been a result of poverty: perhaps they simply had no oil in their house. Perhaps most importantly, Rabbi Hanina ben Dosa is noted throughout the Talmud for his miracle-making capabilities. Though this story does not explicitly state that Rabbi Hanina ben Dosa is

---

1. Exodus 35:3.
2. Talmud.b.Berakhot 31b.

responsible for the vinegar burning for twenty-five hours, it can be added to the many examples of his unwavering faith and mystical accomplishments.

AGGADAH

This story is about what to use for lighting Shabbat candles, and – perhaps more importantly – about how a father responds to his daughter. He notices her distress and responds by aiming to soothe her worry, and educate her in the practice of prayer and faith. Rabbi Hanina ben Dosa's daughter and her father both wish to protect each other from shame.

Rabbi Hanina ben Dosa is a *tzaddik*, a righteous person, and a miracle worker. He has a direct prayer line to the Divine. He is also poor. At times his family does not even have the money to buy bread, let alone extra money for wine and oil for Shabbat.

One Friday, the daughter of Rabbi Hanina ben Dosa was helping to prepare for Shabbat when she found only one bottle where there were usually two. Looking through their small one-room home, she could not find a second bottle. Finally taking the one bottle, which she believed to be vinegar, she decided to pour the liquid into the vessels for Shabbat lights regardless: in doing this, she would spare her father the knowledge that they could not afford new oil for the Shabbat lights.

She told her father that she mistook a jar of vinegar for oil to protect her father from the reality that they did not have enough money for the mitzvah of lighting candles on Shabbat. She loved her father and did not want him to feel guilty or diminished. The daughter believed that her father added greatness to the world, even if they didn't have the material things to show for it.

When Rabbi Hanina ben Dosa looked at his daughter, he saw a girl overcome with grief at the potential of having violated a *mitzvah*. Before responding to her explanation, he looked closely at the vessels of liquid and saw that she was actually mistaken – she *did* in fact fill the Shabbat vessels with oil.

Rather than correct her, he wanted to honor the good that he saw in the mistake she confessed to have made, which was simply confusion itself! Instead of telling his daughter that she actually poured oil in the lamps, he used the situation as a teachable moment. He soothed her worry and demonstrated the practice of prayer and faith.

Rabbi Hanina's daughter knew that her father performed miracles and that his words of prayer had power. What she didn't know is why. The truth of his power is that he saw no distinction between everyday occurrences and miracles. All comes from God, and all is considered a miracle in his experience. This is the teaching he wished to impart to his daughter. He wanted her to see and understand that everything is a blessing: fire from oil is just as much a miracle as fire from vinegar.

In striving to protect her father, the daughter's eyes were opened to the possibility of seeing through a new lens of deeper faith.

PROMPTS

- In this text, lighting Shabbat candles is important. Which of the Jewish rituals hold a special meaning in your life?
- Can you think of a time when you have hidden or obscured something to protect someone you love? How was it helpful? How was it harmful?
- What ordinary occurrence might you transform into seeing as a miracle?

Rabbi Elyssa Joy Austerklein *is an artist, yogi, musician, devoted mother, wife, and congregational rabbi.*

QUICK PICKLED QUINCE

The story of the daughter of Rabbi Hanina ben Dosa is bittersweet. On the one hand, she and her father both strive to protect each other from distress; on the other hand, we know that the family is very poor. To honor the Rabbi's daughter, I have created a recipe that is both sweet and tart: pickled quince. Quince is a fruit that has been cultivated since ancient times and is specifically mentioned in the Talmud. Quince's distinctive aroma makes it a delight to cook with and eat. Throughout the Sephardic world, you will find quince cooked with meat in savory stews or made into rosy-colored jams and jellies.

Here, we cook the quince in vinegar to create a sweet-tart fruit pickle. Serve these spiced, pickled quince slices as an accompaniment to add zing and punch that rounds out any meal.

Prep Time: 30 minutes

Cook Time: 30 minutes

Yield: 3 pints

Tools:

- Cheesecloth
- Ladle
- Large saucepan
- Melon baller
- Sharp knife and cutting board
- Slotted spoon
- 3 pint jars

Ingredients:

- 3⅓ cups apple cider vinegar
- 2¾ cups granulated sugar
- 1 cinnamon stick
- 2 dried red chiles
- Zest of 1 lemon, peeled into strips
- 8 whole cloves
- 12 whole peppercorns
- 4 green cardamom pods
- 3 lbs quince (about 8 quince)

Instructions:

1. Combine the vinegar, sugar, cinnamon stick, chiles, and lemon zest in a large saucepan. Tie the cloves, peppercorns, and cardamom pods in a spice bag or square of cheesecloth and add it to the saucepan as well.

2. Bring the mixture to a boil over medium heat, stirring occasionally to dissolve the sugar.

3. Peel and quarter the quince. Cut off the ends and cores. If any gritty white part remains after removing the core, use a melon baller or spoon to remove it as well. Cut each quarter into two or three slices depending on the size.

4. Add the quince slices to the vinegar brine, turn the heat down to low, cover, and simmer until the quince is tender enough to be pierced by a knife, about 15 minutes. Remove from heat. Pick out and discard the chiles, cinnamon stick, and spice bag.

5. Using a slotted spoon, ladle the quince slices into clean, warm pint jars. Cover with brine and wipe the rims clean. Close and transfer the jars to the refrigerator. (You will likely have brine left over. Use it to flavor beverages or salad dressings.)

6. Allow the jars to cure for one to two weeks before opening.

Emily Paster is a cookbook author, food writer, and culinary instructor specializing in global Jewish cuisine. She lives near Chicago with her husband and children.

THE DAUGHTER OF THE EMPEROR /
ברתיה דקיסר

STORY

The Emperor's daughter has a dynamic relationship with the rabbis.

Upon meeting the renowned Rabbi Yehoshua ben Hananya for the first time, the Emperor's daughter remarks, "Alas for your beautiful wisdom, which has to be contained in such an ugly vessel!" The Rabbi replies, "Does your father keep his wine in clay jars?" and suggests such an exalted family should keep wine in vessels of gold and silver.

Hearing this from his daughter, the Emperor orders all the wine of their household to be put in containers of silver and of gold. In time, all the wine in the new containers goes sour. The Emperor asks his daughter who told her to do it, and he has the Rabbi brought before him to discuss the issue. The Rabbi explains that he said to her the same thing she said to him and he illustrates that finest material is best preserved in the most humble of vessels. The Emperor comments, "But there are handsome people who are wise and learned," to which the Rabbi replies, "Ah, but if they were ugly, just think how much more wise and learned they would be!"

In a second story the Emperor asks Rabban Gamliel, the leader of the Judean community in the Roman Empire, about resurrection, and if "dust comes to life."

The Emperor's daughter interrupts with a parable: "Imagine there are two crafters in our city. One makes bowls out of water, and one makes bowls out of clay. Which one is more impressive?" Her father replied that "of course, the crafter who can make bowls out of water is much more impressive."

His daughter continued, "And a crafter who has the skill to make a bowl from water will of course have the skill to make a bowl from clay! This is how it is with the God of the Jews – if God was able to create the whole world from water, then of course that God will be able to resurrect people from dust."

PASSAGES[1]

Talmud.b.Taanit.7a–7b

CONTEXT

The first story is a digression within a long chain of rabbinic meditations on different metaphors for Torah. Immediately after the end of our story, the Talmud likens Torah to water, wine, and milk, and makes explicit what is implicit in Rabbi Yehoshua's lesson to his imperial family: "Just as water, wine and milk should only be kept in vessels made from the most humble of materials, so, too, Torah learning is best preserved within those people who live life with the most humility" (Talmud.b.Taanit.7b).

The second story comes in the middle of a series of stories wherein the rabbis debate issues of Jewish law, theology, and practice with non-Jewish royalty, including Alexander the Great and Cleopatra. These stories provide an opportunity to show the rabbis engaging as intellectual equals with the elites of their time, and to unfold the reasoning and textual support for some of the most important concepts in Judaism.

At a time when the rabbis were navigating a complex relationship with the Roman government, the Emperor's daughter may have been a safer character to imagine themselves debating with.

AGGADAH

An Instagram influencer started each day by posting a question: mundane, deeply philosophical, or anywhere in between. She asked her followers to message her their answers, and reposted the ones she liked most.

As her audience expanded, so did the kinds of questions she asked. One day, she posted an image of a prominent intellectual who had out-of-proportion and traditionally unattractive facial features. She asked her followers, "Why is such beautiful wisdom contained in such an ugly vessel?"

---

1.   See also, Talmud.b.Sanhedrin.91a, Talmud.b.Taanit.7a–7b, Talmud.b.Hullin.60a, Talmud.b.Megilah.17b.

Soon after, the scholar's name appeared in her DM's. His message simply asked how she stored her wine. She replied, "In the bottles it comes in." The scholar said, "Oh, someone as important as you should store wine in beautiful containers like these silver and gold carafes on Etsy."

She ordered the carafes, and posted all about "wine storage for beautiful people." But when she went to drink the wine, it was sour. She wrote back to the scholar, asking, "Why would you tell me to do something so foolish?" The scholar replied, "Just as wine is best kept in humble containers, so too is wisdom." She took a day to think about it, and then posted their entire text correspondence as the final post in the wine storage series.

After that experience, she began posting deeper and thornier questions, and inviting leading thinkers to answer them with her on Instagram Live. She had a well-known rabbi as a guest, and she read her a question sent by one of her followers: "I don't understand the idea of resurrection of the dead – haven't the dead returned to dust? Does dust come back to life?"

The rabbi took a moment to think, and just as she was about to open her mouth and answer, the influencer jumped in: "Oh! I know this!" Addressing her followers, she said, "Imagine there are two potters – one of them can make bowls from water, and one of them can make bowls from clay. Which one's work is more miraculous?"

Checking the comments on the livestream, she saw that the vast majority agreed the potter who could make bowls out of water was a true miracle worker. "And of course, the one who could make a bowl out of water would be able to make one from clay, right?" Caught up in her excitement about the parable, she rushed on without checking for responses or glancing at her guest, "and God made the whole entire world from water, so of course God can perform the miracle of bringing the dust of humanity back to life!"

Catching her breath, she turned to look at the rabbi, expecting to see a proud smile or at least a pleased expression of agreement. Instead, she saw a slightly puzzled frown. Late that night, rewatching the recording of the livestream, she realized she never heard the rabbi's voice at all.

PROMPTS

- In conversation, what does it mean to be a good ally?
- What choices do we make in order to gain understanding of the world beyond our own "palace" (our home, our city, our country, our comfort zone…)?
- What is the difference between active listening and passive listening?

Rabbi Megan Doherty *(she/her) is Director of Hillel and Campus Jewish Life at Oberlin College. She studies Talmud, Midrash, and chassidic texts for fun.*

RED WINE MUSHROOM SOUP, SERVED IN BAKED SQUASH

The Emperor's daughter learns that wisdom isn't reliant on an attractive exterior. This recipe makes this idea edible by offering a red wine-based soup encased in a baked acorn squash.

This dish is a soup and a bowl all in one!

Prep Time: 20 minutes
Cook Time: 1 hour 20 minutes
Yield: 4 servings

Tools:

- Baking sheet
- Cutting board
- Measuring cups
- Sharp knife
- Soup pot
- Spoon

Ingredients:

- 2 acorn squash
- ½ large onion
- 1 clove garlic
- 5 mushrooms
- 1 14-oz can (400g) diced tomatoes
- 1 cup (240ml) water
- ½ cup (120ml) red wine (recommendation: Merlot)
- Salt
- Pepper
- Red chili flakes
- 1 bay leaf
- Olive oil
- Parsley (optional)

Instructions:

1. Preheat oven to 425° F (220° C).
2. Cut the acorn squash into two halves, scoop out the seeds, and hollow out the centers with a spoon. The seeds can be set aside for optional toasting later.
3. Coat the entire squash halves lightly with oil.
4. Put squash halves on a lined baking sheet, yellow side up, and season with salt and pepper.
5. Bake squash for one hour. Meanwhile, prepare the soup:
6. Dice the onion and crush the garlic, then saute with a little oil in a soup pan until soft.
7. Cut mushroom tops in half and thinly slice. Add them to the soup pot with a small pinch of salt, and stir.
8. Add the can of diced tomatoes and stir.
9. Add the water and wine, a pinch of red chili flakes (to taste), and a bay leaf.
10. Leave soup to simmer for 20 minutes.
11. Remove the cooked squash from the oven and ladle soup into the hollows.
12. Turn the oven down to 350° F (180° C) and return the soup-filled squash to the oven for another 20 minutes.
13. Remove from the oven, garnish with parsley, and serve.

Tani Prell's (she/her) focus is education, arts, and Judaism. She is the Chicago Director for 18Doors, an anti-racism educator and consultant, and brunch connoisseur.

STORY

Donag[1] is a young girl, the daughter of Rav Nahman and Yalta. She is mentioned in the Talmud in the context of an exchange regarding local customs.

The story tells us that Rav Yehuda comes to live for a time in Nehardea, to learn with Rav Shmuel. While there he meets Donag's father, Rav Nahman. As the two rabbis begin to get to know each other, they discuss their local customs and cultures – in particular how they differently interpret the meaning of specific words and Jewish laws.

Later on, when Rav Yehuda is visiting Rav Nahman at home, he says to Rav Yehuda, "My daughter Donag will come pour us a drink." Rav Yehuda is surprised and replies that his teacher Rav Shmuel has said that one may not use women in this way, no matter their age.

The back-and-forth banter continues between these two colleagues, with the next discussion being about whether a man should greet another man's wife, or send greetings to a woman at all.

Meanwhile, Rav Nahman's wife, Yalta, overhears her husband's vexing discussion with Rav Yehuda. Disliking what she hears, she sends a message to her husband asking him to end the meeting, to protect him from becoming linked with an "ignoramus."

PASSAGES

Talmud b. Kiddushin 70a

CONTEXT

Donag appears in a discussion which takes place in her parents' home. Her mother, Yalta, may have been the daughter of an exilarch,[2] and is depicted in the Talmud as strong-willed. Donag's father, Rav Nachman, was an influential judge, whose wealth and privileged connections afforded him power.[3]

---

1. Talmud.b.Kiddushin.70a 16.
2. A nonreligious leader of the Jewish community in Babylonia for the first 12 centuries CE.
3. Sefaria "Rav Nachman."

Upon first reading, the discussion about whether or not Donag may be called on to serve drinks reflects well on Rav Yehuda. However, the Talmudic text surrounding this exchange shows Rav Nachman making several attempts to be hospitable to Rav Yehuda. Rav Yehuda accompanies his rebuttal of each and every offer with references to the teachings of Rav Shmuel – pointing out how they contrast with his host's behavior.

With the mention of Donag, the discussion moves to the proper role of women within the household. Rav Yehuda seems to speak against "using" Donag to serve drinks. The men go on to discuss platonic communication between unmarried men and women, via the suggestion that Rav Yehuda might send greetings to Yalta. Rav Yehuda quotes his teacher and says that men may not speak to women because their voice is considered nakedness.[4]

Initially Donag's story seems to cast Rav Yehuda as an early feminist ally. However, when this excerpt is seen in its broader Talmudic context, an altogether different perspective on Rav Yehuda is revealed. In fact, his objection to Donag serving drinks is not based on concern for female servitude, but rather linked to his belief that men should not communicate or interact with women and girls outside of their own family.

AGGADAH

Donag's story sits within a larger story about how customs vary based on geographical location and culture. In this case, the two male rabbis have different ways of understanding the definition of words and Jewish customs.

Donag's story raises the question of the proper role of women and girls in the household. The particular story about Donag (and Yalta) is about welcoming guests. Rav Nachman, attempting to be hospitable to his guest, offers his guest food and drinks himself. Then he suggests that his daughter could pour them drinks, then mentions that his wife, Yalta, might say hello. Each offer of hospitality is refused.

What are the sentiments behind Rav Nachman's relationship with Donag? Was Rav Nachman including his daughter in the family's custom of welcoming guests, thinking that by serving drinks she would increase the household's hospitality toward Rav Yehuda? Was he

4. Talmud b. Kiddushin.70a: 17.

treating her like a servant asking her to do something he thought was beneath him, or what he thought was the role of women and girls in the home? Or was he reaching out to his daughter and wife for help as he was getting more and more exacerbated by a combative guest who was unrelentlessly trying to one-up him?

We cannot know what was in Rav Nachman's mind or heart when he offered drinks served by Donag. We can infer some from other interactions he had in the Talmud. (See the chapter in this book on Yalta, in which Rav Nachman insists that his wife be given a cup of wine[5] so she can recite a blessing.) We can infer that Rav Nachman was perhaps flummoxed by people's responses to his request for drinks for others, particularly when he attempted to include women.

This story of Donag showcases an enduring truth and a lesson learned. First, the role of girls in the home is determined by family and community customs and norms. Second, if you want to offer a person a drink or food as a gesture of hospitality in your home, it's best to get up and do it yourself no matter your gender or your age.

PROMPTS

- What do you think was in Rav Nachman's heart and mind when he suggested Donag serve drinks?
- Do you think Yalta would have allowed her daughter to serve drinks in their home?
- What did you learn about hospitality toward guests in your family of origin?
- What is your personal approach to hospitality in your home? Do you have any particular customs, and how (if at all) does gender factor into these customs?

Kenden Alfond

---

5. Talmud.b.Berachot 51a–b.

KVASS: FERMENTED RYE BREAD
AND RAISIN BEVERAGE

As a society, we need to ensure that girls' strengths and talents are not wasted. Donag, once released from her serving duty, can share all of her unique talents with the world, not letting them go to waste.

As a society, we also need to reduce our food waste. A fermented drink made from stale bread, Kvass is an authentic no-waste recipe.

This recipe is a classic fermented drink. It is made from dark rye bread, which must contain rye malt. While the assembly of the ingredients is quick, the recipe takes a few days to ferment.

Rich in probiotics, Kvass has a strong fermented taste with a hint of sweetness and is typically served cold.

Prep Time: 10 minutes
Cook Time: 3 hours
Ferment Time: 4 days
Yield: 20–25 glasses

Tools:

- Cheesecloth/kitchen towel
- Large boiling pot
- Toaster/oven
- Large glass container with lid
- Mesh strainer
- Funnel
- Measuring utensils
- Flip-top glass bottles, or glass 2-liter bottle

Ingredients:

- 7–10 slices (400g) dark rye bread
- 2.64 gallons (10 liters) water
- 1 cup (160g) raisins
- 2 tbsp dry active yeast
- 3½ cups (450g) sugar

Instructions:

1. Toast sliced dark rye bread until very dark.

2. Heat water to boiling. Add the toasted rye bread and half the raisins. Turn off the stove and let it sit until the water is warm.

3. Remove the bread. Then, add dry active yeast and sugar to the steeped liquid. Stir, then leave the mixture to sit for 12 hours.

4. Strain the liquid into a large jar. Add the remaining raisins or other dried fruit and let sit for a few days. After a few days the fermented drink should be bubbly.

5. Transfer to bottles and store in the refrigerator for up to 7–10 days.

Alexandra Corwin is mom to Rivka and wife to Jacob. She is an educator, writes poetry, and creates vegan versions of her family's Peruvian recipes.

EM / אם

STORY

Em is a female expert in neonatal care and child development. Her knowledge concerns such topics as the proper management of circumcision wounds, urgent neonatal care, and breastfeeding. She also offers guidance on the appropriate age for boys to begin religious education, and for children to observe fasting. Her expertise is referred to in twenty-six different locations in different Tractates of the Babylonian Talmud, the Bavli.

We never meet Em; we hear about her. Her voice is mediated through male rabbis' voices.[1] The first time she is referred to is in the brief banter between male rabbis concerning who honors their mother more in the Bavli. She is *Em*: mother; a mother perhaps, or a woman named Em. The Bavli defines her as Abaye's foster-mother or nurse (מְרַבִּינְתֵּיה) given that his birth mother had died while birthing him.[2] Abaye was a major Babylonian *Amora*[3] (b.278–d.338 CE), having served as president of the Pumbedita Academy. Abaye refers to her when he wants to impart her expertise and knowledge when useful to the discussion. Ravina also twice refers to a woman called Em.

Em's true identity will be eternally disputed. Em could have been Abaye's foster-mother, his nurse, his aunt, a slave in his uncle's home, or a well-known woman in a position of authority. Whatever the precise nature of Em's relationship to Abaye, it was such that he learned from her while overhearing discussions taking place within his earshot, watching her, or asking her directly. Abaye benefited from Em's knowledge and expertise so much that he readily shared it with other thought leaders of the time, never concealing its origin. The rabbis recorded her expertise in the Babylonian Talmud.

PASSAGES

Shabbat 134a

---

1. Catherine Fonrobert, *Menstrual Purity* (Stanford: Stanford University Press, 2000).
2. Talmud.b.Kiddushin 31b.
3. Refers to Jewish scholars of the period from about 200 to 500 CE, who "said" or "told over" the teachings of the Oral Torah.

CONTEXT

Em's voice is unique in rabbinic literature because of the sheer number of times that she is cited.[4] Her advice is considered useful medicinally, socially, and eventually halachically.[5] Her words are taken so seriously that they are used centuries later in halachic texts and Responsa literature.

In Shabbat 134a:12–14, Em's expertise brings medical wisdom to the discussion of how to care for a circumcision wound. Em "is certainly the person who knows more about the circumcision wound in the Bavli than any other authority."[6] In Talmud.b.Ketubot.50a, Abaye shares Em's child development expertise of when children, particularly young males, are ready to fast and to learn Bible and Mishnah.

These stories are also archival: the later Talmudic editors wanted Abaye's citation of Em's expertise to be readily available to rabbis reading the text. The rabbis and editors of the Babylonian Talmud present Em as an authority, without being preceded or followed by the citation of a parallel remedy or incantation by one of the rabbis.[7]

AGGADAH

Through mimetic tradition, what some would refer to as Oral Torah, Abaye learned from Em, and in turn taught other rabbis how to practice.

Em's expertise – mainly in neonatal care, child development, folk medicine, amulets, and gossip – falls firmly under the rubric of traditional women's occupation.

Throughout history and still today, many make an erroneous assumption that male rabbis in the Bavli learned only from men, and only in a *beit midrash* outside of the home. Em's transmission of knowledge to Abaye illustrates another model of teaching and learning that is not text-based in third-century Babylonia: a wise maternal figure sharing information with a younger (male), most likely in the home and most certainly not in a *beit midrash*.

---

4. Fonrobert.
5. see: Uziel, o.c. 22:13; Ohr Zarua, Volume II, 100:1.
6. Tal Ilan, *Massekhet Hullin: Text, Translation, and Commentary* (Germany: Mohr Siebeck, 2017), 247
7. Fonrobert, 155–56.

During the time of Em and Abaye, the home was the locus of education, healthcare, and religious observance. Since modernity, these areas of life extended outside of the home, taking place in specialized locations: schools, synagogues, hospitals.

As social development enabled women access to life outside of purely domestic positions, the essential role of the home as an arena of religious ritual and education has fundamentally changed. We can ask ourselves: in our modern context, how do we teach and live our Jewish lives in our homes?

Today, men and women can play a role in the mimetic tradition of passing on Torah, just as Em passed it down to Abaye.

PROMPTS

- Are there any particular mitzvot (commandments) or other responsibilities for which you are obligated for your household because you are a woman? If not, do you think that there should be? If not, why not?
- Are there any areas of expertise that belong primarily to women, such as those mastered by Em? Think of today's professions that are dominated by women, such as midwifery, preschool and kindergarten education, assistant roles in medicine and administration. Are women socialized into these roles, or is there some gender-specific expertise or skill?
- What are we missing when we lack a mimetic tradition of Oral Torah to pass down to our daughters and granddaughters? Do we want to, and how can we get this back?
- Is there space today for women's voices and expertise to go undisputed in Judaism, like Em's advice? Do we find today that rabbis and other communal leaders depend on women's advice for practice and observance, like Abaye did with Em? If not, why not?

Rabbi Chasya Uriel Steinbauer, *Founder of the Institute for Holiness: Kehilat Mussar, lives her purpose through Mussar Mindfulness, Torah, the Dharma, and Insight Meditation.*

GRANDMOTHER'S BORSCHT

This recipe is from my grandmother Miryam. It is a sweet and sour, earthy and herby borscht recipe. She brought it with her to the United States from Ukraine in the 1970s. Making and eating this soup instantly takes me back to her, the feeling of being with her in her kitchen.

Like Em, the true origin of borscht is often in dispute. Borscht recipes differ from family to family, but for all Ukrainians this soup is a staple that is often passed down matrilineally. Borscht, like Em, is a source of great nourishment.

Borscht is made of the earth's most nutrient-dense, easy-to-grow ingredients. It is naturally filling and includes immune-boosting ingredients like beetroot, garlic, cabbage, and fresh herbs. It is sweet from beets, and bright and a little sour from tomatoes. I add potatoes to the soup, which turns a simple bowl of borscht into a filling meal. Served with a slice of crusty bread, this is the epitome of old-world comfort food.

The most important part of borscht is to use the recipe as a guide, and to make the soup to your own liking.

Prep Time: 20 minutes

Cook Time: 50–60 minutes

Yield: 6–8 servings

Tools:

- Box grater
- Food processor
- Knife
- Large soup pot

Ingredients:

- 1 lb (450g) beets, about 4 medium
- 1 lb (250g) carrots, about 2 large
- 1 large yellow onion, finely chopped
- 4–6 cloves garlic, finely minced
- ¾ lb (350g) Yukon gold or Dutch gold potatoes, diced into small bite-sized cubes
- 3 cups chopped cabbage and/or kale, chard, beet greens
- 2 tbsp dill stems, chopped fine
- ½ cup dill fronds, roughly chopped, plus more for garnish (a medium handful), or to taste
- ½ cup parsley leaves removed from stem, chopped (a medium handful), or to taste

- 2–3 tbsp oil (sunflower, avocado, or any neutral oil)
- 1 tbsp tomato paste
- ½ cup (100g) chopped fresh tomatoes, or canned plain tomato purée
- 10–12 cups (3 liters) water or homemade vegetable broth
- 1–2 bay leaves
- Juice of 1 lemon, or to taste
- 3 tsp kosher salt, or to taste

Toppings:

- Vegan sour cream (optional)
- Freshly chopped dill

Instructions:

1. Peel the beets and carrots. Finely slice using a food processor fitted with the shredding disc attachment, or using the medium-size hole of a box grater.

2. Prepare the rest of the ingredients: chop the onion, mince the garlic, dice the potatoes, chop the greens, chop the dill stems and fronds, and chop the parsley.

3. Add oil to a large pot on medium heat, then add the shredded beets, carrots, onion, and salt. Sweat the vegetables over medium heat for 8–10 minutes, or until the vegetables are softened.

4. Add the garlic to the pot and cook for 2–3 more minutes, or until the garlic releases its aroma and is no longer raw.

5. Add the tomato paste and tomatoes to the pot, and stir until well combined, another 1–2 minutes.

6. Add the diced potatoes, liquid, and bay leaf. Bring to a boil, then turn down the heat and simmer the borscht for 30 minutes, allowing the flavors to come together.

7. Add the chopped greens and chopped dill stems to the soup. Simmer for 15–20 more minutes, or until the greens and all of the vegetables are completely soft and tender.

8. Turn off heat, remove bay leaves and add chopped dill and parsley. Season to taste with lemon juice, salt and pepper.

9. Serve with a sprinkle of fresh chopped dill, and vegan sour cream if desired.

 Sonya Sanford *is a chef, writer, cooking instructor, and food stylist in Portland, Oregon. She shares recipes on her blog, Instagram, and The Nosher.*

HANNAH, THE WIFE OF RABBI MANI /
חנה אשתו של רבי מני

STORY

A very short story about Hannah, the named wife of Rabbi Mani, is located in an exchange between her husband and the great miracle-worker, Rabbi Yitzchak ben Elyashiv.

Rabbi Mani is fed up with his life circumstances, and approaches Rabbi Yitzchak with grievances about his wife, Hannah, and her family. First, his in-laws are too wealthy, and they cause him anguish because of the power they exert over him. Second, his wife is "unacceptable to him," as her appearance displeases him. When Rabbi Mani complains about his wife's appearance, Rabbi Yitzchak asks for her name, upon which Rabbi Mani simply says: Hannah.

In response to both of Rabbi Mani's complaints, Rabbi Yitzchak reverses the situation: his wife's family becomes poor, and his wife herself becomes beautiful. Rabbi Mani, however, finds no relief. Now his wife's family pesters him because they are poor and need assistance, and, while she's now attractive to him, Hannah has become arrogant due to her good looks. Frustrated, Rabbi Mani comes running back, and the miracle-worker restores the original order – the family to its wealth, and Hannah to her plain appearance.

PASSAGES

Talmud b. Taanit 23b

CONTEXT

Taanit 23a and 23b include stories about people who are able to change the course of nature with their prayers and incantations. Notably, other stories have more to do with miracles in the natural world, like rainfall. But in this story, the miracle-worker Rabbi Yitzchak ben Elyashiv changes a family's financial circumstances and a woman's appearance.

This story is not about Hannah, per se, but the presence of her name in the text is significant. It is not certain why the story was recorded, but it raises a number of questions about

Rabbi Mani's narrative. If his wife is being named here, then maybe the story is more about her and her power than it seems on the surface.

AGGADAH

Hannah (and her parents) are transformed in this story because of Rabbi Mani, a man governed by his grievances. Why does Rabbi Yitzchak ask Rabbi Mani for the name of his wife? After all, the miracle-worker does not ask for the names of the frustrating in-laws; he just works his wonders and reverses their fate without knowing anything about them.

The *Ben Yehoyada* claims that, as a rule, miracle-workers needed to be able to visualize the people that they were praying about. Rabbi Yitzchak may have been able to visualize a father-in-law, for example, since men were so visible and well-known. He may not have needed a name in order to have the right intention for his incantation. But, since women were less present in everyday public life, Rabbi Yitzchak may have needed more specificity about Rabbi Mani's wife in order to direct his prayer appropriately.

But what if there was a different reason that the miracle-worker was asking for her name? Names are humanizing. It can be far more difficult to dismiss, disregard, or dehumanize someone who has a name, than someone anonymous. By asking Rabbi Mani to say his wife's name aloud, Rabbi Yitzchak is, in a sense, challenging Rabbi Mani to confront what he's doing to another human being, a person with whom he is in an intimate relationship.

Furthermore, Hannah's name itself has significance here. In Hebrew, "Hannah" means grace. The Hebrew root of her name can be found alongside the word for beauty, for example in Proverbs 31:30: *"Sheker hachen v'hevel hayofi"* – grace is deceptive and beauty illusory."[1]

Perhaps, by asking Rabbi Mani to utter Hannah's name, Rabbi Yitzchak was pushing him to actually *see* the essence of his wife, and to acknowledge her. Saying her name out loud might remind him that objectification and acting on someone without her consent will only ever cause harm.

---

1. Trans. The JPS Tanakh, 1985. Recovered from: https://www.sefaria.org.il/Proverbs?lang=bi.

On one hand, this is a story about being careful what one wishes for. On the other, it is a cautionary tale about the dangers of looking for quick fixes, such as outsourcing one's relationship problems or family dynamics to a miracle-worker, to real-life problems.

In fact, Rashi notes that the word used for her haughtiness in response to her new appearance is related to the word "*geder,*" a fence, implying that she further cuts herself off from her partner as a result of his intervention. Certainly, as the story of Hannah and Rabbi Mani teaches, trying to change someone will never be a way to mend a relationship or bring people closer together.

PROMPTS

- Has someone ever tried to change you? How do you react when someone refuses to see you for who you really are?
- On the flipside, what are the redemptive possibilities for a relationship when you are truly seen?
- What does your name say about your essence? How does the way you are known to others communicate something central about who you are?

Rabbanit Dasi Fruchter *is the founder and spiritual leader of the South Philadelphia Shtiebel. Rabbanit Fruchter is a passionate educator and community builder.*

SEPHARDIC-STYLE CHILLED CUCUMBER SOUP

R' Mani was not able to accept his wife and her parents as they were. He was not in touch with Hannah as she truly was.

This is a simple dish with a few everyday ingredients to match this Talmudic character. In this soup, you get the real taste of the main ingredient.

Incredibly easy to make, this cucumber soup is perfect for a quick summer lunch or dinner. You can use the whole cucumber. You can also make good use of any leftover stale bread, so it is a completely wasteless recipe. It is refreshing, delicious, and healthy.

Prep Time: 20 minutes

Chill Time: 1–2 hours

Yield: 6 servings

Tools:

- Blender or food processor
- Cutting board
- Kitchen scale
- Large mixing bowl
- Lemon juicer
- Knife
- Spoon

Ingredients:

- 4 slices of stale bread (about 150–200g)
- 2 medium-sized organic cucumbers
- 2 garlic cloves, minced
- ⅓ cup (80ml) olive oil
- ⅓ cup (80ml) fresh lemon juice (the juice of 1½–2 lemons)
- 1 cup (80g) fresh mint leaves, chopped
- Salt and white pepper, to taste
- To garnish: ¼ cup (60ml) olive oil mixed with 1 tsp hot red pepper flakes

Instructions:

1. Soak the bread slices in water until soft. Squeeze dry.

2. Slice the whole cucumbers, skin on. Set aside a few slices to decorate.

3. Put all the ingredients into a food processor or blender and mix until a thick soup consistency is reached. Add some water if necessary.

4. Transfer to a bowl. Cover and chill in the fridge for 1–2 hours.

5. Before serving, decorate the soup with a few slices of cucumber and drizzle with the olive oil and red pepper flakes.

Sibel Pinto *was raised in Istanbul, Turkey. She is passionate about traditional Sephardi recipes, and is an author of a book about Sephardic food history.*

STORY

Hanina's daughter-in-law appears in the Talmud in a story alongside three men: Rabban Gamliel, Rabbi Yehoshua, and Hanina. The focus of the story is the definition of a mother's ritual purity status following a miscarriage. The particular teaching at the center of the story is about the designation of ritual purity depending on the specific type and form of the miscarried fetus.

Hanina, Rabbi Yehoshua's nephew, taught that a woman who miscarried a fetus that looks like a snake is considered *yoledes* (a woman who has given birth).

Rabbi Yehoshua tells Rabban Gamliel that Hanina taught this halacha. At the time, Rabban Gamliel was the *Nasi* and therefore in charge of the Sanhedrin. He had the authority to determine the final ruling of a halacha. Rabban Gamliel ruled that the determination of a miscarried baby as a fetus depended on how closely it resembled a human form. This would in turn determine whether the woman was considered a *yoledes* (a woman who has given birth) and was therefore *tameah* (ritually impure).

Rabban Gamliel requests that Rabbi Yehoshua bring Hanina before him to be reprimanded for his incorrect teaching. As Rabbi Yehoshua is walking to meet Rabban Gamliel, Hanina's daughter-in-law stops him. She calls out to Rabbi Yeshoshua with a question: "My teacher, what is the halacha with regard to a woman who discharges an item that looks like a snake?"

Rabbi Yehoshua, now knowing Rabban Gamliel's understanding of this case, gives the appropriate explanation and explains to Hanina's daughter-in-law that the woman would remain *tahor* (ritually pure), because a snake-like shaped miscarriage discharge does not resemble a miscarried human fetus.

Challenging him, Hanina's daughter-in-law replies, "But my mother-in-law said to me in your name that its mother is impure in such a case, and that you said to her: 'For what reason is she impure? It is because the pupil of a snake is round like that of a human.'"

Hearing her words, Rabbi Yehoshua remembers that he did indeed teach this halacha. He sends a message to Rabban Gamliel that Hanina, his nephew, made his ruling based on a teaching of Rabbi Yehoshua himself, and not based on his own understanding.

PASSAGES

Talmud b. Niddah 24b

CONTEXT

This story is an example of men discussing what happens to a woman's body and determining a halacha that affects a woman. In this story it is two women, Hanina's wife and daughter-in-law, who remind the men of how a halacha was taught and the reasoning behind it.

We learn from this story that it is important for a teacher to always teach the reasoning behind his halacha, along with the halacha itself, as that will ensure that the teacher remembers his halacha correctly.

AGGADAH

It seems that Hanina's daughter-in-law understood that her father-in-law, Hanina, was about to be scolded by Rabban Gamliel for something he had learned from his uncle, and not for a halacha that he had developed himself. She intervenes and defends Hanina by quoting his wife, her mother-in-law.

Hanina's daughter-in-law was learned and confident enough to become involved in this debate. Her intervention shows courage, a commitment to defend those wrongly accused, and her desire to preserve the integrity of the understanding of halacha.

That Hanina's daughter-in-law calls out to Rabbi Yehoshua, "my teacher," brings up some important questions regarding who is teaching whom. Do her words, "my teacher," imply that she learned Jewish law from a man? Yet, Hanina's daughter-in-law states that she learned the halacha from her mother-in-law. So we must ask – who taught Hanina's wife Jewish law?

Hanina's daughter-in-law calls Rabbi Yehoshua the teacher, yet in their subsequent interaction, it is she who teaches him. She reminds him of his own past teaching, and points out that it contradicts what he is telling her on this occasion. Is her choice to refer to him as "my teacher" a tactic to protect his pride, thus enabling her the space to challenge his view?

Hanina's daughter-in-law's story shows us how no matter who is considered to be a teacher at this time, women were also teaching Jewish law because they were learning it. In this story, we see how a teacher's incorrect teaching is rectified only by a student's insistent and bold questioning.

PROMPTS

- Why should women be taught halacha (Jewish law)?
- How is Jewish law practiced differently when women participate in its process?
- What does it say about a teacher when he is willing to take ownership over his own mistakes?

Yardaena Osband, MD, *is Assistant Clinical Professor of Pediatrics at New York Medical College. She resides in New York with her husband and children.*

MISCARRIAGE RECOVERY TEA

After a miscarriage, a woman's entire system needs time, nourishment, and care to recover. During this time, liquids and minerals are required, especially iron. Teas are a great way to give the body fluid along with replenishing many nutrients that have been lost.

The ingredients should all be in dried form and can be found in online organic / natural health stores. The measurements are given as a ratio so that you can adapt how much you make according to your preference.

Brew this tea one cup at a time or by the quartful. Leftover tea should be stored in the refrigerator for up to 2 days. Can be enjoyed warm or cold.

Prep Time: 5 minutes

Cook Time: 20 minutes

Yield: 8 cups of tea

Tools:

- Filtered water
- Measuring cups/spoons
- Medium saucepan with lid
- Non-metal spoon (wood, bamboo)
- Tea strainer

Ingredients:

- ½ cup (or 4 parts) red raspberry leaf
- ½ cup (or 4 parts) red clover
- ½ cup (or 4 parts) nettles
- ¼ cup (or 2 parts) hibiscus
- ¼ cup (or 2 parts) rose hips
- ⅛ cup (or 1 part) rose petals

Instructions:

1. Put all ingredients into a glass jar with a lid. I like to use Ball quart jars.
2. Mix well by shaking the jar or moving it around in circles until the mixture is well distributed.
3. Measure the amount of tea you'd like to brew and put it in a saucepan: use 2 tablespoons of tea mixture per cup of tea.
4. Add filtered water to the saucepan.
5. Bring to a boil, put the lid on the saucepan, and then reduce to a simmer for 5 minutes.
6. After 5 minutes, turn the stove off and let the tea rest for 15 minutes.
7. Strain, allow to cool slightly, and sip slowly.
8. May be sweetened with honey, agave, or your sweetener of choice.

Amy Green is an accomplished nutritious food business owner, magical herbal recipe writer, lover of Gaia. She loves sharing knowledge and bringing joy to the world.

HARUTA / חרותא

STORY

The name Haruta, given to the female protagonist of the story, is not her real name. We have no idea what she was called. She uses the name Haruta to assume a disguise. In the story, she is identified only as a wife of a respected Talmudic sage, Rav Hiyya bar Ashi.

He is a second- and third-generation *amora* from Babylon, which means that he lived around 250 to 320 CE. *Amoraim*, "those who say," were the Sages interpreting the oral tradition transmitted to them from the previous generations of scholars.

The Talmudical narrative starts by describing the Rabbi being concerned about an evil inclination that might lead him astray. His wife overhears him saying the prayer, "may the Merciful One save us from the evil inclination." She is bewildered as to the need for such prayer, since the Rabbi had long ceased having any intimacy with her. Whether desiring to test him or whether sincerely hoping to resume their sex life, she takes an idea from the Hebrew Bible and imitates the behavior of Tamar in Genesis 38.

וירא יהודה ויחשבה לזונה כי כסתה פניה:

When Judah saw her, he took her for a harlot; for she had covered her face.[1]

The wife of Rav Hiyya distracts him from the studies by repeatedly walking past him in the garden. Not realizing her true identity, the Rabbi propositions her and demonstrates the wonders of his agility by reaching for a pomegranate she demands as a payment.

All these interpretations come together in our story, where the supposedly righteous man succumbs to the temptation presented to him by a woman. After the physical intimacy, the wife of Rav Hiyya calmly goes back to her domestic duties. More precisely, she lights an oven, which is a very clear allusion to the power of sexual desire.

Her husband, noticing the fire, sits inside the oven, thus punishing himself for the blatant transgression of the Jewish law. He confesses his misdeed to the wife, while she tries to

---

1. Genesis 38:15.

console him, confessing her true identity. Adamantly insisting on his intention to commit a transgression, he starves himself to death.

PASSAGES

Talmud b. Kiddushin 81b

CONTEXT

The purpose of the story is twofold. Firstly, it serves as a warning against excessive and unnecessary piety, demonstrated by Rav Hiyya. It also can be read as praise of a woman performing a righteous deed, just like the biblical Tamar was praised.

The rabbis wanted to illustrate the shallowness of the outward piety of Rav Hiyya. His wife, taking the matter in her hands to get what is due to her according to the law – a sexual relationship with her husband – is far more righteous than him.

The pomegranate, of course, is a reference to it being the symbol of righteousness, as the rabbis believed it has 613 seeds corresponding to the number of commandments. It is also a symbol of fertility and love as stated in the Song of Songs.

AGGADAH

Of course, it was my idea. Haruta first tried to dissuade me. She said Hiyya would immediately recognize me even in disguise. I just snorted and kindly explained to her that my husband has stopped paying any attention to me a long time ago.

I guess in your day and age you would probably put your profile on Tinder with a picture of some random attractive woman and wait to see whether he takes the bait, but in our time, everything was way simpler.

So, I borrowed my friend's distinctive cloak and jewelry and even used her perfume. Righteous women did not adorn themselves with such trinkets. I should not have used the scent but, sod it, I was tired of righteousness. I had not had sex with my husband in many years. He claimed old age but I was sure that was just a flimsy pretext to avoid me.

I was right. The infamous old age did not prevent him from leaping to the top of a tree for the pomegranate I claimed to be my payment. I was sure he would see through my game there and then. What kind of prostitute takes payments in fruit?

Haruta laughed when I told her about my plan and predicted my utter failure at that stage. Well, she was wrong. Hiyya was so engrossed in catering to my whims that he did not even question my choice of payment.

I had secretly hoped he would recognize me in the end but he still thought he was dealing with the prostitute. Although it was so lovely, amidst the blossoming fruit trees, in the fleeting moment of the short Babylonian spring. I did not regret anything since I hoped he would listen to me afterward.

He rushed into the kitchen like a possessed person and tried to get into the fired-up oven. I expected him to confess the truth, and so he did. I knew he would not be able to hide anything from me. He was, after all, a decent person.

To my dismay, he did not listen, and only when I presented him with the clear signs of my true identity, he realized his mistake. In hindsight, maybe I should not have tricked him, but I was desperate. In the end, his obsession with his ideas of evil inside of himself kept him away from me. I've lost him forever.

PROMPTS

- The poet John Lyly said, "All is fair in love and war." Do you agree with this statement and is Rav Hiyya's wife's behavior fair to him?
- What about the conduct of Rav Hiyya himself? According to Jewish law, he is obligated to be intimate with his wife. In fact, the lack of intimacy is a valid ground for divorce. He clearly still experiences sexual desire. What do you think is behind his behavior?
- What would you do if you faced "Haruta's" dilemma? What would you do differently?

Nelly Shulman is a writer living in Saint Petersburg, Russia.

BEET, POMEGRANATE, AND PARSLEY SALAD

Haruta is willing to bend the truth because of the passion inside her being smothered by the lack of intimacy with her husband.

The deep, rich color of the beets reminds me of the fire burning in Haruta, the passion she was missing. I also included pomegranate – which has so much significance in Judaism.

This dish is citrusy, sweet, and a little bitter. A bit like a telenovela filled with drama and goodness, you just can't walk away from it or put it down.

Prep Time: 20 minutes
Chill Time: 10 minutes before serving
Yield: 4 servings

Tools:

- Cutting board
- Large salad bowl
- Medium prep bowl
- Patience to take out each pomegranate seed

Ingredients:

- 6 beets
- 1 large pomegranate
- 1 bundle chopped parsley
- 1 to 2 garlic cloves (minced)
- ½ lemon
- 1 tbsp apple cider vinegar
- ½ tbsp olive oil
- 1 tbsp raw honey or coconut sugar
- Salt and pepper to taste

Instructions:

1. Boil the beets to a perfect texture of not too soft or too hard. Set aside to cool.
2. Meanwhile, take the seeds out of the pomegranate and place them in a bowl in the refrigerator.
3. Wash the parsley and dry well.
4. Chop the cooled beets into small cubes, slice thinly, or grate according to your texture and presentation preference.
5. Add parsley, minced garlic, lemon, apple cider vinegar, and olive oil and toss gently.
6. Add pomegranate seeds and raw honey or coconut sugar and salt and pepper to your liking.
7. Do final toss at the table.
8. Enjoy. Bon Appétit. B'ta'avon.

Chaya Lev is a breast cancer survivor, storyteller, and dance teacher who made Aliyah.

STORY

There once was a woman whose mother-in-law hated her. The Talmud neither gives us the woman's name, nor the reason for her mother-in-law's hatred.

On a Friday night before Shabbat, the mother-in-law instructed her to use balsam oil to make herself beautiful. She went and adorned herself. When she returned, the mother-in-law ordered her: "Go light the lamp [for Shabbat]." She followed this instruction and, as she lit the lamp, she caught on fire and was consumed by flames.

The Talmud does not clarify whether the burns she suffered were fatal.

PASSAGES

Talmud b. Shabbat 26a

CONTEXT

The story comes in the middle of a Talmudic discussion about which fuels may be used to light the Shabbat lamp. Page 26a is devoted entirely to balsam oil. In the Middle East, balsam was used for both medical and cosmetic purposes and was rare and luxurious.

The Talmud concludes that one may not light on Shabbat with sap from balsam trees. The rabbis wonder why such a specialty item should not be used to celebrate Shabbat. They worry that the smell may tempt people to violate Shabbat by dipping their hands into the pot of oil. Another concern is that it's flammable and too dangerous for lighting. To illustrate this point, the rabbis relate the story of a mother-in-law who knows how dangerous the oil is and intentionally makes her daughter-in-law adorn herself with balsam oil before lighting the Shabbat lamp.

AGGADAH

She sat there, listless, thinking about her life. She monotonously moved through it, barely knowing that she was alive. She *was* alive, but wasn't living. She lived miles away from her family with a husband whom she didn't know and a mother-in-law who resented her. So, to survive, she stopped living. She walked through life in a catatonic state, quietly hoping for it to end.

On the eve of Shabbat, just as the ministering angels were imminently approaching, her silent prayers were answered. Her mother-in-law was orchestrating her death. So, she sat there, thinking of her past and arranging her future. As she obediently anointed her body in balsam oil, the medicine started to heal her. Only dreaming forward, with a nod to her past self, in a trance-like state, she followed her mother-in-law's orders and danced her way to the lamp.

Her dark, penetrating eyes stared at the match and gently struck it against the perfume bottle on the floor. She watched the sky erupt into flames creating the most beautiful candle lighting she had ever seen. And in that moment of eruption, she waved her hands three times over the flame and recited the blessing. As the fire was blazing and the sun was setting, the Shabbat Queen quietly whispered back, "You, who are rising up from this fire's blaze, let your spirit free. I bless you with love and incense."

PROMPTS

- When is a time that you felt like you were just robotically moving through life, without really being alive?
- If you find yourself in an unhealthy relationship with a family member or a person who claims to love you, what can you do?
- When is a time where something traumatic or difficult was followed by a deep healing?

Mollie Andron is an educator, midrashist, and wonderer. She lives in Brooklyn with her husband the clown and her daughter the unicorn.

CURRIED NETTLE VEGAN SAUSAGE ROLLS

The woman in this story is subjected to a singularly cruel fate at the hands of her mother-in-law. But she undergoes a beautiful transformation in the Aggadah. Similarly, this recipe combines vegan mince "meat" with a stinging plant and transforms them into something wonderfully nourishing.

A classic British Isles savory meat pastry gets a vegan edge here. Nettles (Urtica dioica), usually known for stinging, are highly medicinal and nutritious plants.

A golden puff pastry casing surrounds a filling of vegan mince and nettles spiced with curry powder. Nettles can replace spinach in almost any recipe. Their uniquely "woody" taste pairs wonderfully with the warm, complex notes of Indian curry.

Prep Time: 10 minutes
Cook Time: 25 minutes
Yield: approximately 20–25 small sausage rolls

Tools:

- Baking tray
- Baking paper
- Cooling rack
- Large frying pan or wok
- Large mixing bowl and wooden spoon
- Mezzaluna or sharp knife for chopping nettles
- Rubber gloves, scissors, and a bag or large bowl for picking nettles
- Rolling pin
- Pastry brush

Ingredients:

- 750g (26 oz) freshly picked nettles, gently rinsed and left to stand to ensure no tiny insects remain
- 10g (3.5 oz) vegan mince "meat"
- 1 tbsp vegetable oil
- 1 tbsp nutritional yeast flakes
- 1 tsp mild curry powder
- ½ tsp salt
- A good grind of black pepper
- 320g (11 oz) ready-rolled vegan puff pastry (or make your own!)
- ½ cup of any plant-based milk for coating the pastry

Instructions:

1. Wearing rubber gloves, use scissors to cut nettle leaves from your garden or a field – well away from exhaust fumes and litter! Younger, smaller leaves are tastier – don't pick from plants that are flowering as they can be toxic.

2. Gently rinse the nettles, then leave to stand for a while to give any tiny insects the chance to leave the nettles.

3. Preheat oven to 180° C / 350° F.

4. Chop up the nettle leaves with a mezzaluna or sharp knife.

5. Place the vegan mince in a large bowl, add a little water and the chopped nettles, and mix well.

6. Heat a tablespoon of oil of your choice in a large frying pan or wok, add the mince and nettles, the yeast flakes, curry powder, salt, and pepper. Mix and heat gently for five minutes, then set aside to cool for a few minutes.

7. Roll out the vegan pastry to a ¼ inch (½ cm) thick rectangle. Cut long strips, each approximately 3 inches (8 cm) wide.

8. Spoon the filling into a long sausage shape along the length of the center of each pastry strip, taking care to leave ¾ inch (2 cm) gaps on either side for closing the rolls.

9. Brush each edge space with plant milk, then carefully fold the sides over so they cover the filling. Press the edges together gently with your fingertips to seal.

10. Cut the strips into 1½ inch (4 cm) long sausage rolls and brush the tops with plant milk. Impress a fork gently across the top of each to make small furrows.

11. Transfer to a lined baking tray, taking care to leave gaps between all the rolls.

12. Bake on a middle shelf in the oven for 25 minutes, until the rolls are golden on top.

13. Transfer to a cooling rack for 20 minutes.

14. Eat hot or cold! Store in the fridge or freezer.

Jane Smith *is an adoptive mother, a writer, and a psychotherapist by training. She lives in Cheshire, UK, and loves rambling, foraging, and wild swimming.*

STORY

Homa[1] is remembered in the Babylonian Talmud as a woman who was widowed three times. Her last husband was Abaye, one of the leading Sages of the Babylonian Jewish community and head of the academy in Pumpedita. Many of the Sages in the Talmud were inclined to prohibit marrying a woman who had already lost two husbands. They worried that the woman herself had unintentionally caused their deaths, whether because she had bad luck, or because of some inherently harmful physical characteristic. Abaye, however, was not one for such superstitions or paranoia. He married Homa without hesitation.

After Abaye's death, Homa went to collect the material provisions she was owed from her late husband's estate. Rava, her husband's student and successor, provided her with food and shelter, but not wine, as this was a matter of legal dispute. In fact, it is in the very context of this dispute that the Gemara narrates Homa's story.

Unsatisfied, Homa boldly and confidently demanded that Rava apportion her wine as well. Rava incredulously responded that he knew his teacher never drank wine. A woman whose husband didn't drink surely would not have been accustomed to drink wine herself! To the contrary, Homa argued back, and she demonstrated with her hands the size of the glass of wine her husband used to serve her. In the midst of her gesture, Homa's sleeve slipped back and her arm was revealed in the courtroom. The Gemara describes how at this very moment, it was as if the room had been filled with a beautiful light.

Rava, seemingly aroused by this incident, goes home and tries to entice his wife to have sex with him. Suspicious, his wife asks who was in court that day. Rava tells her about Homa. With this information, Rava's wife storms out of the house and finds Homa. She begins physically assaulting Homa, and chastises her, "You have already killed three men, now you mean to kill a fourth?" Ultimately she drives Homa out of the city of Mehoza. Thus, Rava's

---

1. Homa is mentioned in the Talmud here: Talmud.b.Yevamot.64b, Talmud.b.Ketubot 65a.

wife gives voice to a fear other Sages had expressed regarding the danger of women who were widowed one too many times.

PASSAGES

Talmud b. Ketubot 65a

CONTEXT

Homa's demand that she be apportioned wine is situated in the midst of a rabbinic debate about whether or not it is appropriate to include wine in a wife's material provisions. While the Mishnah does not include wine in its list, a rivaling *baraita* is cited, explaining that women who are accustomed to drink wine should be provided with wine. Homa's story is cited as evidence of this practice.

The debate over serving women wine seems to be animated by a deeper anxiety about female sexuality and women's bodies. One *baraita* goes so far as suggesting that a woman who is served more than three glasses of wine will lose all sense of decency to the point that she would even be willing to sleep with a donkey. Nevertheless, in the story recorded in Tractate Ketubot, it is not Homa, but Rava – a sober sage and trusted leader – who is portrayed as unable to control his sexual appetite.

AGGADAH

Homa may have been remembered in the Talmud for her short-lived marriages, but the story recorded in Ketubot offers insight into her unique partnership with Abaye. Typically in Babylonia, women would only drink wine *if and when* their husbands drank. A woman drinking alone, it seems, could not be trusted to behave modestly.

Abaye, however, was not one for kowtowing to conventional social norms. He married Homa, in spite of paranoid attitudes toward twice-widowed women. In marriage as well, Abaye was not plagued by anxieties that his wife would act inappropriately. He served her as much wine as she pleased, even if he wasn't interested in drinking himself. Abaye did not fear Homa; he trusted her. He treated her as an equal, and not as a liability.

The love and respect upon which Homa and Abaye built their marriage can be heard in Homa's voice as she recounts her memories to Rava in the courtroom. She doesn't simply tell Rava that she was accustomed to drinking wine with her husband. Overcome with love and appreciation for how much her husband took care of her, she gets swept up in recreating the size of the glass Abaye used to pour for her. He was a husband who catered to her *wants* as much as her *needs*. Homa knew that she deserved nothing less, and was bold enough to say so directly to the head of the court.

Homa's fond memories of drinking wine beside her husband give voice to a countercurrent in Ketubot's discussion about policing women's alcohol consumption. For all the voices that denigrate women who drink, one tradition suggests that it is perfectly appropriate for women to drink freely with their husbands, as it will encourage a healthy sex life!

Homa and Abaye's marriage models a partnership unencumbered by convention and built on mutual trust and care for each other's happiness. Homa's willingness to insist that she be apportioned wine also teaches us how to advocate for our own needs, irrespective of marriage. As traditional caretakers, women have a tendency to put other people's needs before their own. We sacrifice rest, time spent on work, and even food preferences to make sure our loved ones are happy and fulfilled. We spend so much time catching up on our basic needs, who has time to even consider self-care?

I imagine Homa would counter that it is our own job as much as it is the job of our loved ones to make sure we find opportunities to relax and enjoy ourselves. Perhaps that much-needed act of self-care is enjoying a large glass of wine – with or without your spouse. Perhaps it's partaking in another favorite food, an evening reading a book, watching TV, carving out time for exercise, or spending time with friends. Whatever that activity may be, Homa teaches us that we should never let the expectations of others get in the way of tending to our own happiness.

PROMPTS

- What does the Gemara mean when it says that the courtroom filled with light when Homa's arm was exposed? Is it a criticism of her immodesty, praise for her beauty, or something else altogether?
- Why was Rava's wife so troubled by Homa's presence in the courtroom? Whose responsibility was it to protect Homa as she was being assaulted and driven out of the city?
- Ketubot discusses the material dimensions of what a husband must provide for his wife. What do you consider to be your basic needs – physical or otherwise – to lead a healthy and happy life? How would you go about securing these needs in a relationship with your partner?

Shira Eliassian *is a PhD candidate at Yale. Her work focuses on religious innovation, identity formation, and the politics of orthodoxy.*

FIERY FUDGY BROWNIES

Homa and Abaye's marriage was an inspiring partnership.

I offer a recipe that reflects the characteristics of their marriage – sexy and indulgent. These rich brownies use a dynamic duo ingredient partnership to uplift the flavor profile of a common baked treat. The combination of chili and chocolate is ancient, going back to the Aztecs.

These fiery and fudgy brownies are oil-free. They are spiced with a kick of cayenne and a touch of musky cinnamon for a cakey brownie that is light, moist, airy, and delicious. Make a double batch because these brownies go from cakey to fudgy when stored in an airtight container for a few days.

Prep Time: 10 minutes
Cook Time: 30 minutes
Yield: 16 brownies

Tools:

- Rectangular baking pan 8"×8" (20×20 cm) brownie pan
- Kitchen scale
- Mixing bowls
- Measuring cups and spoons
- Silicone spatula

Ingredients:

- 6 oz (170g) vegan chocolate, preferably refined sugar free
- 2 tbsp ground flaxseed
- 6 tbsp water
- 1 cup (180g) coconut sugar
- ¼ cup (60g) unsweetened applesauce
- 1 tsp vanilla extract
- 1 cup (125g) all-purpose flour
- 2 tbsp cocoa powder, preferably Dutch process
- 1 tsp baking powder
- ½ tsp cinnamon
- ¼ tsp cayenne pepper
- ¼ tsp salt

Instructions:

1. Preheat the oven to 350° F (175° C). Line an 8″×8″ (20×20 cm) brownie pan with parchment paper.

2. Place the chocolate chips in a double boiler or in a heatproof bowl over a pot of boiling water. Stir with a silicone spatula and melt until smooth. Take the chocolate off the heat and set aside.

3. Add the ground flaxseeds and water to a medium mixing bowl and whisk together. Set aside to allow the flaxseeds to absorb the water for 5 minutes.

4. Add the coconut sugar, applesauce, and vanilla extract to the ground flaxseed mixture. Whisk to combine. Fold in the melted chocolate. Set aside.

5. Add the flour, cocoa powder, baking powder, cinnamon, cayenne pepper, and salt to a big mixing bowl. Whisk to combine.

6. Add the wet ingredients to the dry ingredients. Mix until the batter comes together. It will be thick. Turn the batter out into the brownie pan and press it to the edges. Use a spatula or spoon to even it out.

7. Bake for 30 minutes or until a skewer comes out clean. Let the brownies cool in the pan for 10 minutes, then lift out by the parchment. Transfer to a cooling rack and cool completely before cutting into squares.

Lisa Dawn Angerame *is the author of* Wait, That's Vegan?! *and* The Vegan ABCs Cookbook. *She lives in New York with her husband and son.*

STORY

Hova is mentioned twice in the Talmud, when her husband and his learning partner are discussing Jewish laws. She incurs a terrible and tragic curse: the death of her children for actions she may not realize are transgressive.

The first time we encounter Hova is in Tractate Nazir. In this story, her husband, Rav Huna, is talking to Rav Adda bar Ahava about rulings regarding cutting young boys' hair. Traditionally, one does not cut the hair on the corners of one's head; this comes from a prohibition in Leviticus 19:27 as it tells us, "do not round the corners of your head…," which prohibits removing the hair that grows in this spot. Rav Huna gives a stringent ruling that the person who does not follow this law and shaves the head (rounds out the sides) is liable to receive lashes.

Then Rav Adda bar Ahava makes the conversation about the law personal, asking Rav Huna who shaves his son's hair. And Rav Huna replies, "My wife, Hova, shaves his head since she is not included in this prohibition." In anger, Rav Adda bar Ahava responds with an exclamation: "Hova should bury her sons!"

The second story appears in Tractate Bava Kamma. Similar to the first story, it occurs when Rav Huna and Rav Adda bar Ahava are learning. They are discussing laws around raising small domesticated animals and grazing flocks. Rav Adda bar Ahava asks Rav Huna who watches and raises his flocks. And Rav Huna says, "My wife, Hova, watches and raises my flocks." Rav Huna claims that since she is a woman, she is not obligated in such laws. Again, Rav Adda exclaims, "Hova should bury her sons!"

The Gemara tells us that while Rav Adda bar Ahava was alive, none of Hova's children survived.

PASSAGES

Talmud b. Nazir 57b and Talmud b. Bava Kamma 80a

CONTEXT

The two episodes of Hova's story illustrate a disconnect between Rav Huna's theoretical legal rulings, and his application of this knowledge in his own family.

The section directly before the first story mentioning Hova discusses the laws surrounding men's haircuts. The Sages are debating the idea of פאת ראשכם, literally rounding of the head. As we learn, Jewish law forbids a man from rounding, or removing the hair around, his head and from shaving his beard. These prohibitions do not apply to women, since they do not have beards, nor do they apply to children. Nevertheless, Rav Huna teaches that an adult who cuts a child's hair in the forbidden manner will be held liable.

In Tractate Bava Kamma, the Sages are focusing on the laws of agriculture, specifically flocks and grazing. Prior to Hova's story, Rav Huna and Rav Adda bar Ahava are discussing halacha; they are looking at the prohibitions against raising certain animals and allowing animals to graze in others' fields. Rav Adda bar Ahava asks Rav Huna if he raises such animals and where he allows them to graze. Rav Huna replies that Hova, his wife, is the one who raises and watches the animals. Again, Rav Adda bar Ahava seemingly curses Hova and her children.

This story serves as a moral lesson of responsibility; it showcases the importance of being aware of how rabbinic rulings may impact others. While one should be wary of straying far from Torah, when making halachot (Jewish laws), the rabbis must take into consideration how others may be affected.

This story is a reminder that refusal to take responsibility has dire consequences for other people. Rav Huna tries to hide from his obligation by placing responsibility and thus blame on his wife. But we see that by ignoring his responsibility and obligation to halacha, he condemns his entire family.

AGGADAH

Hova's story is one of pain. She is, intentionally or not, scapegoated by her husband. It is not entirely clear whether his hypocrisy is malicious: does he intentionally use his wife as a pawn to "bend the rules," perhaps purposefully keeping her unaware of the halachic context

of her actions? Or does he really believe that she is free from certain legal obligations and therefore will suffer no consequences?

Hova's name offers a way to reclaim her and her children, through its different meanings:[1, 2]

חבה ,חבא ,חבי – to cover or hide.
חובה ,חובא – sin or guilt.
חובה f. (חוב) – obligation or duty.
חובות – condemnation or doom.

With these definitions in mind, Rav Adda bar Ahava's curse can be read as condemning Rav Huna's lack of responsibility. As the head of his house, Rav Huna should recognize that even his wife has a responsibility to keep halacha. Rav Adda bar Ahava recognizes the hypocrisy of shifting responsibility onto Hova, and he curses Hova to show that rulings impact all household members, not just the men. Rav Huna hides behind his wife, pushing off the blame. In doing so, he ignores his own familial obligations and his own duty to safeguard them, and condemns his family to death.

Hova's story is full of injustice. Let's rewrite her story:

Two *chevrutas* (partners), Rav Huna and Rav Adda bar Ahava, come to debate halachot. In the heat of the debate, Rav Adda bar Ahava recognizes the hypocrisy of Rav Huna's stringency when it comes to theoretical legal rulings. Rav Adda bar Ahava is aware that, in practice, Rav Huna does not apply such stringency to matters concerning his own family life. Hova, Rav Huna's wife, cuts their children's hair and watches and raises the flocks. Yet this dutiful wife is seemingly unaware that her husband has simultaneously halachically ruled against her actions, yet neglected to intervene to stop her or teach her Jewish law.

Hoping for Rav Huna to recognize his hypocrisy and acknowledge the work his wife does, Rav Adda bar Ahava asks his friend: Who cuts your son's hair? Who raises and watches the

---

1. Marcus Jastrow, *Dictionary of Targumim, Talmud and Midrashic Literature* (The Judaica Press, 1996), 452–455.
2. Ruhama Weiss and Avner HaCohen, *Mothers in Therapy* (Miskal-Yedioth Ahronoth Books and Chemed Books, 2012), 132–150.

flock? Rav Huna replies that it is Hova. Furthermore since it is Hova, his wife, a woman, she is not truly liable for punishment, despite his previous rulings.

Rav Adda bar Ahava, incensed at Rav Huna's deflection of responsibility, exclaims: "You are hiding behind your wife and ignoring your responsibility to your family. In secrecy you can hide no more! You shall not merit any more children until you take responsibility. Recognize the impact of your stringencies and your denial!"

We are then told that until Rav Huna's rulings eventually match his practices, he is unable to connect with his family or have any more children with Hova.

PROMPTS

- Which responsibilities do you hide from, when, and why? What is a responsibility that somebody else hides from, and how does that impact you?
- How do our actions connect or disconnect us from those we are close to?
- Rav Huna was dogmatic about the law in theory, yet somewhat flexible in its application. His "hypocrisy" reveals the inflexibility of a dogmatic approach to life. Reflect on aspects of your own values and actions which clash: if our actions are sometimes imperfect, does it mean we should altogether abandon our better ideals? Or does it point to the fact that we need to be more flexible and not so binary?

Hannah Greenberg *is a Jewish educator who studied at Pardes's Center for Jewish Education. Her M.Ed. is in Exceptional Children & Youth from the University of Delaware.*

BOURBON CINNAMON PECAN PIE

In families, we share food as one of the tangible ways of expressing our love. One food that is best shared with others is pie. I would like to imagine that things had gone differently for Hova, and she could bake and enjoy this pie, piece by piece, with her sons.

This delicious pecan pie is spiced with bourbon and a hint of cinnamon. It is dairy-free and refined sugar-free. It is not overly sweet and has a very gooey texture and nutty flavor from the pecans. The pie is also very simple to prepare – you don't need to cook the filling and you don't need to prebake the crust.

You can also replace the cinnamon and vanilla with ¼ cup crystalized ginger for a flavor variation with a kick.

Prep Time: 40 minutes
Cook Time: 35 minutes
Yield: one 9-inch pecan pie

Tools:

- Large mixing bowl
- Medium mixing bowl
- 9-inch tart pan or a pie plate
- Whisk

Ingredients:

- 4 tbsp (25g) ground flaxseed
- 4 tbsp (60ml) water
- ½ cup (120ml) maple syrup
- ½ cup (120ml) agave nectar (or more maple syrup)
- 3 tbsp (45g) tahini
- 3 tbsp (45ml) bourbon
- 1 tsp vanilla extract
- ½ tsp ground cinnamon
- 1½ cups (200g) chopped pecans (plus more for garnish, if desired)
- 1½ cups + 3 tbsp (210g) all-purpose flour
- A pinch of salt
- ½ cup (120ml) olive oil
- 2 tbsp (30ml) unsweetened soy milk

Instructions:

1. Mix ground flaxseed and water in a large mixing bowl.
2. Add maple syrup, agave, tahini, bourbon, vanilla, cinnamon, and pecans to the bowl. Whisk until well-combined. Place pecan filling in the fridge for at least 30 minutes.
3. Add flour, salt, olive oil, and soy milk to a medium bowl and mix with a fork until combined. The mixture will be smooth and pliable.
4. Press dough into a tart pan or a pie plate.
5. Preheat the oven to 350° F / 175° C and pour the filling over the pie crust.
6. Place pecan pie into the preheated oven and bake for 30 minutes. Turn off the oven and let the pecan pie sit in the oven for an additional 15 minutes.
7. Set aside to cool completely before serving. Enjoy!

From the Jewish Food Hero Kitchen

STORY

The Talmud is not a history book; its stories are not historical events. However, some of the characters in the Talmud were based on historical figures.

Ifra Hurmiz might have been based on the historical character of the Zoroastrian[1] queen, wife of the King Hormizd II, and mother of the Iranian King Shapur II. She was a member of the Imperial Sasanian family, which ruled from 224 to 651 CE.[2]

In the Talmud, several anecdotes are told about Ifra Hurmiz's long-standing friendship with a leading Talmudic Sage named Rava.

In Tractate Taanit we learn that her son, King Shapur II, tried to intervene in Rava's court. Ifra protected the Sage, telling her son, "Do not interfere with the Jews, as whatever they request from their Master (G-d), He gives them."

In Tractate Niddah, the Talmud tells us of another story where Ifra Hurmiz sent bloodstains to Rava for proper identification. In the diverse Sasanian Empire, most religious groups, including the Zoroastrian rulers, observed stringencies surrounding menstruation. Bloodstains were relevant to Jews, to their non-Jewish neighbors, and to royalty. Rava correctly identified the type of blood on the stain Ifra Hurmiz sent, but King Shapur suggested it was just a lucky guess, "like a blind man who escapes from a chimney."

Ifra Hurmiz then sent Rava sixty different bloodstains as a test. Rava correctly identified all of them, until the very last one. Fortunately for Rava, he sent it back with a gift of a lice comb – and indeed, the blood was louse blood. Ifra Hurmiz's respect for Rava and the Jews was confirmed, as she concluded: "Jews, you dwell in the chamber of hearts."

---

1. Zoroastrianism is one of the world's oldest continuously practiced religions. It follows the teaching of the ancient Iranian prophet Zoroaster.
2. They were the last Persian Imperial dynasty before the arrival of Islam in the mid-seventh century CE.

In another instance, recorded in Tractate Zevachim, Ifra Hurmiz not only speaks respectfully of Jews, but actually even sends Rava an animal to sacrifice "for the sake of Heaven." Jews are no longer permitted to sacrifice outside of the Temple Mount. But at the time, they could instruct non-Jews on how to bring sacrifices appropriately. Rava arranged for Ifra Hurmiz's sacrifice to be carried out in a beautiful and respectful way, true to her intentions and in accordance with Jewish law.

PASSAGES

Talmud.b.Niddah.20b

CONTEXT

Queen Ifra's story shows a non-Jewish woman in a position of power, who was sympathetic to, and even respectful of, the Jewish faith. Ifra Hurmiz was one of several individuals in the Imperial Sasanian family who positively impacted the relations between the Sasanian Empire and the Jews. However, her story is really a device to tell us about the Talmudic Sage Rava.

We can speculate that stories about Rava's respectful relationship with the king's mother are intended to affirm the brilliance of Rava. He was an established leader of the Jewish community, so extraordinary that even non-Jewish royalty recognized his stature.

There is of course a possibility that this relationship was real – that Ifra Hurmiz and Rava did in fact have a relationship. The rabbis of the Talmud were also interested in positioning themselves as experts in bloodstains, so stories about non-Jewish women coming to them would showcase their expertise.

AGGADAH

"Ifra Hurmiz then sent Rava sixty different types of blood."

Imagine a world in which menstrual blood couldn't possibly be private. A world without sanitary supplies, but also without shame. Menstrual blood plays a ritual role, surely, but it is not disgusting or unusual. Impurity is just a regular part of life – even for a queen. The Queen Mother sends a tricky bloodstain to a Rabbi for inspection just because it is an interesting kind of stain: can he identify it? He inspects it publicly, before his students. She

is so impressed that she sends him sixty more. She wants to test his knowledge and capabilities. She might as well be asking whether he can taste the difference between Coca-Cola and Pepsi. Can he smell the difference between white roses and red ones? How clever are these Jews anyway? How blessed are they by their God?

Nobody today would play games with her bloodstains. But imagine a world in which we did. A world without period shaming. Where women's opinions or emotions are never undermined by the ever-subverting misogyny of "are you having your period or something?" Where leaks are laundry problems, same as a coffee spill, and nothing more.

In a world in which menstruation was just one of the many normal, natural fluids of life, girls would not feel ashamed to speak about their cramps, to ask permission to leave class, to seek medical attention if needed. Bathrooms would stock pads and tampons the way they stock toilet paper and soap. Menstruation might still be painful, but without shame, the pain would be addressed and the emotional burden would be lightened.

PROMPTS

- What can you do to help build a world without period shame?
- Are there regal, non-Jewish women who inspire your Judaism?
- Do you have as comfortable a relationship with any Rabbi as Ifra Hurmiz had with Rava?

Rabbanit Leah Sarna is an energetic Jewish educator and Halakha enthusiast. Ordained by Yeshivat Maharat, she lives and works in the United States.

DANDELION-PUMPKIN SEED PESTO

Ifra Hurmiz (and every woman) can strengthen her body after the menses with the bitter herb, dandelion (Taraxacum officinale).

Dandelion-pumpkin seed pesto is a nourishing food that helps support immunity, digestion, the liver, and the natural hormonal loops of the body. The female body can especially benefit from this because it includes natural sources of calcium that are so vital for women's bone health.

This pesto is easy to prepare, vegan, and also nut-free. It is a hearty pesto that also tastes decadent. All of the dry ingredients are easy to find in the gluten-free, natural food, or bulk grocery section of most grocery stores.

You can forage for dandelions in the spring, or find them in specialty supermarkets or Asian stores. If you cannot find any, try substituting rocket (arugula), frisee, chicory, or radicchio.

Prep Time: 3 minutes
Cook Time: 3 minutes
Yield: 1½ cups of pesto

Tools:

- Blender (at least 900 watts)
- Knife and cutting board
- Spatula

Ingredients:

- 1 cup (128g) fresh dandelion greens, chopped (*Taraxacum officinale*)
- 1 cup (128g) toasted hulled pumpkin seeds (pepitas)
- ½ cup (64g) nutritional yeast
- 1–2 cloves fresh garlic, coarsely chopped (*Allium sativum*)
- ½ fresh lemon, squeezed
- ¼ cup (59ml) extra virgin olive oil
- Salt to taste
- Pinch of flaxseed powder
- 1 tbsp filtered water

Instructions:

1. Combine all the ingredients in a blender, slowly adding in the olive oil until all ingredients are broken down into a nice paste.
2. Serve immediately, store in the fridge for 4 days, or freeze for 3 months.

Laura Baum is an herbalist and childcare specialist and the founder of *Laura's Botanicals. She supports families and children in her local Jewish community center.*

IKKU / איכו

STORY

Ikku appears in a text about the miracles that the impoverished Rabbi Hanina ben Dosa performs through the power of his deep belief in God and his prayers. He was said to be so righteous and his prayer so powerful that he was able to perform miracles: making a small amount of inferior food nourish his family for a whole week, filling his wife's kneading bowl and oven with bread, and helping Ikku.

Ikku, who was a neighbor of the Rabbi and his wife, was in the process of building a house. She discovered halfway through that the beams were not long enough to reach from one wall to another. She appealed to the great Rabbi for advice, and the Rabbi performed another miracle. The beams grew to an extent that they reached the walls and then some. Ikku was able to live her life in a secure house as a result of this remarkable miracle.

PASSAGES

Talmud b. Taanit 25a

CONTEXT

The purpose of the story is to maintain that miracles can happen if one has a strong enough faith, including lengthening the size of beams so that one can live securely in her home.

Rabbi Hanina ben Dosa was a man who was known for his deep commitment to prayer, and through prayer, his ability to perform miracles. He is said to have been a humble man, but he appeared to have a dramatic flair. He was first encountered in Tractate Berakhot (33a) when he brought a poisonous snake to a study hall to demonstrate that it could not harm someone who is free of transgression. He appeared again in Tractate Pesachim (112b) when he offered Agrat, daughter of Mahalat, safe passage through spaces inhabited by dangerous spirits. In Bava Kamma (50a), he rescued a woman who had fallen through a ditch. He was a humble man of limited means, and in all these cases it was his power of prayer that led to the miracles.

AGGADAH

Many women in the Talmud appear as secondary characters, often without names.[1] Ikku is mentioned by name, and in connection to her own home, under construction. Notably, there is no appearance or mention of her husband or any other male family member in connection to her name or home. Even though her status as a property owner was not central to the theme of this text, it is a central factor in any modern reading of Ikku's story.

Ikku has a name, a house, a lead role in getting her house built, and the wisdom to ask for help. I like to imagine Ikku as either a single woman building her own home, or as a married woman who is responsible for overseeing a family project.

Things are not going as expected, which is often the case with construction projects. Perhaps the builders got the measurements wrong and she received beams that were too short. Perhaps the building team tried to cut corners by delivering substandard beams. Maybe they thought Ikku would not notice this technical detail. The discovery of the wrongly cut beams leaves Ikku anguished. Without the right materials to support the roof of her home, it would all come tumbling down on top of her.

Ikku asks for help from Rabbi Hanina ben Dosa, known for finding solutions to the most difficult of problems. When Ikku appeared with her problem, we can imagine that Rabbi Hanina ben Dosa and his wife saw something good in Ikku. The three of them sat down together and prayed over the beams. It is unclear how the beams became right-sized. The text records that they lengthened overnight, so that Ikku's roof could be secured.

If a woman has a secure roof over her head, she has a literal place and one foundational piece of a secure life. The roof and beams of this house were Ikku's safe place – they were *her* roof and beams and walls. This is the true miracle of Ikku's house.

Today, Jewish women like Ikku are digging in and building a literal and figurative space to learn and teach Talmud.

---

1. The story of Yalta in Tractate Berachot stands out as one example of a female primary Talmudic character.

PROMPTS

- What is the significance of Ikku's appeal to the Rabbi and his wife for help with the construction of her home?
- Have you ever felt that people underestimated your technical capacity or intelligence in areas stereotypically gendered male? What is the most effective way to remedy these types of situations?
- What key material items do you need to ensure your own sense of security? Who could/did/will support you to get them?

Penny Cagan *is a published poet and writer who lives in New York City and supports herself as a risk manager.*

ELLEN'S FOUR-BEAN SALAD WITH DRY MUSTARD VINAIGRETTE

When I told my mother Ikku's story over the phone, my mother suggested that Ikku was busy and needed simple recipes that would keep for a few days.

This was my grandmother Ellen's recipe, and one of the first salads my mother learned how to make when she got married. Most weeks, my mother makes this dish and she and my father eat it over a few days. The dressing is my grandmother's and mother's signature vinaigrette.

Prep Time: 10 minutes
Yield: 8 servings

Tools:

- Blender (a powerful one is best)
- Colander
- Large salad bowl
- Food processor with slicing blade (or a sharp knife)

Ingredients:

For the salad:

- 1 medium onion, sliced extra thin
- 14 oz (400g) can chickpeas
- 14 oz (400g) can cannellini beans
- 14 oz (400g) can kidney beans
- 14 oz (400g) can black beans

For the dressing:

- ¾ cup (175ml) white vinegar, 5% alcohol
- 10–12 garlic cloves
- 1 tsp salt
- 1 tsp dry mustard powder
- 2 tsp sugar
- 1½ cups (350ml) corn oil (such as Mazola)

Instructions:

Make the dressing:

1. Place the vinegar, garlic cloves, salt, dry mustard, and sugar in a blender. Blend on high until completely smooth.

2. Add the corn oil slowly while the blender is on. The dressing should become white and creamy as it emulsifies.

3. Taste to check seasoning and consistency. Add ¼ cup more water to thin out or reduce the garlic taste.

4. Pour into a glass jar and set aside. This dressing will keep in the refrigerator for 10 days (beware the garlic flavor will intensify with time!).

Make the salad:

5. Peel and cut the onion in half, then slice it as thinly as possible. You can do this by hand or with a food processor.

6. Place all the beans into a colander and rinse well with cold water.

7. Transfer beans and onion to a serving bowl, dress the salad to taste, and mix well.

8. Cover with plastic or beeswax wrap and allow to sit for 3 hours or overnight before serving. This salad is better the second day as the beans and onions marinate in the dressing.

From the Jewish Food Hero Kitchen

STORY

Imma Shalom is mentioned by name in the Babylonian Talmud. Her name means "Mother Peace." She was surrounded by prominent Sages: her husband, Rabbi Eliezer ben Hurkanos, was among the most prominent Sages of the Mishnah, and her brother, Rabban Gamliel, was president of the Sanhedrin (*Nasi*). Mentions of her in the Talmud define her largely through her relationship with these two men, and, in one instance, her attempt to mediate tensions that arose between them.

The first time Imma Shalom is mentioned in the Talmud is in Tractate Eruvin 63a. The story concerns her husband's accurate prediction of the death of a student. Rabbi Eliezer had a student who was brazen enough to issue a legal ruling in his presence. Rabbi Eliezer confided to his wife that he did not think that this man was going to last a year. Imma Shalom asked him: "Are you a prophet?" He told her that he was "neither a prophet nor the son of a prophet"[1] – but that his knowledge came from the tradition that, "anyone who issues a legal ruling in his teacher's presence is liable to receive the death penalty." The student died.

The second story is recounted in Tractate Bava Metsia 59b:

Rabbi Eliezar is emotionally distraught and grieving. His Jewish legal ruling rejected, he was dismissed from the Sanhedrin. Rabban Gamliel thinks he is carrying out God's will and that discharging Rabbi Eliezer from the Sanhedrin will prevent the proliferation of legal disputes in Israel.

Consequently, Imma insists her husband abstain from praying *tachanun*, the prayer of supplication, for fear that his pain and sorrow would result in the death of her brother.

There are two versions of what happens next. Both involve Imma briefly leaving her husband unattended, while she goes to give a poor person a loaf of bread. One version explains that she thought it was safe to leave her husband, as she had mistaken the date for Rosh Chodesh (the New Moon), a day on which people do not usually recite supplication prayers.

---

1. Amos 7:14.

When she returned, she saw that he had prayed *tachanun*, and cried out: "Rise! For you have killed my brother." The shofar blew at the exact same time, announcing that Rabban Gamliel had died.

The exchange that follows offers a mirror image of the former story. Rabbi Eliezer asks her: "How did you know that he was going to die?" She answers: "This is the tradition I have received from my grandfather's house: 'though all the Gates of Heaven be locked, the Gates will open to those who suffer.'"[2]

PASSAGES[3]

Talmud b. Bava Metsia 59b

CONTEXT

The story highlights the Talmud's insistence that prayer is an extremely powerful tool, which can either save or kill, depending on its implicit intentions. Therefore, a person must be very careful what they pray for. The death of the Rabban Gamliel following Rabbi Eliezer's prayers points to the idea that even hidden motives and underlying feelings have consequences.

This may be an aggadic extension of the halachic (legal) principle that one should not pray while in a state of moral affliction. This narrative serves as a cautionary tale providing a form of moral instruction (*mussar*). Prayer should be used to repair the world, not to cause more harm, and our intentions as we pray should reflect this.

Imma Shalom's story also suggests that knowledge of tradition provides foresight of future events. Just as her husband was able to predict the death of the student, Imma knows that her husband's strong emotions have the potential to hasten her brother's death. As the tragic story unfolds, there is a sense of inevitability. Ultimately Imma Shalom's attempts to intervene are futile not because of her own failings, but due to the power of our emotions to manifest through prayer.

---

2. My translation of Bava Metsia 59b.
3. See also, Shabbat 116a, Eruvin 63a, Bava Metsia 59b, Nedarim 20a.

AGGADAH

In both these stories Imma Shalom attempts to mitigate the intensity of emotion felt by her husband. First, by quietly questioning him; in the second by desperately imploring him to modify his behavior.

The narratives are tragic (in the classical sense of the word) because it relies on a sense of inevitability. There was nothing Imma Shalom could do to stop her husband from crying his heart out in prayer. The sense of tragedy is heightened by the fact that her own intentions were explicitly good: she rose only to give a poor man a loaf of bread. It is hard to understand how her generous act led to such horrifying implications.[4]

Imma Shalom's story illustrates the fact that women in the times of the Talmud were not kept apart from the chain of family traditions and teachings. A teaching imparted by a man (the tradition of her grandfather) is mediated by a woman – his granddaughter, Imma Shalom. This story confirms that women were recipients and carriers of wisdom within the household. It is implied that these pious, knowledgeable women were never silenced by their husbands. Quite the contrary – our tradition simply implies that they were right.

Individual intuition and knowledge are fundamental to understanding the consequences of thought and action. However, one cannot but wonder what would have happened if Imma Shalom had shared her grandfather's teaching with her husband more directly and explicitly, before the death of Rabban Gamliel.[5] If Imma Shalom had transmitted this teaching to Rabbi Eliezer, he might have been able to restrain himself from praying out of respect and compassion.

As the story happens, Rabbi Eliezer's prayers open the Gates of Heaven and set in motion direct punitive justice that hurts everybody involved. Sometimes, it would perhaps be better if the Gates of Heaven remain locked.

---

4. In Shabbat 156b, the daughter of Rabbi Akiva, whose death was foretold by soothsayers, escapes her tragic fate by rising from a banquet and offering bread to a person in need who was knocking at the door. *Tsedaka*, Rabbi Akiva concludes, will save you from death. This beautiful story is ironically mirrored in the second version of Imma Shalom's lapse of awareness: how could it be that Imma Shalom's *tsedaka* had such horrifying implications?

5. Imma Shalom was known to be witty in her encounters with heretics. In Shabbat 116a, along with her brother, she exposes the hypocrisy of a so-called philosopher.

PROMPTS

- What did Rabbi Eliezer stand to gain from his brother-in-law's death?
- How does peace find a voice when conflict runs deep in a group?
- How can we go beyond the politics of damage control to a more assertive expression of compassion and justice?

Myriam Ackermann-Sommer is a rabbinical student at Yeshivat Maharat. A lover of teaching and Torah, she created the first women's kollel in France.

VEGAN CHOCOLATE BABKA

I connected Imma Shalom's story with bread because she gives bread as charity in her story. For me, babka is a luxurious and indulgent type of bread.

The key ingredient in this babka is the chocolate. If the chocolate spread on the inside of the babka is not delicious, your babka will be worth nothing. When I have time, I make my own chocolate blend. When making your babka, you need to make sure the dough has enough time to grow, but not too much.

A good babka is heavenly in the mouth; melting, crunchy, and sweet.

Prep Time: 20 minutes plus 2 hours to rise (depending on the weather)
Cook Time: 40 minutes
Yield: 6 servings

Tools:

- Stand mixer with dough hook (optional)
- Kitchen scale
- Large bowl
- Loaf pan
- Small bowl
- Spatula

Ingredients:

For the dough:

- 3 cups + 2 tbsp (500g) flour
- 3 tbsp (21g) fresh yeast or 2 tbsp (14g) dried yeast
- 1 cup (240ml) water
- 1 tbsp maple syrup
- ¼ cup (60ml) sunflower oil
- ½ cup plant-based butter (113g / 4 oz / 1 stick)
- 4.2 oz (125ml) soy yogurt
- ½ cup (100g) caster sugar
- 1 pinch salt

For the filling:

- A handful of hazelnuts
- 1 tsp cinnamon
- 3 or 4 tbsp (30g) cocoa
- 1 tbsp (12g) caster sugar
- 2 tbsp sunflower oil
- 1 cup (170g) vegan chocolate chips

For the glaze:

- ¼ cup (50g) sugar
- ⅛ tbsp (50ml) water

Instructions:

1. Mix yeast with water and maple syrup to activate. Leave to stand for 5–10 minutes until the surface is bubbly.
2. Combine all other dough ingredients in a large mixing bowl. Knead the mixture by hand for 10 minutes. Alternatively, use a stand mixer with the dough hook attached. The dough is ready when it forms a soft but not sticky ball.
3. Rest the dough in a covered bowl for one hour.
4. Meanwhile, prepare the filling, blending all ingredients (besides the chocolate chips) till smooth.
5. Roll out the rested dough to a ½-cm-thickness rectangle shape.
6. Spread the chocolate filling on top of the dough, then sprinkle with chocolate chips.
7. Roll the dough lengthways (Swiss roll style) and cut into two. Twist the two lengths together to shape and place in a loaf pan. Cover and leave to rise for 1 hour, or until doubled in size.
8. Heat the oven to 190° C (375° F).
9. Before cooking, sprinkle extra chocolate chips and chopped hazelnut pieces on top of the bread (optional).
10. Bake the babka for 30 minutes.
11. Meanwhile, melt ¼ cup sugar into ⅛ tbsp water and let boil until it becomes sticky.
12. Remove the browned babka from the oven and brush immediately with the sugar syrup mixture. Cool before serving.

Azelma Moscati is an Italian mother of four. A freelancer who loves reading and baking. Fresh cakes are always available in her kitchen.

STORY

Immarta bat Talei makes her only appearance in the Talmud in a story about her wrongful execution and/or her wrongfully performed execution. She was the daughter of a *kohein* (priest), and had committed adultery. According to Torah law, the adulterous daughter of a *kohein* is punishable by *sereifa*, literally "burning." For *sereifa*, the executioners would light a wick and put it into the person's mouth to burn their insides. But when Immarta bat Talei was executed, she was burned at the stake – wrapped in bundles of branches and set ablaze.[1]

Rav Yosef argues that the court that executed Immarta, led by Hama bar Tovia, made two critical errors. The first is that they performed the execution incorrectly. They should have poured a lit wick down her throat instead of burning her at the stake. But more critically, Rav Yosef claims that they had no right to execute Immarta in the first place. A judiciary can only carry out capital punishment when the Temple stands, and this incident took place after the fall of the Temple. This execution never should have happened.

PASSAGES

Talmud.b.Sanhedrin.52a-b

CONTEXT

The mishnah preceding Immarta's story discusses how *sereifa* is done. Yet, within the mishnah itself, there is some concern that the wick approach might be mistaken: Rabbi Elazar bar Tzadok cites the case of the (unnamed) daughter of a priest[2] who had committed adultery and was burned at the stake rather than burned via proper *sereifa*. In the Mishnah, Rabbi Elazar is assured that this does not undermine rabbinic definitions of *sereifa* but instead must have been the workings of an ignorant court. In the Gemara, the rabbis claim that

---

1. It is unclear whether burning at the stake was considered more or less humane as a form of execution. See Talmud.b.Sanhedrin.52b where it seems that if enough bundles are added, it might be a more humane form of execution than pouring a burning wick down someone's throat.
2. The Gemara understands this case as separate from the Immarta bat Talei case.

perhaps Rabbi Elazar's example came from a Sadducean (i.e., anti-Rabbinic) court, or that maybe he misremembered because he was young at the time.[3]

In the Talmudic section immediately preceding Immarta's case, the rabbis offer Scriptural origins for their unique version of *sereifa*. This explains why Rav Yosef's first objection to Immarta bat Talei's story is about *the way* her execution was performed, rather than the fact that it had been performed at all.

Nonetheless, Rav Yosef has another critique: Rabbi Hama bar Tovia did not have the authority to perform this execution. This should have been reserved only for the time when the Temple stood. It is unclear whether Rav Yosef's statement is primarily about rabbinic judicial authority, the importance of the Temple, or a discomfort with use of the death penalty more generally. Scholars debate the degree to which the rabbis supported capital punishment.[4]

AGGADAH

After the fall of the Temple in Jerusalem in 70 CE, leadership became decentralized, and power changed hands from the priests to the rabbis (with ample tension). With the loss of Jewish infrastructure, the rabbis argued about which laws and customs would remain, and what would be changed. In the uncertainty of that transition, as in all times of transition, some things were done that should not have been done. This is the case with Immarta bat Talei, a priest's daughter convicted of committing adultery.

At the time, some rabbis were sure that the death penalty was one of the practices that should continue from Temple times. After all, how else could they keep Jewish society from falling apart, from becoming a new Sodom and Gomorrah? Other rabbis must have disagreed. Surely there are some practices meant for only the kind of authority that a Temple can bring. But did those who objected speak up? Did those who faced the death penalty like Immarta speak up? Who even knew of the controversy, and how was it decided? We do not know. But in the meantime Immarta burned.

---

3. Talmud.b.Sanhedrin.52b.
4. See Beth Berkowitz, *Execution and Invention: Death Penalty Discourse in Early Rabbinic and Christian Cultures* (Oxford University Press, 2006), and Devora Steinmetz, *Punishment and Freedom: The Rabbinic Construction of Criminal Law* (University of Pennsylvania Press, 2008).

Centuries later, in a different time and a different place, Rav Yosef bar Hiyya read of what had happened and, with his twenty-twenty hindsight, lamented the court's overreach.

In addition to the questions that the story raises about transition, power, and controversy, for the contemporary reader, there are two additional nuances to consider. The first is about gender. To modern readers, the gender dynamics in the story are stark. Immarta bat Talei's status is a result of being the daughter of a male priest; she is put to death for committing sexual impropriety with a man against her male husband; and she is sentenced and killed by a male judge. It is worth asking whether this would have played out in quite this way had the gender dynamics been otherwise.

And the second issue relates to how the story is told: legal discourse can decenter the impact on the parties involved in favor of focusing on the laws of the institutions themselves. For this reason, we do not know much about Immarta's life and about the impact of an execution that should not have happened. Thus, it is worth asking the various ways this story could have been told if the focus was not specifically on the legal manner of carrying of *sereifa*.

PROMPTS

- What do you think about the death penalty? What do you think about the neater ritualization of the death penalty presented in rabbinic sources?
- How do you feel about Immarta? Do you feel pity for her? Or do you consider her to be deserving of her fate? How does this track with your perspective on the death penalty in general?
- If each of the characters in this story – Immarta, Hama bar Tovia, Rav Yosef – could speak today, what do you think each would say?

Elana Stein Hain, PhD, is Director of Faculty at the Shalom Hartman Institute of North America. She is working on a book on rabbinic jurisprudence.

CALM YOUR NERVOUS SYSTEM TONIC

The story of Immarta bat Talei is hard to read: a woman, killed. While the Mishnah speaks of her execution being performed wrongly, it is hard to think there was a right way of doing it. Many of us know women, maybe even ourselves, who have experienced violence.

Hearing about, reading about, and experiencing violence causes mental, emotional, and physical stress and anxiety in our minds and bodies.

This herbal remedy is a simple tincture, made by dissolving herbs in alcohol. It is an antidote for stress and anxiety and supports an overall calmer mood. The ingredients for this remedy can be found in your local food store or online.

Please note that this remedy is NOT to be used during the first trimester of pregnancy.

Prep Time: 2 minutes
Steep Time: 2–4 weeks
Yield: 200ml

Tools:

- 250ml glass jar
- Strainer
- Large bowl or measuring cup
- Cheesecloth
- 50ml brown or blue bottle with a dropper dispenser

Ingredients:

- ¼ cup (20g) Valeriana
- ¼ cup (20g) *scutellaria lateriflora* (skullcap)
- ¼ cup (20g) *passiflora incarnata* (passion flower)
- 1 cup (250ml) vodka

Instructions:

1. Place herbs and vodka in a jar and stir well. It is okay if the herbs are not fully covered; just make sure that everything is saturated.

2. Label the jar with the date and the ingredients.

3. Store the jar in a cool place, out of direct sunlight. Shake the jar daily for 2–4 weeks.

4. Place a strainer lined with cheesecloth over a large bowl or measuring cup. Pour the tincture through the cheesecloth. Squeeze all of the liquid out of the herbs, and compost the herbs.

5. Pour the tincture into a brown-colored glass tincture bottle. Label the tincture with the date and ingredients.

6. Keep your tinctures in a cool, dark place, such as a medicine cabinet or kitchen cupboard. I recommend using alcohol-based herbal tinctures within two years.

7. You now have a tincture that is ready to use. Start with 30 drops as needed. If needed, take up to 1 teaspoon each time.

Nicole Cohen Yechezkel is a passionate herbalist, naturopath, and the owner of Shoresh Body and Soul. She lives in Neve Tzuf, Israel, with her three boys.

STORY

Jonah's wife is referenced in a long and technical discussion in the Talmud about the wearing of *t'fillin* on Shabbat. A question arises as to whether women can wear *t'fillin*, if it is a time-bound mitzvah, and whether women can wear *t'fillin*, even if they are not obligated to do so. Traditionally, women do not participate in time-bound mitzvot.

Proof is brought that, although she was not obligated to do so, Jonah's wife would go up to Jerusalem during the Festival pilgrimage – a time-bound mitzvah.

The passages continue to emphasize again: it was known that Jonah's wife would go up to Jerusalem during the Festival pilgrimage; and that the Sages did not reprimand her. The Gemara then states a question: "Is there anyone who says that the mitzvah of Festival pilgrimage is not a time-bound positive mitzvah and that women are obligated to fulfill it?"

They then state that Jonah's wife did not go on the pilgrimage as an obligation, but that it was optional for her, thus showing that it is possible for women to participate in optional mitzvot.

PASSAGES

Talmud b. Eruvin 96:a

CONTEXT

A positive time-bound commandment is defined as one that could be physically fulfilled at any time, but that the Torah has mandated is to be done only at specific times. When a mitzvah is dependent on time, women are not obligated to fulfill them.

The key question here is – can one carry out a "bonus" mitzvah, even when not obligated to do so? What if one is a woman? The rabbis argue this point thoroughly. Some say women are able to do optional mitzvot, others say, "of course not!"

The Rabbi's use of Jonah's wife as an exemplar in a highly technical discussion about time-bound mitzvot may be no coincidence. Her husband ran away from his obligation to serve God. In contrast, his wife wanted to fulfill and exceed her duty, choosing to do additional, optional mitzvot.

AGGADAH

Consider the story of Jonah's wife in the context of her marital relationship. Her husband's approach to responsibility toward higher power and community differs from his wife's quite fundamentally.

God commands his prophet Jonah to take definitive action on humanity's behalf – *kum, lech, vekera* – get up, go and call out.[1] Jonah not only refrains from warning the people but worse, he is actively opposed to intervening. The command was to get up, to arise. But Jonah's response is to descend, to run away. In contrast, Jonah's wife ascends up to Jerusalem on a regular basis. She actively serves God, and goes above and beyond in her duty, becoming an active member of society and joining the community in the Festival pilgrimage.

Both Jonah and his wife carried out dangerous journeys. Jonah travelled by boat away from God to escape his obligations. Yet his wife regularly travelled, perhaps alone as a vulnerable woman without the protection of her husband, to Jerusalem on a long and tiring journey to visit the Temple and fulfill an optional obligation for God.

Jonah's wife is an example to her husband and to us. She teaches us that we can and must go beyond the fulfillment of basic obligations, even if we are surrounded by people who avoid responsibility, or limit their potential.

---

1. Jonah 1:2.

PROMPTS

- Do you think Jonah's wife chose to carry out the optional Festival pilgrimage in protest against her husband's cowardice?
- Might Jonah have been inspired by his wife's dedication to religious obligations? How have you been positively influenced by others' behavior, religious or otherwise?
- Do you surround yourself with people who bring you down or raise you up? Which of your relationships provide space for you to relax your expectations? Who challenges you to grow?
- Do you do the bare minimum or go beyond?

Hannah Gaventa *specializes in post-disaster resiliency and climate adaptation. Currently, Hannah works on a UK government program targeting education and skills development.*

VEGAN YAKITORI

Jonah's wife would go up to Jerusalem during the Festival pilgrimage, and she probably packed food for her journey. I made a vegan yakitori for Jonah's wife because I wanted to offer her a simple recipe that travels well, and combines my Japanese and Jewish identity and heritage.

In traditional yakitori, various cuts of chicken are prepared into bite-sized pieces, marinated in a savory-sweet sauce, and cooked over a hot grill.

Today, chicken-style tofu can be used as a substitute for meat. This vegan recipe uses two different types of vegan "chicken" nuggets marinated in a homemade Japanese tare sauce, along with sweet potato and spring green onions. This vegan yakitori is delicious hot or cold, at home or on a journey.

Prep Time: 10 minutes +
30 minutes marination
Cook Time: 5 minutes
Yield: about 12 skewers

Tools:

- Grill
- Prep bowl
- Soup pot
- Wooden skewers, 1 pack

Ingredients:

- 1 packet of plant-based soy nuggets
- 1 packet of tofu nuggets
- 3 large spring onions
- 2 large Japanese yams (Satsumaimo) (substitute sweet potatoes)
- Za'atar seasoning for a light marinade and coating

For the tare sauce:

- ¼ cup (60ml) soy sauce
- ¼ cup (60ml) mirin
- ⅛ cup (30ml) sake
- ⅛ cup (25g) brown sugar
- ¾ tbsp rice vinegar
- 1 tsp black pepper
- 1 tsp minced garlic
- 1 green scallion, sliced
- 1½ tsp grated ginger

Instructions:

1. Soak the skewers in warm water for 20 minutes before using to stop them from burning during cooking.
2. Combine all the tare sauce ingredients in a bowl, mix until smooth, and set aside.
3. Cut the soy and tofu nuggets into triangles and squares, and transfer into the tare sauce to marinate for at least 10 minutes.
4. Wash and slice the green spring onions into thick slices.
5. Peel the sweet potatoes and dice into 2–3-inch squares. Parboil for 5–8 minutes until a little more than al dente. Rinse in cold water and drain.
6. Thread the yakitori ingredients onto the skewers, alternating between pieces of tofu, soy nuggets, onions, and sweet potato squares.
7. Gently sprinkle the vegetables and tofu with za'atar.
8. Heat the griddle pan and brush with oil.
9. Place loaded skewers on the hot grill and brush the top side with tare sauce.
10. After a few minutes, flip and brush with tare sauce again.
11. Repeat flipping and brushing every few minutes until golden brown on all sides. It will take about 8–10 minutes.

Dee Sanae, writer and social justice activist, focuses on making an inclusive and tolerant society through community and coalition building. She founded the Mosaic Visions Organization.

STORY

Kimchit[1] is remembered as a modest woman who was the mother of High Priests. In a way her story remains hidden, but is inferred through her sons' spiritual standing and positions, and by the response she gives to a question from the Sages.

Her son Yishmael, a High Priest at the *Beit HaMikdash*, is referred to as the "son of Kimchit."[2] One of Yishmael's duties was to prepare the incense and offer it at the Golden Altar on Yom Kippur. Yishmael would fill his hands with incense and transfer it into a large spoon, then enter the inner sanctum of the Temple with a shovel of coals in his right hand and the spoon of incense in his left. The Gemara relates that Yishmael had exceptionally large hands and could fill his spoon with so much incense it weighed as much as the coals.

When Yishmael scooped the incense, he stated: "All the mothers selected the best, the selection of my mother rose to the top."[3] With these words, Yishmael seems to credit his mother for his impressive physical stature.

Similarly, it seems that the Gemara credits Kimchit with her son's spiritual standing, as Yishmael is known by his matronym "son of Kimchit."[4]

We then learn that when Yishmael was unable to fulfill his duties as High Priest his brother filled in for him, and thus Kimchit saw two of her sons serve as High Priest on the same

---

1. Talmud.b.Yoma 47a, Talmud.y.Yoma17b.
2. This is highly unusual, compounded by the fact that the priestly caste, as all tribal affiliations, is transmitted by the father's line and not the mother. We know nothing about Kimchit's family before she was married, her husband's lineage, or even his name. As opposed to the priestly affiliation, her personal significance is not inherited; it appears to be based on her own merit. This passage also implies that Kimchit is the head of this family, at least in a spiritual sense.
3. As his language is vague, the Gemara offers two possible explanations – either Yishmael is referring to the special flour his mother ate while she was pregnant to ensure her son's future health, or it is a euphemism for the sperm which her womb chose to fertilize her egg. Either way, Yishmael credits his mother for his impressive stature.
4. This impression is reinforced as the Gemara further relates two occasions when Yishmael was ritually unclean and temporarily unable to perform the duties of the High Priest. In both cases, one of his brothers served in his place. The Gemara concludes both these stories with the statement, "Thus their mother [Kimchit] saw two [of her sons] serve as High Priest on the same day."

day. The Gemara relates that Kimchit had seven sons and all of them served as High Priest in the Temple, presumably filling in for one another when necessary.

The Sages ask Kimchit directly what she did to merit seven sons who all served as High Priests. She responds: "In all my days the beams of my house have not seen the braids of my hair." The Sages end with a comment that many women have done the same without any advantage.

This is the story the Talmud tells about Kimchit.

PASSAGES

Talmud b. Yoma 47a

CONTEXT

The meaning of Kimchit's story is open to polarized readings. Either the Sages are holding her up as a paragon of modesty, or rejecting her behavior as unnecessary. Either the Talmud is presenting Kimchit as a virtuous matriarch who birthed a dynasty of spiritual leaders, or as a superficially pious woman whose sons are emblematic of the problematic priestly leadership of the latter portion of the Second Temple period.

The story is read one way or the other depending on how the reader answers the following questions:

Were the sons of Kimchit pious, and to what degree?

It is believed that the story of Kimchit and her sons takes place at some point in the last 200 years of the Second Temple. Both religious and secular sources from this era often critique the High Priests of this time as not particularly pious, and often corrupt. A symptom of this corruption was the turnover rate of High Priests, turning a position that had formerly been a lifetime appointment into a political commodity bought and sold at an alarming rate.

In this light, this story could be read as critical of Kimchit's behavior.

There are those who read this story as a cautionary tale of a woman who valued cosmetic and frivolous modesty and thus instilled her sons with a superficial spirituality that led to later corrupt behavior. They are another example of corrupt leaders at the end of the Second Temple period. This popular interpretation may fit well with the time period this story is set in, but it clashes with the language of the Gemara, which is overwhelmingly positive when discussing both Kimchit and her sons.

Is it positive to have seven sons from the same family serve as High Priest?

Throughout the First Temple period, the position of High Priest was both hereditary and a lifetime appointment. Though this seems to be the case for much of the Second Temple period as well, it changed at some point during the Hasmonean dynasty, when the position became a political appointment with established term lengths.

So, why were seven of Kimchit's sons eligible to serve as High Priest? Were they dealing the position like a commodity, as many did in that time? Or perhaps, as the Gemara indicates, all of Kimchit's sons were as meticulous and pious as their mother – careful to observe the laws of ritual purity as it seems she observed her modesty.

What standards of modesty were expected from women during Kimchit's time, and is Kimchit's story a benchmark for Jewish modesty standards?

The Gemara in Ketubot 72a–b relates that the Torah prohibits a woman from going out of the home with her hair completely uncovered, and that there are further cultural norms that dictate the extent of hair covering outside the home. Yet nowhere in the Gemara is there discussion of hair covering inside the home. However, generations of rabbinic Sages have debated whether the description of Kimchit's hair covering was utterly rejected by the rabbinic leadership of her time, or whether it is a standard that all women should continue to strive to attain.

AGGADAH

One must begin with the obvious – Kimchit's statement about her hair cannot be understood literally. At the very least she must have uncovered her hair to bathe. This was probably done relatively frequently, as one can assume she meticulously observed the laws of ritual purity that were especially relevant to the priestly class at that time, which necessitated frequent bathing.

It seems that the Sages' inquiry is sincere. They truly want to know what she did to raise such exemplary sons. They are not asking how she raised corrupt leaders. Her answer, though, is curious. Are we meant to believe that Kimchit herself attributed the spiritual achievements of her sons to her extreme zealotry regarding the laws of modesty? More specifically hair covering? This seems unlikely and reductionistic.

Kimchit's son Yishmael dodges flattery of his physical stature with the words: "I owe everything to my mother." This is a man who understands that he did not achieve his lofty spiritual position on his merit alone. He understands that he is subject to God's authority. He is willing to step down from his position, albeit temporarily, and share the limelight with his brother when mandated by God's law. He is both meticulous and humble – welcome traits in a spiritual leader. Traits that both he and the Sages attribute to his mother.

Perhaps Kimchit's statement about covering her hair at all times is another form of modesty. The Sages ask her to detail her merits; she demurs. One of the more charitable explanations of the halachic obligation of a married woman to cover her hair is to leave some things private, between a woman and her spouse. Perhaps Kimchit is telling the Sages that just as she does not flaunt her physical beauty, so too she will not flaunt her spiritual beauty. There are some things a woman keeps to herself.

Many rabbinic calls to female modesty sound dated and patriarchal. In this day and age it sounds tone deaf to claim that women should dress for the male gaze. Feminism is about choice; each individual woman should get to choose what they wish to reveal, when, and to whom.

And yet it often feels like modesty is a lost art. Not the modesty of policing dress and measuring hemlines, but the modesty of choosing to keep some things private, of concealing the external so that the internal and spiritual are more clearly seen.

PROMPTS

- What place does modesty have in our modern world? For women? For men? For humans?
- Kimchit chooses to stay hidden – Is her modesty a form of patriarchal oppression? Is it a personal choice or one imposed on her by society? Can these things ever be separated?
- Do virtuous people have a special responsibility to share their story so others may learn from them?

Rabbanit Debbie Zimmerman *graduated from the first cohort of Hilkhata – Matan's Advanced Halakhic Institute in Jerusalem. Debbie lives in Jerusalem.*

SPICED ACORN SQUASH BREAKFAST BAKE

Kimchit had to prepare breakfast every day for her seven sons. I imagine Kimchit quadrupling this recipe and placing a deep, steaming baking dish on the family breakfast table.

Like Kimchit, the mother of High Priests, the acorn squash is modest, concealing its earthy, colorful, delightful flesh under an unremarkable green skin.

This recipe will show you the joys of eating vegetables for breakfast, and can double up as a sugar-free dessert. This baked acorn dish combines the creamy flesh of the squash and vegan yogurt with the tartness of apples, the crunch of walnuts, and the melted sweetness of dates.

Prep Time: 1 hour
Cook Time: 50 minutes
Yield: 2 servings

Tools:

- Knife
- Deep-sided baking dish
- Aluminum foil
- Soup spoon
- Measuring spoons and cups

Ingredients:

- 1 acorn squash
- ½ tsp ground cinnamon (more or less to your taste)
- ¼ tsp ground cardamom
- ¼ tsp sea salt
- 1 apple, cored and chopped into small pieces
- 3 dates, pitted and chopped
- ¼ cup (55g) chopped walnuts
- ½ cup (120ml) nondairy, unsweetened yogurt (plain or vanilla)
- Tiny bit of oil to rub on pan
- 1 tbsp hemp seeds or 1 tsp ground flaxseeds

Instructions:

1. Preheat the oven to 400° F (200° C).
2. Line a deep-sided baking dish with tinfoil. Rub with a tiny bit of oil.
3. Cut squash in half widthwise to make two little squash boats.
4. Using a soup spoon, scoop out the seeds. Either discard them or set aside to clean and roast later.
5. Rub the fleshy part of the squash with cinnamon, cardamom, and a bit of sea salt.
6. Place squash on pan flesh side down, adding a little water to prevent burning.
7. Bake for about 40 minutes, or until squash is soft and can be pierced with a fork.
8. Flip the squash over. To the hollowed-out middles, add the apples, dates, walnuts, and yogurt, and put back in the oven for about 10 minutes.
9. Take out and sprinkle with hemp seeds or ground flax. Serve warm.

Karyn Moskowitz is a food justice organizer and social entrepreneur, working in the Ohio River Valley. She is a mom to a veggie-loving daughter.

LIKHLUKHIT / לכלוכית

STORY

There was once a woman whose husband was repulsed by her. He made a legally binding declaration: Just as the consecrated sacrifices in the Temple are off-limits to me, so too you are "*konam*," forbidden to me, unless Rabbi Yishmael the son of Yosei can identify even a single redeeming feature in you.

The woman came before Rabbi Yishmael, who was known to believe that creating harmony between a husband and a wife was a social priority.

He brought her before his students. Studiously, they assessed this woman trying to find something…anything…beautiful about her. Her head was dismissed as being too round and her hair was found to be stiff, like strands of flax. Her eyes were rejected as too narrow while her ears were thought to be too large. Her nose was too stubby and her lips too thick. Her neck was too short while her stomach was deemed swollen. Even her legs were critiqued for being as thick as the legs of a goose. At this point, Rabbi Yishmael and his students were stumped.

Rabbi Yishmael, who was a peacemaker for married couples and an advocate of Jewish women's beauty, was unable to find a single redemptive feature in this woman. At their seeming wit's end, the rabbis wondered about her name. Using a pun, they said "*shema* (perhaps) *shema* (her name)?" – "Is it possible that we might find some quality in her name that is beautiful?" At this point her name is revealed to the rabbis and the reader as Likhlukhit, from the root of *likhlukh*, meaning dirty. Rabbi Yishmael then says, "Aha, finally we have come upon a beautiful feature of this woman. Her name is *yafeh* (beautiful or fitting). She is called Likhlukhit (meaning dirty) for she is dirty with blemishes."

Upon establishing that her name was Likhlukhit's beautiful feature, the rabbis declare that her husband's vow is indeed invalid for it was conditional on Likhlukhit being entirely ugly. Likhlukhit remained protected by the parameters of her marriage contract.

PASSAGES

Talmud b. Nedarim 66b

CONTEXT

The story of Likhlukhit is found in the context of a discussion about vows, *nedarim*, that have been taken by men in relation to their wives or betrothed. A person's vow is considered to be binding. Generally, the rabbis were disapproving of people taking on extra vows because extricating oneself from a vow is a tricky business.

There is a section in Tractate Nedarim that talks specifically about men who seek to use a vow in order to disavow themselves from their duties and obligations to their wives. They cite a formula in order to do this, saying "you are *konam* to me." "*Konam*" is a play on the word *korban,* meaning Temple sacrifice. In using this formula, a man effectively says, "you, my wife, are as disconnected from me as the forbidden food of the Temple sacrifice." In this tractate, we find a collection of anecdotes about men who sought to take this vow because they found their wives to be unattractive or even repulsive. This served as a justification for saying, "she is *konam* to me, as forbidden to me as a Temple sacrifice." Because vows were considered to be binding, one could not easily dismiss them. However, allowing these vows to take effect was equally problematic, as it would leave a woman without the protection of her marriage contract. These vows were a disruption of the social order, with concrete social and economic consequences for the women involved.

AGGADAH

Likhlukhit petitions the rabbis to assist her by rendering her husband's disavowal vow invalid. The rabbis go through an ardent process to invalidate Likhlukhit's husband's vow by showing the contingent claim of the husband to be untrue. In seeking loopholes to assist Likhlukhit, the rabbis raise questions about beauty and ugliness. The rabbis – the halachic interpreters of the law – assume a very different role in this *sugya*: it is as if our wise, thoughtful Sages are presiding at a kind of ancient beauty pageant set in a courtroom. This beauty pageant involved a dehumanizing and most likely deeply humiliating experience for Likhlukhit – being paraded in front of Rabbi Yishmael and his students and having them name all her physical flaws out loud.

On one level, the story of Likhlukhit suggests that vows about our most intimate relationships are, simply put, not a good idea. It reflects badly on a man or a woman to summarily vow a disconnection from their partner based on feelings about their physical features. A society that seeks to protect the more vulnerable members – including women, widows, and orphans – suffers if a wife loses her status because of something as subjective as her appearance.

On a deeper level, perhaps the rabbis are sending out a message about the value of marriage. The Talmud and the Midrash claim that God cares about love and marriage and therefore the rabbis should care about it too.[1] On the one hand, feeling repulsed by one's partner could be valid grounds for divorce, since a couple with no physical attraction should not be compelled to stay together in a loveless and un-erotic marriage. At the same time, the rabbis in this story advocate for the idea of working on a marriage, and model this by searching for a redemptive feature in Likhlukhit. Perhaps they are showing the men of their time that while the fiery passion of the first period of falling in love disappears, the work of marriage requires that we make an effort to find and connect with the external and internal beauty in our partner.

Finally, performative speech is key to this story. Just as words affect the binding nature of a vow, Likhlukhit's name (itself a word) engenders the creation or revelation of her beauty. The husband attempts to use words to escape his marital vow; in turn, the rabbis use words to strengthen the marriage contract.

Likhlukhit's name serves as a vow or testament of her congruence. That her name matches her essence or reflects "truth" is an ironic contrast to her unnamed husband's words: his claim is neither truthful nor congruent. The story presents a countercultural comment: sometimes the dispossessed and disempowered in society display more congruence in their being than the person with more power.

---

1. See for instance, Vayikra Rabah 8:1, where it tells a story of a Roman Matron who asked Rabbi Yosei bar Chalafta what God has been doing since He created the world. Rabbi Yosei answers that God makes marriages. In answering thus, Rabbi Yosei conveys that from the rabbinic point of view, God cares deeply about love and marriage and indeed sees love and marriage as holding a weight that is equivalent to the task of the creation of the world.

This story is recorded about a woman because men could take vows about objects or things they had acquired. On the most technical level, in the legal act of marriage women are acquired as wives, rendering them their husband's property. However, the marriage contract obligates the husband to protect his wife. By recording this story about a woman – the so-called property of the man in the halachic system – the tale provides a subtle critique of the system, and warns men not to take advantage of the women they marry. The law may situate a woman as property but the rabbis see the woman as human. She is a sentient being with feelings, thoughts, and agency, who is legally entitled to be treated in an ethical manner.

PROMPTS

- Likhlukhit goes to Rabbi Yishmael for support when her husband tries to break his marriage vows. What did Rabbi Yishmael do for the legal rights of Likhlukhit and all women at this time?
- There are so many ways in which our society attempts to define what is beautiful. What do you think we should teach girls and women about inner and outer beauty?
- In Kabbalah, *Tiferet* (Glory) could be understood as the quality of beauty that is defined as the perfect balance of *Chesed* (Kindness) and *Gevurah* (Strength or Boundaries). How would you explain beauty as the integration of these two qualities?[2]

Adina Roth *is a Jewish educator, psychologist, aspiring runner, yogi, lover of nature, Jewish texts, and stories. She is also a student at Maharat.*

---

2. With thanks to my friend Shannon Walbran for sparking this question.

ZOHARIT SKIN, HAIR, AND GUT SUPPORT

This non-edible skin cleanser and hair rinse morning elixir would have helped Likhlukhit care for her own body: her straw-like hair, the spots on her face, and her swollen stomach.

Skin and Hair:

Apple cider vinegar and tea tree oil are great for all skin types and hair. This concoction treats acne and spot-prone skin, improves complexion, and boosts overall skin health. For the hair, it is a natural hair softener and is also an effective treatment for dandruff.

Gut Health:

Consuming apple cider vinegar is medicinal for our guts and reduces bloating.

Prep Time: 15 minutes
Cook Time: 0

Tools:

- Cotton pads
- Mixing bowl
- Spoon
- 50ml jar

Ingredients:

For hair and skin remedy:

- 2 tbsp (25ml) organic apple cider vinegar
- 10 drops tea tree essential oil
- 2 tbsp (25ml) filtered water

For apple cider vinegar morning elixir:

- 1 tbsp (15ml) apple cider vinegar
- 8 oz (240ml) fresh water

Instructions for hair and skin remedy:

1. Pour the apple cider vinegar into a mixing bowl.
2. Add the tea tree oil and mix.
3. Add water and mix.
4. Pour into a clean 50ml jar and store out of direct sunlight.

How to use:

For face (morning and/or evening):

Douse a cotton pad and massage your clean face in a circular motion. Douse another cotton pad and clean behind the ears and neck.

For hair:

Use as a rinse after shampoo, as a substitute for conditioner. Pour the mixture over hair evenly, working into the scalp. Let it sit for a couple of minutes before rinsing clean with water.

Instructions for apple cider vinegar morning elixir:

Dilute apple cider vinegar in a glass of water each morning or evening as an enjoyable drink that reduces bloating.

__Chanita Golomb__ is a daughter of hippies and grew up in a colorful, lively home where aromatherapy was commonplace. She is the founder of Chanita's Naturals.

LILITH[1] / לילית

STORY

Lilith, our night-demon, threads her way through the Talmud leaving her violent and deadly mark as she goes. While in the Tanakh, she is only referenced once as a night-demon, she comes to life in the Talmud.[2]

Yet we catch only glimpses of Lilith in the Talmud, leaving space for many questions. Mostly Lilith is seen in the dangerous and transitional moments of birth or sexual relations. In one Talmudic passage, we are brought into the story of a woman's labor. She gives birth to a fetus in the form of a lilith, whom Rashi, the medieval commentator, says has a human face and wings.[3] Another passage explains that Adam, after his exile from the Garden of Eden, bore spirits, demons, and night-demons (liliths).[4]

But it is in Tractate Shabbat of the Babylonian Talmud that we come across the real might and danger of Lilith. Rabbi Chanina makes a pronouncement that "it is prohibited to sleep alone in a house, and anyone who sleeps alone in a house will be seized by Lilith."[5] Apart from other scant mentions of liliths, much is left to our imagination.[6]

It is later in our tradition, within these spaces left by the Talmud, that Lilith becomes a fully formed, dangerous creature who preys on babies during the night. The Midrash of the Alphabet of Ben Sira, from the Geonic period, gave us Lilith's origin story as the first wife to Adam, who fled after he denied her the equality she was entitled to.[7] In this satirical work, Lilith utters God's ineffable name and flies away, wings and all. In a heated discussion with

---

1. Lilith is mentioned in Talmud.b.Eruvin.100b, Talmud.b.Niddah.24b, Talmud.b.Shabbat.151b, Talmud.b.Bava Batra. 73a–b, Talmud.b.Eruvin. 18b and in Talmud.b.Pesachim 112a.

2. Isaiah 34, 14. And see the Encyclopedia Judaica's entry on Lilith for other sightings of Lilith across other traditions. Fred Skolnik and Michael Berenbaum (eds.), *Encyclopaedia Judaica, Second Edition, Volume 13* (Detroit: Thomson Gale, 2007) 17–20.

3. Talmud.b.Niddah.24b.

4. Talmud.b.Eruvin. 18b.

5. Talmud.b.Shabbat.151b.

6. Talmud.b.Bava Batra. 73a–b where Lilith's son Hurman is mentioned and Talmud.b.Pesachim 112a, which includes a warning not to drink from water at night, the abode of night demons.

7. Alphabet of Ben Sira 78.

God's angels she refuses to return and announces that her purpose in creation is to sicken babies – explaining the use of amulets during childbirth to keep Lilith at bay.

Throughout the ages, and many kabbalistic renderings, Lilith, the night-demon, is born. Said to be wife to Satan and linked to the Queen of Sheba, her demon babies continue to roam our world threatening the safety of men, women in labor, and babies.

PASSAGES

Talmud.b.Eruvin.100b, Talmud.b.Pesachim 112a, Talmud.b.Shabbat.151b

CONTEXT

Demons are universally present in religion, occultism, literature, fiction, mythology, and folklore.

Although other Near Eastern, polytheistic religions assigned roles to particular demons, some with godlike characteristics, the Torah marked a move away from demonology and toward monotheism. Yet traces of beliefs in demons survived in the Torah, where we see them living in isolated places, coming out at night and causing chaos.[8] References to demons continue in rabbinic literature as we read that, for example, Rabbi Yochanan ben Zakkai was proficient in the "speech of the *shedim* (demons)."[9] While the Jerusalem Talmud is relatively free of references to demons, the Babylonian Talmud is replete with stories of these evil spirits. Later Jewish thinkers, such as Maimonides and Abraham Ibn Ezra, rejected these traditions. The demons of old were dismissed and forgotten about.

Perhaps Lilith, a female night-demon, bent on disrupting births and lurking in the shadows, was an attempt at understanding the cruel nature of death and of the dangers of childbirth. The warnings may have helped the rabbis have a sense of control over events that were seemingly all-powerful and terrifying. Perhaps demons were also a device to help them place human tragedies with a larger struggle between good and evil.

---

8. See Leviticus 16:10, Isaiah 31:32, 34:14 and 1 Samuel 16:15, 23 for some examples.
9. Talmud.b.Sukkot.28a.

It is not surprising that it was a female demon who disrupted and killed. Women are often demonized, dehumanized and sidelined as a way of strengthening male power and authority.

AGGADAH

The woman who came after me was named the Mother Of All Life. They have wrongly cast me as the Mother Of All Death. My name has been sullied and I have been held responsible for the premature ending of infant lives. People's fear of childbirth, death, and sickness have led them to construct false stories, and they seek to exile me. How little they know of my true power and story.

I fled the Garden of Eden to protect the principles of equality and justice, and I am so grateful that I left. Many years after I fled Adam, I was curious to see what had become of him, and so I broke through those gates to the Garden of Eden and saw her. I returned for her over and over again. I observed Eve. She was so trapped in that garden, hemmed in and disconnected from her own power, desires, and needs. She had no voice and no connection with God. She was walking about in a daze, unable to see the possibilities before her. I saw myself in her. But I knew her path could be different to mine. If only I could teach her, then she could break out and bring Adam with her – she could do things differently.

I wanted to make more direct contact with Eve, so I spoke words of encouragement to her through the gaze of the serpent. I showed her how to live a life of curiosity, how to ask questions and not trust the words of those men. I taught her how to fill her belly, how to be nourished, and how to take pleasure through those juicy figs. I broke her out of the Garden of Eden and taught her how to give birth to her children and her own needs. Yes, I brought into the world pain, death, struggle, tears, blood, grief, and growth, but that was necessary so that her naming and owning herself could be unleashed. I taught her to disrupt and how to find peace.

My power, for some, feels terrifying. They call it evil – the work of devils. Yet I teach about life, gratitude, and the power of the woman. I lurk in the shadows, on the margins, in the darkness. Women feel me close to them when they are most vulnerable and beginning to collapse under the weight of patriarchy. Like when they awaken in the middle of night engulfed by self-sabotaging thoughts and are almost ready to give up on themselves.

I attached myself to Eve and have stayed close to women ever since. I provoke them to find their own power and use their voices. I am beside them as they negotiate and break cracks in and chip away at the systems of power that hold them back.

I keep watch.
I am a deep, wild, unstoppable force.
For I am Lilith.

PROMPTS

- What lurks in the shadows for you?
- Are you able to feel the deep power within yourself? How can you step into that power?
- What would it mean for you to uphold the principles of equality and justice?

Rabbi Robyn Ashworth-Steen is a community rabbi in Manchester, UK, who is committed to co-creating relational, textured, spiritual, and activist communities.

MILLET CORIANDER CROQUETTES WITH PUMPKIN TRUFFLE CREAM SAUCE

I wanted to offer a dish that responded to the anger I see in Lilith. I created this dish to give her calming and grounding foods to heal her angry liver and support her spleen.

The recipe is easy to prepare and can be served in variations. It can be fried or baked. Before forming the patties it can be served as a delicious alternative to mashed potatoes.

Both millet and cauliflower are grounding foods, and in the preparation, we are invited to connect to mother earth. The sweetness of cauliflower and pumpkin supports the pancreas. In Chinese medicine these vegetables are prescribed to strengthen women's Hara (localized at the navel, thought of as the source of "Qi" or vital life energy).

This dish is a baked savory delight, bathed in a delicious, nutritious, hearty sauce with a touch of luxury truffle oil.

Prep Time: 20 minutes
Cook Time: 20 minutes
Yield: 12 patties

Tools:

- Stainless steel pot with lid
- Baking tray or frying pan
- Large mixing bowl
- Cutting board
- Sharp knife

Ingredients:

For the croquettes:

- 1 cup washed millet
- 1 cup cauliflower, washed and cut into florets
- 1 tsp Himalaya or sea salt
- 4 cups water
- 1 bunch coriander, finely chopped
- 1 large onion, finely chopped
- Sunflower oil, for frying

For the sauce:

- 1 cup pumpkin, roughly chopped (preferably sweet like kabocha or butternut squash)
- 1 medium onion, roughly chopped
- ½ tsp sweet paprika powder
- ½ tsp garlic powder
- ½ tsp coriander powder
- ½ tsp onion powder
- Cayenne pepper to taste
- ½ cup plant-based cream such as soy, almond, cashew, or coconut

Instructions:

To make the patties:

1. Add millet, cauliflower, and salt to a pan of boiling water. When the water comes back to the boil, reduce the heat to very low, cover, and cook for 30 minutes. When all water has been absorbed, transfer the millet to a large mixing bowl and add the chopped onions and coriander. Season with salt and mix well.
2. Using wet hands, form round or oval patties – do not flatten.
3. Fry in sunflower oil till golden brown, or pat with olive oil and bake in a 350° F (180° C) oven for 20 minutes, then turn the heat up high for a final 5 minutes.

To make the sauce:

1. Boil the pumpkin and onion in water seasoned with salt and spices, until soft.
2. Drain and puree with an immersion blender. Add in the cream until the sauce is your desired shade of orange.

To serve:

Place 3 or more cooked croquettes on a semi-deep plate and pour the pumpkin orange sauce around it to half cover the croquettes. Garnish with chopped coriander.

Liat Solomon *is an alternative medicine practitioner. Her methods are based on Chinese medicine, Oriental diagnosis, alternative medicine, Jewish mysticism, macrobiotics, and intuitive reading.*

THE MAIDEN WHO PRAYS
CONSTANTLY / בתולה צליינית

STORY

As our rabbis consider examples of people who erode the world, the maiden who prays constantly is listed as one such person, along with the abstinent woman, the overly friendly widow, and the child who did not complete their gestation period.

Our rabbis were troubled by the suggestion that a woman devoted to prayer could cause decay to the world, asking, "Could it really be so?" On the contrary, Rabbi Yohanan taught that we can all learn the values of awe and fear of wrongdoing from maidens.

Our maiden was once overheard by Rabbi Yohanan as she fell on her face in spontaneous prayer, crying out to the Divine in hopes that she would not cause a single human being to stumble or do any wrong.

PASSAGES

Talmud.b. Sotah 22a

CONTEXT

In our *sugya* the rabbis are concerned about which people cause the world to dissolve or decay – presumably in addition to the woman who commits adultery.

If you're thinking, *How could a woman devoted to prayer possibly cause decay to our world?*, you're not alone! The rabbis were perplexed and made uncomfortable by this suggestion too.

The rabbis suggest possible culprits for the erosion of the world, only to flip the suggestions on their head, proving the exact opposite! The rhetorical style of the rabbis is often to propose absurdities in order to cause the reader to step back, reflect, and ultimately come to the opposite conclusion. The rabbis of the Talmud might have wanted us to ask, "Really? Can this be so?"

Where at first glance our *sugya* seems to promote the rabbis' reluctance to accept women's religiosity, and perhaps even their desire to moderate the behavior of women by elevating the value of modesty, a deeper inspection of the rabbis' proposal and rejection tells us quite the opposite.

AGGADAH

Why does our maiden *fall on her face* in prayer? What does falling on one's face symbolize? Throughout the *Tanach*, falling on one's face is reflective of a wide spectrum of human emotions that include deep joy,[1] humility,[2] remorse,[3] shame,[4] and even relief.[5] Falling on one's face describes a powerful, spontaneous, and emotional prayer that comes from the depths of the soul.

How can we learn the quality of יראת חטא – *yira'at chet*, awe and fear of wrongdoing – from our maiden? When commenting on "those who erode the world," Rashi remarks that this can only refer to women who are adulterous, sorcerous, or *those who see themselves as overly righteous.*

For the rabbis, there is a fine line between just the right amount of piety and too much piety. Prayer that erodes the world, according to Rashi, is inauthentic, haughty, arrogant, and perhaps even self-serving. Could it really be that our maiden, whose prayer was infused with humility and concern for others, is among such overly righteous pray-ers?

On the contrary! By using the biblical expression of "falling on one's face" to describe our maiden's prayer, and by teaching that we learn the qualities of awe and fear of wrongdoing from our maiden, the rabbis of the Talmud imply that those whose prayer is spontaneous, authentic, awe-inspired, and selfless are the truly righteous ones. The story of our maiden suggests that people who pray genuinely and from the depths of their heart – women who bring awe into the world – serve not to erode the world, but to enhance it.

---

1. Avraham in Genesis 17:17.
2. Ruth in Ruth 2:10.
3. Abigail in 1 Samuel 25:23.
4. Moses in Numbers 16:4.
5. Joseph in Genesis 50:1.

PROMPTS

- What is the difference between a righteous and overly righteous person?
- Have you ever prayed a "fall-on-your-face," spontaneous, from the depth of your soul kind of prayer? If so, what prompted this prayer? If not, what factors might be holding you back?
- When do you feel a sense of awe, or ירא (fear)?

Lara Rodin is a student at the Jewish Theological Seminary. When she's not in the classroom, you can find her hiking or cycling near Calgary.

VEGAN NUTTY CHOCOLATE CHIP COOKIES

This story makes me think about how our food choices might make us fall on our faces. Sometimes, we neglect our own nourishment by eating too little, eating too much, or eating foods that are not beneficial to us.

This is especially true with sweets. This chocolate chip cookie recipe hits the taste points and will not make us fall on our faces.

These cookies are Pesach friendly and you can make them with either white beans or sweet potatoes depending on your dietary preference. Sweet potatoes are naturally caramel-flavored, intensely sweet, and full of natural fiber. If you eat Kitniyot during Passover, the beans increase the protein in these cookies.

Prep Time: 20 minutes
Cook Time: 20–24 minutes
Yield: One dozen cookies

Tools:

- Food processor
- Measuring cups and spoons
- Medium bowl
- Parchment paper
- Rubber spatula
- Two baking sheets

Ingredients:

- 1¼ cups (230g) cooked great northern or cannellini beans or 1¼ cups (280g) cooked sweet potato puree (depending on which you eat during the holiday)
- ¼ cup natural almond butter
- 1 tsp vanilla extract
- 2 tbsp (25g) soft light or dark brown sugar
- 1 tsp baking powder
- ¼ tsp salt
- ½ cup (48g) almond flour or matzo meal
- 3 tbsp vegan chocolate chips

Instructions:

1. Preheat the oven to 350° F (180° C) and line two baking sheets with parchment paper.
2. If using, make the sweet potato puree by steaming (don't boil!) peeled, chunked sweet potato and mashing until smooth.
3. Alternatively, rinse the white beans multiple times in the colander.
4. Put white beans or sweet potato puree, almond butter, vanilla, sugar, baking powder, and salt into a food processor.
5. Mix until very smooth, scraping down the sides of the container when necessary.
6. Add the matzo meal or almond flour and pulse a few times – do not overmix.
7. Transfer the dough into a mixing bowl and fold in the chocolate chips.
8. Place rounded tablespoons of the dough evenly spaced 2 inches apart on the baking sheets.
9. Bake for approximately 20–24 minutes, or until they turn golden brown.
10. Remove the cookies from the baking sheet and allow them to cool before serving or storing.

From the Jewish Food Hero Kitchen

MAR SHMUEL'S DAUGHTERS /
בנתיה דמר שמואל

STORY

Mar Shmuel was a name given to Samuel of Nehardea, or Samuel bar Abba, a Jewish *amora* of the first generation. He was a head of a yeshiva in Babylonia. He was, among other subjects, a teacher of halacha. He had two daughters and no sons.

During the war with the Romans, Mar Shmuel's daughters were captured by Roman soldiers. From Babylon, they traveled with their captors until they reached the shores of the Land of Israel. In addition to the emotional experience of being kidnapped, they had an intellectual understanding of how being taken captive could ruin their reputation, and therefore their marriage prospects. They steered their captors to a *beit midrash* to visit their grandfather, Rav Hanina. They wanted to affirm that they had not been raped, but proving that was complex. They came up with a strategic plan to navigate their delicate legal situation, and to prove that they had not been raped while being held captive.

Once they arrived, they left their kidnappers outside the *beit midrash*, and entered alone. If their captors entered with them to affirm their capture, they would immediately have been assumed to have been raped. The daughters knew that they would be believed if they revealed their entire predicament. Following the guidance given to witnesses in the Mishnah, "the mouth that forbids is the same mouth that permits,"[1] a court either believes both parts of a statement, or none. If they told their grandfather that they were taken captive, but not raped, they could leave with their reputations intact.

Each daughter presented herself to Rav Hanina, but was careful to not reveal her identity. "I was taken captive, but I was not violated," the first one stated. Her sister relayed the same. Rav Hanina replied that they were believed in full; they were captured, but had not been raped. He continued: so reliable was their word, that they could marry into the priesthood if they so chose.

---

1. Conservative Yeshiva commentary on Ketubot 18b, retreived from https://www.sefaria.org/Daf_Shevui_to_Ketubot.18b.

They were still in the *beit midrash* when their captors entered, perhaps wondering what was taking so long. Rav Hanina realized that the daughters had purposely kept their captors outside the *beit midrash*, to ensure that he would say they were pure. So precise and legalistic was their ruse, that Rav Hanina whelped, "These are the daughters of a scholar!" It was then whispered across the room that, in fact, these were the daughters of Mar Shmuel.

PASSAGES[2]

Talmud b. Ketubot 23a

CONTEXT

This story is included in a discussion of the credibility of declarations made in a court of law. If a person reveals damaging information about themselves and a remedy for the damage in one breath, both parts of the statement are believed. But if a witness comes to affirm the damaging information, the defendant is no longer believed for the remedy.

This story showcases how a person can argue a case for their own benefit. Mar Shmuel's daughters steered their case right to the court because they knew they must be the first and only witnesses in their case. They knew if their captors were the first to stand as witnesses, their claims that they had not been raped would be deemed unreliable. So they selectively timed and showcased the elements of their case for a positive outcome.

However, this idea of applying legal principles for personal benefit could have been illustrated in other ways. Why use Mar Shmuel's daughters in particular? Scholars suggest that this story also showcases how Mar Shmuel taught his daughters Torah. Their case was complicated, yet these women knew Jewish laws well enough to leave their captors behind. When Rav Hanina says that these are "daughters of a scholar," he is "suggesting that scholars teach halacha to their daughters on many subjects, not just those related to household management."[3]

These daughters symbolize that Torah study permeated the lives of women in Talmudic times. So much so, they could apply intricate legal categories to their lived experience.

---

2. See also, Talmud y. Ketubot 2:6.
3. Hauptman, Judith, "A New View of Women and Torah Study in the Talmudic Period" (JSIJ9, 2010) 249–292.

AGGADAH

The trial of Mar Shmuel's daughters is a Talmudic heist tale that unfolds like a film. These women are cool, calm, and collected. They have a mission to accomplish, and by hell or high water, they are going to see it through. Don't get me wrong, these women were in a complicated situation. We aren't given the details of the hows, whens, or whys of the kidnapping. We don't know how long they've been gone, or how they convinced their captors to listen to their demands. Like the protagonists in a crime thriller, they want to live their lives unhindered by past experiences. They want to be free to marry whomever they choose.

The small details given in the Talmud allow the imaginative modern reader to envision these women as protagonists in a movie. Gutsy women who, amidst a bad situation, decide their own fate.

Every step of their escape is choreographed. They con their captors to become their unknowing accomplices, as they see their plan through. They convince their captors to take them to Israel, or even just to the *beit midrash* of Rav Hanina in a scene that is a masterpiece of negotiation. With guts and guile, they instruct the men to stay outside while they go to Rav Hanina.

The pièce de résistance in the film is the scene when Mar Shmuel's daughters present their case to Rav Hanina. They arrive (in sunglasses, in my head, but not necessarily in yours) sliding into the *beit midrash*, past rows and rows of men staring as they walk down the aisle. They're out of place, but claim the space as their own.

After Rav Hanina looks at both and says, "you are believed!" the daughters exhale, bursting with emotion over their accomplishment. As they strut out of the room, someone notices the strange men outside, and deduces who they are: the captors. Rav Hanina smacks his head, "They're daughters of a wise man!" They knew how to play the long game. But the daughters never heard Rav Hanina's assessment of them. They had already ridden off into the sunset.

PROMPTS

- What does it mean for a person to use their agency to negotiate situations to their advantage?
- Reflect on a time when you behaved in a way that effectively demonstrated your knowledge and skill.
- How do you embody the legacy of your parents?

Zissy Turner *serves on the Judaic Studies faculty at S.A.R. High School. She is certified as a Yoetzet Halakha/Nishmat's Miriam Glaubach Center.*

APPLE SAGE MUFFINS

A sage is profoundly wise, just like the daughters of Mar Shmuel.

These Apple Sage Muffins highlight the wisdom of Mar Shmuel's daughters with a hint of earthy, peppery flavor from the sage underneath the sweetness of the apple.

Perfect for breakfast or a snack, these muffins can be stored in an airtight container for five days.

Prep Time: 10 minutes
Cook Time: 20–22 minutes
Yield: approximately 18 muffins

Tools:

- Box grater
- Measuring cups and spoons
- Mixing bowls, large and small
- Muffin baking pans

Ingredients:

- 1 cup (240ml) almond milk
- 2 tbsp ground chia seeds
- 1 tbsp apple cider vinegar
- 2 cups all-purpose flour
- 1 tsp baking soda
- 1 tsp baking powder
- Pinch salt
- ¾ cup (150g) brown sugar
- 3½ tbsp fresh sage, finely chopped
- 1 heaping packed cup of grated Fuji apples (approximately 2 apples)
- 1 tbsp juice from apples
- 1½ tbsp vanilla extract
- ¼ cup (60ml) olive oil

Instructions:

1. Position an oven rack just above the center of the oven and preheat to 375° F (190° C).

2. Grease the bottoms and sides of the muffin tins well.

3. Mix together the almond milk and ground chia in the small mixing bowl. Add the apple cider vinegar and let sit for at least 5 minutes.

4. Sift the flour, baking soda, baking powder, and salt into the large mixing bowl. Add the brown sugar and sage and whisk everything together.

5. Grate two apples and then squeeze the grated apple gently to expel most of the juice into a small bowl.

6. Measure the grated and squeezed apple.

7. Add the grated apple, apple juice, vanilla, and olive oil to the milk, chia, and vinegar mixture. Whisk until well combined.

8. Pour the wet mixture into the dry and fold together until just combined. Do not overmix.

9. Spoon the batter into the muffin tins, about two tablespoons in each spot (a cookie scoop works well here).

10. Bake in the preheated oven for 20–22 minutes, or until a toothpick comes out clean.

11. Remove the tins from the oven and immediately transfer to a wire rack to cool completely before serving.

Maddie Reich *is a Jewish vegan blogger, recipe creator, and food photographer. She is a cofounder of Jewish Vegan Life.*

STORY

There was a poor man in Mar Ukva's neighborhood. Every day, he would toss four *dinars* through a gap in the (poor man's) door.

One day, the poor man said, "I'll go and see who my benefactor is."

That day, Mar Ukva was delayed in the study hall, and his wife accompanied him.

As (the poor man) heard someone opening his door he ran out to see who it was. Mar Ukva and his wife dashed out of the way and hid in a raked-out furnace. Mar Ukva's legs were singed (by the residual heat). His wife said to him, "Set your legs on mine, they are not burning."

He felt faint. How is it that for all his charity, he was still singed by the fire, and yet his wife merited miraculously unharmed feet?

She said, "I provide food and company for the poor from my home. The benefit they receive from me is direct."

PASSAGES

Talmud b. Ketubot 67b

CONTEXT

Mar Ukva's wife's story is one of several that appear in Talmud b. Ketubot 67b, illustrating the Mishnah's teaching on communal *tzedakah* funds: the amount distributed should enable the needy to maintain their dignity.

This particular aggadah focuses on the value of delivering charity in the form of goods rather than money. Mar Ukva's wife gives charity in the form of a home-cooked meal that immediately satisfies, while her husband's coins are but one of many more steps on the way to the same outcome.

AGGADAH

ומאי כולי האי? דאמר מר זוטרא בר טוביה אמר רב ואמרי לה אמר רב הונא בר ביזנא אמר
ר״ש חסידא ואמרי לה א״ר יוחנן משום רבי שמעון בן יוחי נוח לו לאדם שימסור עצמו לתוך
כבשן האש ואל ילבין פני חברו ברבים

At the conclusion of the story the Gemara asks: And what was all this effort (to remain anonymous) for? As Mar Zutra bar Toviya said that Rav said, and some say that Rav Huna bar Bizna said that Rabbi Shimon Hasida said, and some say that Rabbi Yohanan said in the name of Rabbi Shimon ben Yohai: "*It is preferable for a person to jump into a fiery furnace rather than embarrass his fellow in public.*"

(Talmud B Ketubot 67b)

It appears that the rabbis drew a different conclusion from the story. Mar Ukva indeed tries really hard to avoid embarrassing the recipient of his *tzedakah*. But as he jumps into the still-hot oven to hide, Mar Ukva is dismayed to discover that all his Torah and good deeds do not protect him from feeling the heat, while his own wife's merit protects her.

She, at home, welcomes people in need. She cooks and shares meals at her kitchen table. Her *tzedakah*, delivered face-to-face, creates community. It is a shared meal and conversation. Hunger is satisfied, and souls are nourished by her caring. The recipients feel recognized, their human dignity restored.

Mar Ukva's wife's *tzedakah* reminds us that *tzedakah* can be simple and direct. Her husband's anonymous *tzedakah* is following the letter of the law and bound up with notions of shame, to the extent that he instinctively jumps to hide himself inside an oven rather than be seen.

The fact that Mar Ukva's wife's feet do not feel the sensation of heat within the oven teaches us that there are important and meaningful exceptions to giving *tzedakah* anonymously. Mar Ukva's wife shows us that *tzedakah* is not only giving money anonymously. *Tzedakah* also means giving time, energy, hospitality, and kindness in face-to-face situations.

PROMPTS

- What makes us uncomfortable about coming face-to-face with need and vulnerability?
- How does human connection factor in your own *tzedakah*?
- Think about a woman you know who behaves like Mar Ukva's wife. What does she do right?

Rabba Dina Brawer *is a thought leader and podcaster. Her interests: social change, the nexus between religion and gender, values within halakhah, and meaningful prayer.*

WHITE BEAN KALE STEW WITH MATZO BALLS

I think of Mar Ukva's wife's soft, gentle, and comforting characteristics. I chose to make a stew with matzo balls because it's healing, warm, and filling. This recipe is nourishing for the body and soul – which is what Mar Ukva's wife was about. She connected with the physical in a very spiritual way.

The dish is made with dill, rosemary, and thyme to help nurture the body and support the immune system.

A unique ingredient in the matzo balls is black Himalayan salt. It contains sulfur and gives the vegan matzo balls an egg-like taste.

Prep Time: 25 minutes

Cook Time: 50 minutes

Yield: 6 servings

Tools:

- Cutting board
- Knife
- Ladle
- Large soup pot
- Medium-size bowl
- Measuring cups and spoons

Ingredients:

For the stew:

- 3 cloves garlic, minced
- 1 yellow onion, diced small
- 5 cups (1200ml) vegetable broth
- 2 sticks celery, sliced thin
- 2 medium carrots, diced
- 15 oz (425g) can white beans, such as cannellini
- 2 large handfuls kale
- ¼ tsp cumin powder
- ¼ tsp sea salt
- ½ cup (4.45g) fresh dill
- 1 tsp fresh rosemary, minced
- ¼ tsp fresh thyme

For the matzo balls:

- 1 cup (100g) matzo meal
- ½ tbsp potato starch
- ¼ tsp baking soda
- ¼ tsp baking powder
- ½ tsp black salt (can substitute ¼ tsp sea salt)
- ½ tsp garlic powder
- 1 flax egg (1 tbsp flax meal mixed with 2½ tbsp water, set aside for at least 5 minutes)
- ½ tbsp avocado oil (can substitute canola oil)
- ¾ cup (180ml) water

Instructions:

1. Wash and prepare all the vegetables.
2. In the soup pot, saute the minced garlic and diced onions in a bit of vegetable broth to prevent sticking.
3. Add the celery and carrots, and continue to cook for about 5 minutes.
4. Add in the drained white beans with the rest of the vegetable broth.
5. Cover and bring the soup to a boil. Then, reduce heat to a simmer and cook for 35 minutes.
6. Add in the chopped kale, cumin, salt, and fresh herbs. Let cook for another 10 minutes.

Make the matzo balls:

1. Bring a pot of water to a boil.
2. Combine all the dry ingredients in a mixing bowl: matzo meal, potato starch, baking soda, baking powder, salt, garlic powder. Mix well.
3. Make the flax egg by mixing 1 tablespoon flax meal with 2½ tablespoons water; set aside for at least 5 minutes.
4. Add the flax egg, oil, and water to the dry ingredients. Make sure everything is mixed together well.
5. Roll ping-pong-sized matzo balls and place in the pot of boiling water.
6. Cover and boil for about 8–10 minutes. Scoop them out if you have more to put in the pot. Repeat until done.
7. Assemble just before serving: ladle a few scoops of bean and kale stew into bowls, topping each with 3–5 matzo balls.

Natalya Fisher *is the plant-based chef behind the Little Leaf Kitchen in New York City. Natalya's cooking is influenced by her background in art and aromatherapy.*

MARTA BAT BEITUS / מרתא בת בייתוס

STORY

In Jerusalem, during the time of the siege by the Romans in 70 CE, the population suffered from violence and hunger, as there was fighting and a famine.

At that time, there was a rich woman who lived in Jerusalem called Marta bat Beitus. She sent her servant to buy some fine wheat flour. Although the servant searched extensively, he was unable to find the fine flour she requested. He returned to Marta bat Beitus's house and advised her that only regular white flour was available.

Marta instructed him to buy the regular white flour, but by the time he went the white flour had sold out. He returned a second time and told her there was no white flour, but only dark flour available.

She sent him again, this time to buy her dark flour. And again, by the time he went out, this too had sold out. He came back a third time and told her there was no more dark flour, only barley flour.

She told him to go and get the barley flour for her, but of course, by the time he went back, even the barley flour had sold out.

In desperation, Marta left her house to see if she could find anything else to eat. As she left her house, she stepped in some dung and died of shock. Rabban Yochanan ben Zakkai thus applied to her the biblical verse, "The tender and delicate woman among you who would not adventure to set the sole of her foot upon the ground" (Deuteronomy 28:56).

Some contend that her death was not from stepping on dung but rather from eating a fig. This was not an ordinary fig. It was a fig discarded by Rabbi Tzadok, who observed fasts for 40 years in order that Jerusalem might not be destroyed. When he wanted to restore himself, they used to bring him a fig. He would suck the juice and discard the remaining fruit.

It was recorded that, prior to her death, Marta brought out all her gold and silver and threw it in the street, saying, "What is the good of this to me," thus giving effect to the verse, "they shall cast their silver in the streets."[1]

PASSAGE[2]

Talmud b. Gittin 56a

CONTEXT

Marta's story is a moral instruction about the potential social and personal consequences of personal wealth. Her focus was on obtaining the best flour for herself irrespective of the social circumstances. Her story takes place against the backdrop of the three-year Roman siege on Jerusalem. This wealthy woman's behavior is in unfavorable contrast with that of three wealthy men in Jerusalem at the time.

Nakdimon Ben Guri'on, Ben Kalba Savu'a, and Ben Tzitzit HaKesat promised to pay for the food supply for the city of Jerusalem for as long as the siege lasted. Their three storehouses could have provided for the city of Jerusalem for 21 years. However, the *Biryonim*, a group of Jewish zealots, decided to fight the Romans rather than adhere to the siege. The rabbis preferred to negotiate directly with the Romans. The *Biryonim* set fire to the city's storehouses, causing widespread famine to spread across Jerusalem.

In contrast, Marta used her wealth to secure personal glory rather than to help others. It is recorded that after her first husband died she paid King Yannai a huge sum of money to nominate her new husband to become *Kohein Gadol*. This was despite the fact that he was neither suitable nor elected to the post by the relevant Sanhedrin.

During the most difficult days of the Jewish people, Marta did not use her wealth to help, and perhaps it is for this reason she dies and experiences such a cruel fate.

---

1. Ezekiel 7:19.
2. See also, Talmud.b. Gittin 56a, Talmud.b. Ketubot 104a, Mishnah Yevamot 6:4, Talmud.b. Yoma 18a, Talmud.b. Yevamot 61a.

AGGADAH

The story of Marta is meant to teach us a lesson. Marta is a Talmudic character who comes face-to-face with a timeless conflict: morality and materialism. Her exaggerated material concern is for her own comfort, pleasure, and reputation, during a time of intense suffering for the Jewish people. Ultimately, her materialism leads to her humiliating death.

Marta's priority at the beginning of the story is to buy the best possible flour available in the marketplace for her household. As this becomes successively impossible, she goes through an almost comic series of attempts to buy the next best flour until she realizes her folly and it is too late. After such a cosseted life, when Marta finally does step onto the street to attempt to find food for herself, contact with the real world kills her.

Other stories build the case against Marta as self-centered and precious. The midrash (Eichah Rabbah 1) relates that when Marta wished to see her husband read from the Torah in the *Beit HaMikdash* on Yom Kippur, she had the streets leading from her home to the *Beit HaMikdash* lined with carpets. This was so she would not have to have her feet come too close to contact with the road.

Another example is recorded of Marta's obsession with social status. After her first husband died she paid King Yannai a huge sum of money to nominate her new husband to become *Kohein Gadol.* This was despite the fact that he was neither suitable nor elected to the post by the relevant Sanhedrin.

Today we know that there is no historical record of Marta as a benefactor of the city of Jerusalem. People who do for other people often remain in the historical record via writings or inscriptions dedicated to them. The fact that there are none about Marta may show that she was not particularly generous.

In the real world, materialism – even excessive – rarely leads to actual death. However, Marta's story shows us that materialism leads to a type of spiritual and relational death where there is not much room for worship of God or compassion for others, and destroys your legacy.

PROMPTS

- How does wealth contribute to people losing sight of what is important?
- Is this portrayal of a wealthy woman in the Talmud specific to her gender, or is it interlinked with her actions?
- What can one do to ensure that they realize their privilege and not squander opportunities?

Nomi Kaltmann *is from Melbourne, Australia, where she specializes in charities and not-for-profit law. Nomi is the president of the Jewish Orthodox Feminist Alliance in Australia.*

TURKISH SAND COOKIES

This cookie recipe might have saved Marta bat Beitus' life, since they are humble cookies that use basic items that you probably already have at home.

Also known as Kurabiyes, these sweet, nutty shortbread-like biscuits have a melt-in-the-mouth texture. Versions of the sand cookie are found in countries that were part of the Ottoman Empire. Early recipes similar to Kurabiyes were recorded in the tenth century, but officially arrived in Ottoman cuisine in the fifteenth century.

This recipe is updated with spices, nut butter, and a gluten-free option. As it melts in the mouth, the spices become aromatic.

Prep Time: 10 minutes
Cook Time: 20–24 minutes
Yield: 16–20 cookies

Tools:

- Cookie baking sheets
- Measuring cups and spoons
- Mixing bowl
- Mixing spoon
- Parchment paper

Ingredients:

- 1 cup (250ml) canola vegetable oil
- 1 cup (200g) white sugar
- 1 tbsp creamy peanut butter (or nut butter of your choice)
- 2¼ cups (280g) all-purpose flour (for gluten-free, use 2 cups gluten-free flour blend and ½ cup coconut or almond flour)
- ¼ cup (45g) semolina or cream of wheat
- ½ tsp cinnamon
- ¼–½ tsp cardamom, optional
- ¼ tsp salt
- powdered sugar
- 16–20 raw walnut halves of whole raw almonds

Instructions:

1. Preheat the oven to 325° F (160° C) and line a large baking sheet with parchment paper.
2. Combine the flour, semolina and spices, then add the oil, sugar, and peanut butter. Stir slowly by hand, or with an electric mixer on low speed.
3. If the dough looks dry, add a little more peanut butter.
4. Shape the dough into walnut-sized balls. Place them about 1 inch apart on the lined baking sheet. Flatten the cookies slightly and press a nut into the center of each.
5. Bake cookies on the middle rack of the oven until set and light brown – around 20–24 minutes.
6. Remove from the oven. They will harden as they cool on a wire rack.
7. Sprinkle with powdered sugar while still warm.

Marlene Souriano-Vinikoor is a first-generation American. She was raised on Sephardic cuisine. Marlene lives in Seattle, with three grown children and five grandchildren.

MATRON HEALER FROM TIBERIAS / תימטינוס ברתיה דדימיטינוס

STORY

The story of Matron Healer From Tiberias is recorded in both the Jerusalem and the Babylonian Talmuds. The story is mentioned during a discussion about how severe an illness must be in order to warrant breaking Shabbat to treat it.

Rabbi Yochanan suffered from *tzafdina* (a tooth ailment according to Rashi), and sought treatment from Timtinis in Tiberias on Thursday and then again on Friday. On Friday he asked Timtinis, "What should I do about treatment tomorrow (on Shabbat)?" She replied, "You will not need treatment." But Rabbi Yochanan persisted, "If I do need treatment, what should I do?" Timtinis revealed her remedy to Rabbi Yochanan, but insisted that he commit not to share it with anyone else.

The next day, however, he taught the remedy in his public lecture. In the Babylonian Talmud the story ends here, and the Talmud goes on only to explore whether Rabbi Yochanan had actually sworn not to tell, and the legal implications of procuring the remedy.

The story appears twice in the Jerusalem Talmud. In Tractate Shabbat, the Talmud suggests two possible epilogues to the story: "some say Timtinis choked herself and some say she converted to Judaism." In Tractate Avodah Zara, the alternative reactions are phrased differently. The story ends: "The next day he went and expounded it in the house of study. She heard and choked herself. Some say she converted to Judaism." This telling suggests that her death by suicide might be closer to the true version of events.

PASSAGES[1]

Talmud.b.Avodah Zarah 28a

---

1.   See also, Talmud.y.Shabbat.14:4,14d, Talmud.b.Avodah Zarah 28a, Talmud.y.Avodah Zarah 2:2, 40d.

CONTEXT

The story of Matron Healer From Tiberias may have served two separate legal purposes. In Tractate Shabbat, the direct purpose of the story is to elucidate in what cases using healing treatments on Shabbat is permissible. In Tractate Avodah Zarah, the purpose of the story is to explore the permissibility of receiving healing from gentiles. In Avodah Zarah, the Gemara digresses to question Rabbi Yochanan's actions, eventually reaching the conclusion that he had not breached his promise to Timtinis of Tiberias.

The literary transformation of the character from the Jerusalem Talmud to the Babylonian is noteworthy. In Avodah Zarah of the Jerusalem Talmud, the doctor is called Matron Healer From Tiberias, while in Shabbat of the Jerusalem Talmud she is referred to as the "daughter of Domitianus." The scribe for the Babylonian Avodah Zarah significantly downplays the centrality of Timtinis by referring to her by no name at all, but only by her occupation.

In Tractate Shabbat the Gemara lays out three lessons one can learn from the anecdote: first, that *sifduna* is life-threatening; second, that one may receive treatment for ailments from the lips inward; and third, "if the practitioner is an *expert* physician [the healing] is permitted." This third lesson is profound in its assumption that a woman (at the time) may be considered an *expert* physician. Israeli historian Tal Ilan suggests that because the gender of the doctor is neither commented upon in any important way, nor concealed, we can assume that it was not unusual for a woman to be a distinguished and skilled doctor at the time.[2]

AGGADAH

Trotula of Salerno was a twelfth-century physician, often regarded as the world's first gynecologist, whose work provided the bedrock of women's health science today. Trotula was a victim of historiographical misogyny – skepticism arose as to whether Trotula was actually a woman, and eventually the doubt conveniently paved the way for her manuscripts to be attributed to men. One might question whether a similar phenomenon occurred in the story of Timtinis.

---

2. Tal Ilan, *Silencing the Queen: The Literary Histories of Shelamzion and Other Jewish Women* (Mohr Siebeck, 2006), 168.

Timtinis insisted that Rabbi Yohanan protect the confidentiality of her treatment, and yet he expounded upon it in public anyway. One epilogue of the story suggests that Timtinis choked herself when she heard that her remedy had been aired to the public – is this because her self-worth and life project had been stolen from her?

An alternative to the epilogue of suicide is the suggestion that Rabbi Yohanan divulging her secret remedy inspired her to convert to Judaism. While one may find that this version of events is an ironic historical revisioning of the immoral actions of Rabbi Yohanan, there is something to be learned from this epilogue too.

In the past few hundred years, many countries have developed intellectual property law to protect the rights of individuals and ensure they receive the credit for and benefit of their innovations. While the utility of patents and ownership rights speaks for itself, one should question whether we as a society have lost our ability to share. Jewish thinking straddles a fine line between possession rights and the doctrine that nothing in this world truly belongs to us as individuals. While knowledge might be attained through hard work and intellectual rigor, it should also reasonably benefit as many people as possible. Homo sapiens are the most intelligent animals not because of the size or strength of individual minds, but because of our ability to collaborate and build lasting empires of knowledge together.

Perhaps Timtinis swore Rabbi Yohanan to secrecy because she was concerned that he would sell the recipe for his own financial benefit.[3] She might have been impressed and inspired when she found out that his motives were not selfish or money-seeking but rather he was motivated by the public good.

Women throughout history have contributed to public life and have achieved great things for the benefit of humanity. By revising our stories and assumptions, we can ensure that credit is attributed appropriately and give voice to historically silenced women.

---

3. *Yefei Einayim, Yoma* 84a.

PROMPTS

- Why do you think Timtinis swore Rabbi Yohanan to secrecy?
- Why are tragic endings a common theme in the Talmud's stories about women?
- Is the Talmud appropriately critical of Rabbi Yohanan's actions? Is this a type of historiographical misogyny?

Chaya Herszberg is a Juris Doctor candidate at the University of Melbourne. She is passionate about poetry, philosophy, and Jewish life.

MEDICINAL ELDERBERRY SYRUP

Just as Timtinis offered a healing remedy to Rabbi Yohanan, I am offering this elderberry syrup packed with potent medicine, antioxidants, and vitamins that boost immunity.

Elderberries are anti-inflammatory, supportive to the immune system, and help protect us from bacterial and viral infections.

This syrup is delicious and loved by both children and adults.

Suggested Use:

> *Adults: take one tablespoon per day for maintenance*

> *Children: one teaspoon per day*

Multiply the dose by 4 when a person is feeling unwell.

Please note: Homemade elderberry syrup is not thick like syrup; the consistency is more like elderberry juice.

Prep Time: 10 minutes
Cook Time: 1 hour
Yield: 24 fl. oz

Tools:

- Medium to large stainless steel stock pot
- Large stainless steel spoon
- Nut milk bag, cheesecloth, or fine-mesh strainer
- Measuring cups and spoons or kitchen scale

Ingredients:

- ¾ cup (85g) dried organic elderberries
- 3 cups (700ml) filtered or spring water
- 1–2 organic cinnamon sticks
- 1 tbsp organic ginger, peeled
- 1 tsp organic whole cloves
- ¾–1 cup (180–240ml) organic raw honey

Instructions:

1. In a large saucepan, bring the elderberries, water, cinnamon sticks, ginger, and cloves to a boil.
2. Cover and reduce heat to low. Allow to simmer for 50–60 minutes.
3. Cool the syrup base until it is lukewarm.
4. Mash the berries with a fork while still in the pan.
5. Drain the liquid using a nut milk bag, cheesecloth, or fine-mesh strainer. Be sure to press all of the liquid out of the berries.
6. Add the raw honey and mix well.
7. Pour into sterilized, airtight glass containers or jars. Store in the refrigerator for up to three months or freeze immediately for up to a year.

Mitten Lowe lives in Boulder, Colorado, and is a mother of two, and a wife. She is a biologist, clinical herbalist, and owner of Journey to Wellness.

MATUN / מתון

STORY

Matun merits seven sentences in the vast corpus of the Talmud.

She walks into the marketplace one day and Rav Adda bar Ahava sees that she is wearing a garment made of a forbidden mixture of wool and linen. He rips the garment off of her, leaving her naked. When it is discovered that she is not Jewish, the Rabbi, Rav Adda bar Ahava, is taken to court for the shame he caused her.

The court forces him to pay her four hundred *zuz* – a significant sum (in comparison, two hundred *zuz* was the amount a woman would be paid upon divorce and is about 1000 grams of silver). At this point, Rav Adda bar Ahava turns to her and asks her what her name is. She replies, Matun.

Her name means slow, careful, or considerate, all things Rav Adda bar Ahava was not. He replies, "Matun, Matun, is worth four hundred *zuz*." This can either mean being slow is worth four hundred *zuz* (i.e., if he had not rushed to judgment he would not have been fined) or it can be a play on the Aramaic word for two hundred – (*matun*), which when said twice is four hundred.

That is where the incident ends. We never hear of Matun again.

PASSAGES

Talmud b. Berakhot 20a

CONTEXT

This story is told in the midst of a discussion about how previous generations were more pious than the current generation. Rav Abba bar Ahava is a second-generation *Amora*, a student of Rav, one of the greatest of the *Amoriam*. He was known as an incredibly pious man.

The story of Matun shows how extreme Rav Adda bar Ahava's actions were. Without a word of discussion or warning, he assumes the right to physically take control of another person in a public place.

The fact that the rabbis fine him severely is indicative of the rabbis' critical position on ill-considered action taken in the name of piety.

The fact that this story is about a woman increases its impact. Women's bodies were more highly regulated than men's bodies in Talmudic times. We can wonder how Rav Adda bar Ahava would have responded if he saw a man wearing linen and wool. We can also wonder how the Jewish court would have responded if Matun had been Jewish.

AGGADAH

This story demonstrates the embarrassment and hurt caused when a seemingly pious person forces their piety onto others.

In the context of the Talmud, it is clear that Rav Adda bar Ahava is a pious person, yet his zealousness is not wholly condemned. The text seems to suggest that his mistake was not in stripping a woman naked in public, but in not checking to make sure she was an Israelite before carrying out such an extreme act.

In a modern context, we can read this story as a cautionary tale of what happens when one religion attempts to police all people, even those who are not believers. Today, we increasingly see attempts to bring the values of one religion (or one branch of one religion) into the public sphere. In the Talmud, the rabbis sanction one of their own for his breach of protocol. He is punished for imposing Jewish rules on a non-Jewish woman, and humiliating her in the process.

The story of Matun calls on us to make sure that we are not forcing others to follow our religious values. It falls on us to take responsibility for calling out people in our community when they cross that line.

Furthermore, this story reminds us that we all can make mistakes. If Rav Adda bar Ahava, one of the most pious of all the ancient rabbis, could give in to emotion and act too quickly, so too we can act rashly. The lesson of Matun is contained in her name – be slow, careful, and considerate in your actions. As we learn in the text Pirkei Avot, "be deliberate in judgment."[1]

PROMPTS

- When have you acted rashly and been quick to judge others?
- Do community leaders need to be held publicly accountable for their actions? What if that accountability is ultimately made to reflect badly on a whole minority group or community (Jews, Muslims, people of color, etc.)? Does that change your feelings about public accountability?
- Matun receives financial compensation for harm done to her. Is that enough? What are other elements needed to have a truly restorative justice model? What responsibility does our society have to those whom we have treated wrongfully in the name of law and order?

Erica Seager Asch is the rabbi of Temple Beth El in Augusta, Maine. She enjoys hiking, cooking, and spending time with her family.

---

1.   Pirkei Avot 1:1 Trans. Dr. Joshua Kulp.

ROASTED GARLIC SOUP

This soup is my Jewish penicillin for when I feel I need a comforting food for self-healing. The shaming of Matun surely created physiological stress for her. This soup will help Matun's body, mind, and soul regain a healthy balance.

The taste is smooth, with a hint of fennel flavor mixed with garlic, but can be altered easily to serve your own taste buds. The roasted/baked garlic puree in the recipe below will produce a very mild flavor. Adding grated raw garlic just before serving gives a punch and will further enhance the healing properties.

Prep Time: 20 minutes
Cook Time: 30 minutes
Yield: 4 servings

Tools:

- Grater (optional)
- Kitchen scale
- Knife
- Large sieve
- 2 small soup pots

Ingredients:

- 1 small bulb garlic
- 4 cups (950ml) of water
- 4 oz (113g) thinly sliced fennel (roughly ½ to 1 whole fennel bulb)
- 1 inch (2.5cm) piece fresh turmeric
- 1 leek, thinly sliced
- 1 dried bay leaf
- Salt and pepper to taste

Garnish:

- Finely chopped coriander

Instructions:

1. Wrap the garlic bulb in foil and bake at 375° F (190° C) for 1 hour. Alternatively, roast in an air fryer for about 10 minutes. It is done when you can pierce through the bulb with a sharp knife. Set aside and allow to cool.

2. Bring the water to a simmering boil in a large soup pot. Add the sliced fennel, turmeric, leek, and bay leaf. Simmer for 15 minutes, then remove from the heat and allow to sit for 5 minutes.

3. Slice top off the cooled roasted garlic bulb. Squeeze into a small bowl. Remove 4 teaspoons and set aside for the soup.

4. Remove the turmeric and bay leaf from the soup.

5. Strain the soup through a sieve to achieve a smooth broth. Either discard the strained ingredients or, alternatively, blend them until smooth and add back into the broth.

6. Gently heat the broth over very low heat and stir through the 4 teaspoons of roasted garlic paste.

7. Bring the soup to a simmer; turn off the heat.

8. Season, sprinkle with chopped coriander, and serve.

Variation: Use a blender to blend ½ cup of roasted cashews with ¼ cup of almond milk, and add the strained ingredients minus the bay leaf and turmeric. Pour into the finished soup and stir until it looks like a thin, creamy mixture.

Sylvie Waxman is a plant-based transition health coach and author of soon-to-be-published book Tikkun Olam in the Kitchen.

STORY

Michal bat Kushi[1] was the daughter of Ahinoam and King Saul, the first king of the United Kingdom of Israel.

Michal, King Saul's youngest daughter, appears throughout the book of 1 Samuel.[2] We learn that Michal falls in love with David, who we know to be the future king of Israel, marries him, and helps David to escape her father when King Saul attempts to kill him.

We also find Michal bat Kushi, Michal, daughter of King Saul, in the Talmud in the Tractate Eruvin. Here we learn that she wore *t'fillin*. In the Babylonian Talmud, the rabbis do not object to her practice, implying that she was permitted to do so.

Later on, the Sages learn about Michal's practice and assume that if she – a woman, and therefore not obligated to do time-bound mitzvot – was permitted to wrap *t'fillin*, then the mitzvah of wrapping *t'fillin* must not be time-bound. However, in the Jerusalem Talmud one Rabbi accounts that the rabbis objected to Michal's practice.

Following Michal's story, the rabbis go on to raise the possibility that a woman can *choose* to fulfill positive, time-bound mitzvot that they are not obligated to do.[3]

PASSAGES

Talmud.b.Eruvin.96a

CONTEXT

The Talmud is trying to answer the following question: does one wear *t'fillin* on Shabbat? It answers this question indirectly, using the example of a woman who wrapped *t'fillin*, Michal bat Kushi. Halacha famously exempts women from positive, time-bound commandments.

---

1. Michal bat Kushi appears in Talmud.b.Eruvin.96a, Talmud.y.Berakhot.14b, Talmud.b.Megillah 15a, Talmud.b.Sanhedrin 19b, Talmud.b.Sanhedrin 21a.
2. Michal appears in 1 Samuel 14:49, 1 Samuel 18:20–28, 1 Samuel 19:11–17, and 1 Samuel 25:44.
3. Rabbanit Michelle Cohen Farber. Daf Yomi for Women (Podcast) Hadran. November 13, 2020.

Michal bat Kushi's story is included here because she did indeed wear *t'fillin*, and so, the Talmud is hoping to conclude that the mitzvah of wearing *t'fillin* is not time-bound, and therefore women are obligated to wear them and they should be donned seven days of the week, including on Shabbat.

By bringing the example of Michal bat Kushi, the rabbis open up another possibility: perhaps women can choose to opt into positive, time-bound mitzvot, like *t'fillin*, even when they are not obligated.

AGGADAH

The other day during weekly Shabbat Torah study, we were discussing different rituals of Shabbat. One person asked the Rabbi, "Rabbi, should we wrap *t'fillin* on Shabbat?"

The Rabbi thought about this and replied, "There are a few questions here. First, by asking if we should wrap *t'fillin* on Shabbat, you could be asking whether or not the mitzvah to put on *t'fillin* is time-bound. If it is not time-bound, then the answer would, of course, be yes – we should also wear *t'fillin* on Shabbat.

"However, by asking this question, and knowing our community," a good-humored smile flickered across the Rabbi's face, "it seems to me that you are asking this question because there are a variety of customs in our congregation. Some people put on *t'fillin* for morning prayer, some wear them whenever possible, and others never don them at all. So, I turn this question to all of you, if you choose to, why do you wrap *t'fillin*?"

My hand shot up immediately. "Because," I said, "Deuteronomy 6:8, the *Shema*, clearly states that we should bind these words on our hands and between our eyes. This is a mitzvah. I learned these words from a young age, watched all of my older siblings fulfill this mitzvah through wrapping *t'fillin*, and I choose to do the same. Through this act, I am a part of the same covenant as my ancestors, I am connected to God, to Torah, and to the Jewish people."

The Rabbi smiled. "You choose to do this mitzvah, Michal, because you feel commanded to, not just by God and Torah, but because it is one way that you keep the covenant and connect with your family and our collective Jewish story. Each of us is searching for connection and meaning, and in the practice of wrapping *t'fillin*, you have found just that."

PROMPTS

■ What rituals or Jewish practices most connect you to your Jewish faith, history, etc.?

■ Who are some of your Jewish role models?

■ What can the Talmud teach us about the diversity of our Jewish ancestors?

Rabbi Jade Sank Ross *serves the Community Synagogue in Port Washington, NY. She lives with her husband, Rabbi Dan Ross, and their dog, Rashi.*

GLUTEN-FREE AMARETTO CAKE

It is written that Michal bat Kushi would watch as David gave out cakes and breads.4 The daughter of a king, she was likely surrounded by all the finest things, including liquor. This cake is flavored with the almond-infused liquor, amaretto.

Another reason I felt drawn to share this recipe is that we are told to teach our children about the mitzvah of t'fillin. Michal wore t'fillin despite not being obligated to.

This recipe was taught to me by my mother, who learned it from her mother, and is one that I hope to teach to my children one day. Though we are not obligated to pass down recipes, in my family it is a special tradition and one that holds great meaning for me.

Amaretto cake can be dressed up with different toppings like roasted nuts. On Rosh Hashanah, I make it with chopped apples and extra honey. The amaretto gives the cake a sweet almond taste, which accents the fluffy cake perfectly.

Prep Time: 20 minutes
Cook Time: 50 minutes
Yield: 8 servings

Tools:

- Bundt pan
- Measuring cups and spoons
- 2 mixing bowls
- Whisk

Ingredients:

For the cake:

- 2 cups (300g) gluten-free all-purpose flour (or regular flour)
- ½ cup (55g) almond flour
- 1 tsp salt
- 1½ tsp baking powder
- ½ tsp baking soda
- 1 cup (200g) sugar
- 1 cup (200g) brown sugar
- 1 cup (180g) margarine or oil
- 1⅓ cups (320ml) plant-based milk
- 1 tsp vanilla
- ½ cup (120ml) Amaretto
- ¾ cup (125g) applesauce (or 4 eggs)

For the topping:

- ½ cup (65g) powdered sugar
- 1 tbsp Amaretto
- ¼ cup (60ml) plant-based milk
- 1 cup (110g) slivered almonds, toasted
- 1 tbsp honey (optional)

---

4. 1 Samuel 6:16–23.

Instructions:

1. Preheat oven to 390° F / 200° C.
2. Combine the flour, almond flour, salt, baking soda, and baking powder in a large bowl.
3. In another bowl, combine the sugars, margarine or oil, milk, vanilla extract, and Amaretto. Add in the applesauce slowly and mix until smooth.
4. Pour the wet ingredients into the dry and combine briefly.
5. Pour the batter into a silicone Bundt pan and bake for 50 minutes.
6. While the cake bakes, combine the powdered sugar, Amaretto, and milk. Place in the fridge for about 30 minutes to thicken.
7. Remove the baked cake from the oven and let it cool.
8. Pour the chilled, thickened glaze over the cooled cake and sprinkle on the toasted almonds. (Alternatively, poke holes in the still-warm cake and pour the glaze over top so it seeps into the entire cake.)

Jazzie Morgan runs an English resource platform on Gluten-Free Israel: The Israel Bites. She accredits her grandparents for her love of baking.

MIRIAM BAT BILGAH / מרים בת בילגה

STORY

We first learn about the Clan of Bilgah in a Mishnaic teaching,[1] which states that they are habitually mistreated and hampered in their Temple duties – their tools are damaged, storage spaces blocked off; they are even chronically short-changed in their showbread allotment.

The Gemara offers an explanation that hinges on the behavior of a clanswoman, Miriam bat Bilgah, who leaves the community and marries a Greek soldier. She then returns to the Temple to chastise God when the Temple appears about to fall into the hands of the Greek army.

PASSAGES

Talmud b. Sukkah 56b

CONTEXT

While this text was probably initially understood as a polemic against intermarriage (or perhaps against women assaulting God and the Temple altar), it's easy to view it as a narrative of a brave woman speaking truth to power.

AGGADAH

Raised in the priestly caste, observing the daily Temple practices, Miriam bat Bilgah *hiemira datah*[2] – changes her religion – *before* she "goes out" (a transgressive act in and of itself) and marries a Greek soldier.

Even after this act of apostasy, she is no stranger to God and the Jewish people: she returns to the Temple, physically striking the altar and accusing God (to whom sheep were daily sacrificed) of being a consuming wolf. Demanding that God not stand by during the Greek invasion, Miriam bat Bilgah follows a long tradition of outspoken Jewish women: criticizing

---

1. M. Sukkah 5:8.
2. While *heimira* (המירה) does mean to change, it is almost certainly a play on the word bitter – *mar* (מר), the base of the name Miriam – i.e., Miriam bat Bilgah is a woman who became embittered about her religion.

and questioning God when male leaders refuse to do so (and taking on the whole sacrificial cult system to boot!).

Miriam bat Bilgah has a lot to teach us about mixed marriage, communal sanctions, and personal relationships with God. While she may change her *dat*, her religion, she retains a strong sense of Jewish identity, and does not feel that conversion precludes her right to be in dialogue with God on behalf of the Jewish people.

So why is the entire clan punished? According to the Talmud, it's because of the principle that the opinions that a child expresses publicly must be those learned in the home: Miriam's behavior only mirrored that which she had been taught. The Clan of Bilgah raised a strong, independent woman who wasn't afraid to rail against God (in God's own house, no less!) and to leave a religious institution that she found meaningless and hypocritical.

PROMPTS

- Do today's institutions (Jewish or secular) do a better job of welcoming and retaining those with critiques and dissenting opinions?
- How are we encouraging future generations to think critically about infrastructures and institutions that may be meaningful to us, but may seem obsolete and harmful to others?
- How do we understand ourselves to be in dialogue with the Divine? Is it a one-time personal interaction, or a communal conversation extending over millennia? And if the latter, how comfortable do we feel/how do we enter that conversation stream?

Rabbi Dena Bodian is Wellesley College's Associate Chaplain and Rabbi. She has plucked chickens, chased goats, davened in a blizzard, and compiled a machzor.

WILD RED RICE ROASTED VEGETABLE PLATTER WITH POMEGRANATE MOLASSES AND FRESH HERBS

This platter features wild red rice, roasted sweet potato, butternut squash, eggplant, and zucchini topped with fresh herbs, pomegranate molasses dressing, and dried cranberries.

Miriam teaches us to be brave and strong, to speak up in the face of injustice and to ensure that we respect everyone no matter their religious or cultural origins. This recipe is unique like her and combines different grains, starches, and vegetables into a delicious dish, perfect for the vibrant Miriam bat Bilgah.

Prep Time: 30 minutes
Cook Time: 20 minutes
Yield: 8 servings

Tools:

- Baking tray
- Colander
- Cutting board
- Large mixing bowl
- Saucepan
- Sharp knife

Ingredients:

- 2 cups (250g) wild red rice
- 2 sweet potatoes, peeled and cubed
- 1 butternut squash, peeled and cubed
- 1 eggplant, cubed
- 1 zucchini, cubed
- 1 tbsp pomegranate molasses
- 1 tbsp soy sauce
- 1 tbsp olive oil
- 1 tbsp white wine vinegar
- ½ tsp Dijon mustard
- Salt and pepper to taste
- Handful dried cranberries
- Zest of 1 orange
- Handful fresh coriander, chopped
- Handful fresh parsley, chopped
- Handful fresh basil, chopped
- Handful fresh dill, chopped
- Handful almonds, chopped

Instructions:

1. Preheat the oven to 350° F (180° C).

2. Cook the rice by boiling in salted water for approximately 20 minutes. Drain and set aside.

3. Meanwhile, scatter the chopped sweet potatoes, butternut squash, eggplant, and zucchini on a baking tray, drizzle with olive oil, season, and roast for 45 minutes.

4. Prepare the dressing by mixing the pomegranate molasses, soy sauce, remaining olive oil, vinegar, and mustard together.

5. Assemble the dish by placing the cooked rice, roasted vegetables, and fresh chopped herbs on a large serving plate.

6. Dress and season before scattering the orange zest, cranberries, and chopped almonds on top to serve.

Allegra Benitah is a corporate tax lawyer turned TV chef in London, England. Allegra shares her recipes and challah bread designs on social media.

STORY

The Talmud relates that Miriam of Tarmod was a Nazirite, a person who has taken a vow to refrain from alcohol, from cutting one's hair, and from becoming ritually impure through contact with a dead body, all for a certain length of time.

Miriam was living at the time of the Second Temple and wanted to bring some sacrifices to the Temple in Jerusalem. She had brought some of them initially, but was then called home because her daughter had fallen critically ill. Upon arrival, Miriam realized that her daughter had died, thus rendering Miriam ritually impure by having had contact with a dead body; this type of impurity is called *tum'at met* (טומאת מת). Therefore, a question arose as to the validity of her previous sacrifices – were they, and those still awaiting sacrifice, still "valid," if the person making the offering had contracted impurity due to contact with a corpse? The rabbis ultimately ruled that in such circumstances, contact with the dead does not interfere with the person making the offering's status *qua* Nazirite, nor with the validity of her sacrifices. In fact, she may proceed to have the rest of her offerings sacrificed and to regain her purity in doing so.

PASSAGES

Talmud b. Nazir 47a

CONTEXT

The main question guiding the Mishnah and Gemara's discussion here is: Can someone who is a Nazirite and is bringing a series of sacrifices to the Temple continue to do so if they accidentally become impure, thus violating their Nazirite vows? What would be at stake in becoming impure: their Nazirite status, and/or their sacrifices? Ultimately, this story demonstrates that the status of a Nazirite is not invalidated, nor are the sacrifices invalidated, in such circumstances.

The story features not one but two women: Miriam of Tarmod *and her daughter*. We see Miriam of Tarmod encounter a conflict between her Nazirite identity and her maternal identity: her daughter is ailing and she is offering sacrifices. Interestingly, the story describes

Miriam of Tarmod's daughter as *m'sukenet* (מסוכנת), or "in danger," i.e., sick enough as to be verging on death. Miriam of Tarmod therefore leaves her sacrificing *knowing* she might very well contract ritual impurity through contact with a dead body.

The story is not one about Miriam's hesitation, but rather about halachic concerns. Ultimately, the law follows the more lenient approach of the rabbis, who validate both her Nazirite status as well as the sacrifices given by the now-impure Nazirite. In this sense, we see this story to be one about law functioning as an expression of compassion, when it is broken in the name of compassion. We see the masculine framing of the law (the rabbis and Rabbi Eliezer), needing to respond to questions emerging from what is framed as the feminine domain of the home, signaled by the sick daughter and the mother. Ultimately, there is a meeting of these gendered spheres found in the sympathetic ruling of the rabbis.

AGGADAH

Imagine: Women sit at a table, surrounded by quiet, by calm, by texts and thoughts. They are studying and discussing the fine points of law. A theoretical question arises: What if a man, a Nazirite, is in the middle of offering sacrifices, but midway through somehow encounters a dead body? Do we say this invalidates all his sacrifices? Does he continue offering the remaining sacrifices and become purified?

As with many legal discussions in this calm, quiet space, the stakes are high in terms of divining what is desired by the Holy One, Blessed be He; until reality breaks through. This decision is both holy and important, but also theoretical. Until...

In runs a man, his clothes in tatters, ashes on his head, tears streaming down his face. Here we see the lived "halachic man" face his esoteric leaders. He cries out: "*Gott in Himmel!* Was it all for nothing?!" The women on the court look down at the supplicant. Chaos has disrupted the pristine and silent hall. "Explain yourself," the head rabbanit says.

The man explains: "I am a Nazir, and I was offering my sacrifices at the Beit HaMikdash, when I heard terrible news: my child, my dear Avinoam, had fallen deathly ill at home. Without any delay, I hastened home, desperate to find him in good health; alas, it was not to be. My dear boy has gone on to the World to Come. I am distraught. In my grief, I know I have contracted *tum'at met*, but I am eager to regain my purity and continue offering my sacrifices. Indeed, I labored to purchase and fatten my offerings, and the hardship that will be caused should they be invalidated is an additional layer of disaster I cannot bear!"

These women, so intellectual, so theoretical, so quiet, feel reality flood their chamber: true life, of suffering, of desperation, and of an endless desire to serve God. They bear witness to one eager to serve God, both by caring for God's dying creations, and by worshipping God through sacrifice.

The rabbaniyot deliberate. They realize: If we believe in the efficacy of *korbanot*, of sacrifice, and in a parent's love and obligations toward their child, how can we obviate one because of the other?

Thus did these women rule that sacrifices can be resumed in such a situation to restore purity.

Let us expand our *halachic empathy* by walking many miles, from Tarmod to Jerusalem, in the shoes of someone else.

PROMPTS

While many of the story's details seem contextually limited, Miriam of Tarmod's narrative raises a number of timeless questions for all of us to consider:

- What is *n'zirut*, Nazirite vow and its restrictions, all about? Why is it a sign of righteousness to abstain from wine, the cutting of hair, and contact with a corpse?
- How might this story contribute to our understanding of death in Judaism? While contact with death can seemingly disrupt the Nazirite's vows, this story also teaches us about the possibility of laxity and of the resumption of ritual purity in certain circumstances. What are those circumstances, and why might they change the outcome?
- Miriam of Tarmod is significant as a female Nazirite. How does Miriam of Tarmod expand this category as a woman and a mother, and what does it mean to consider *n'zirut* an avenue open to both men and women?

Rachel Slutsky *is completing her PhD in Religion at Harvard University. She will be the 2022 Oesterreicher Professor of Jewish Studies at Seton Hall University.*

CHAROSET RUGELACH

Miriam of Tarmod is a Nazirite and a bereaved mother.

I wanted to offer Miriam a comforting, traditional Jewish food; I decided to create a twist on the classic Jewish Ashkenazi pastry, rugelach, by giving it a Sephardic charoset filling.

Nuts and dried fruit are customarily given as part of a shivah platter, are easy to prepare and nourishing. Wine is omitted from the traditional charoset recipe to recognize Miriam's abstention from alcohol. This recipe contains no added sugar in the dough or filling because the fruits satisfy our desire for something sweet.

Prep Time: 1 hour + overnight soaking and chilling time
Cook Time: 20 minutes
Yield: 16 cookies

Tools:

- Cookie sheet
- Immersion blender
- Kitchen mixer
- Large mixing bowl
- Parchment paper
- Pizza wheel
- Rolling pin

Ingredients:

For the dough:

- 4 oz (112g) vegan butter sticks, at room temperature
- 4 oz (112g) vegan cream cheese, at room temperature
- 4 oz (112g) all-purpose flour

For the filling:

- 8 oz (250g) pitted dates
- 8 oz (250g) dried apricots
- 2 oz (50g) finely chopped walnuts or pistachios
- Powdered sugar for the work surface

Instructions:

Start the day before you want to bake and serve the rugelach.

To make the dough:
1. In the bowl of a stand mixer, combine vegan butter sticks and vegan cream cheese at medium speed until completely smooth.
2. Slowly add the flour until the dough comes together – it will be very sticky.
3. Divide the dough in half and spread each half on plastic wrap or wax paper, making a disk that is roughly 1 inch (2.5 cm) thick.
4. Wrap the dough and refrigerate overnight (dough can be frozen for future use).

To make the charoset filling:
1. Place the dates and apricots in a large bowl, cover with water, and leave to soak overnight.
2. Pour the soaked fruits and water into a saucepan, place over high heat, and bring to a boil. Turn down to simmer; stir intermittently until a thick paste is formed.
3. Using an immersion blender, make into a smooth paste.
4. Stir in the walnuts or pistachios.

To assemble:
1. Remove one disk of dough at a time from the refrigerator and let rest for 2 minutes.
2. Dust work surface and rolling pin with powdered sugar and roll out the dough into a ⅛ inch (4 mm) thick circle.
3. Spread the filling on top of the dough.
4. Cut the dough into small (or tiny) pizza slices.
5. Roll rugelach from the outside in and sprinkle the tops with walnuts or pistachios. Place on a lined baking sheet and repeat. Refrigerate for 30 minutes to prevent them from spreading during baking.
6. Repeat with the remaining disk of dough.
7. Bake at 375° F (190° c) for 20 minutes or until golden.

Nathalie Ross *is a doctoral student focusing on Sephardic Jewish foodways and identity. She is a wife, mother, and avid baker.*

THE MOTHER FROM TZIPPORI /
אשה מהלכת בשוק ובנה אחריה

STORY

In Tractate Sanhedrin 19a there is a horrible story about a mother from the city of Tzippori. The story is told like this: In the town of Tzippori there was a mother who walked to the market one day with her son following her. As the child walked behind his mother, bandits abducted him.

Rashi commented on this story: the bandits placed the boy in a house, and when the mother realized that her son had been abducted, she began to scream and cry. One of the bandits told her to follow him. She followed him, and then the bandits raped her.

Following this event, Rabbi Yosei instituted two municipal regulations:

A mother should not walk to the market with her child following behind her, rather the child should walk in front of his/her mother.

Women should speak to one another in secluded women's bathrooms since men would be less likely to assault women if they were in groups in women-only places.

PASSAGES

Talmud b. Sanhedrin 19a

CONTEXT

This story falls in Tractate Sanhedrin (סנהדרין), one of the ten tractates in Seder Nezikin. This section of the Talmud focuses on civil and criminal proceedings that result from damages.

The section surrounding the story of the mother from Tzippori digs deep into the details and explores the correct rules, order, and movement of people during and after a burial. The rabbis discuss the correct way a high priest should participate in a burial procession when his relative dies and the correct way that mourners should line up on public streets to console bereaved family members following a burial service.[1] In this discussion, the rabbis go back and forth about if and when the high priest should emerge from the Temple, debating how strict the rules need to be in order to keep the high priest separate from the corpse. The main concern seems to be that his grief about the death of a close family member might lead him to disregard his professional restrictions and touch the corpse. The Gemara comments: Rabbi Yehuda opinion, that the Priest did not leave the temple at all, was consistent with the straightforward meaning of the verse in Leviticus 21:12, "and from the Temple he shall not emerge."[2]

The story about the mother from Tzippori shows the opposite reality to the extreme; instead of people following laws and social customs that create and maintain public order, violence unfolds in the streets of Tzippori when a group of bandits, overcome by their own desires to control and dominate, assault and victimize a woman and child. In this case, the conclusion is drawn that the town needs a more restrictive regimen to keep women and children safe.

AGGADAH

The story is so horrific and distressing. How many of us read this story and are instantly reminded of too many other stories – our own, each other's, those we read about in the news. Even today, violence against women and girls remains a widespread human rights violation.

Violence against women and girls exists in all communities and is one of the consequences of gender inequality and discrimination, and unequal power relations between men and women.

This particular story about gender-based violence pivots on the vulnerability of motherhood, making it even more sinister and deplorable. Abducting a woman's child is an excruciatingly violent act. Luring her into a secluded house with the promise of saving her child, only then to gang rape her is an act of pure evil. What mother would not follow a bandit into a house to rescue her child?

---

1. Rashi commentary on לא יטמא בעמיו in Leviticus 21:1; In Parshat Emor, it is written that the High Priest is restricted from coming into contact with a corpse (considered ritually impure) in all cases, even when the deceased is a family member, except in instances where the High Priest is the only Jewish person in the vicinity.
2. Sanhedrin 19a.

The mother from Tzippori's story points to an age-old formula following violence against women: focusing on women's actions and restricting their movement outside of the home as the primary prevention against male violence. Rabbi Yosei's response is to put in place a more restrictive regimen that will keep women safe from violence; "and from the home, she shall not emerge."

The story of the Mother from Tzippori begs the question: why, thousands of years after this story, do authorities continue to demand sacrifices of women, rather than forcing society and men to change to end violence?

PROMPTS

- What social and family norms and behavior need to change to prevent violence against women?
- How can people gain more awareness about the impact of gender-based violence on individuals, families, and society?
- How can society increase women's political participation, and how might this contribute to the prevention of violence against women?

Kenden Alfond

MAGNESIUM-BOOSTING SMOOTHIE

A preliminary note:

There is no food which can remedy sexual violence. There are many things that rape survivors urgently need, including medical treatment, psychological and emotional support, and sensitive and safe support from the criminal justice and legal systems.

I wanted to create a recipe which provides a large dose of magnesium-rich foods. Magnesium is a highly calming mineral which helps relax muscles and regulate the nervous system.

In this distressing story, both mother and son have been subjected to terrifying circumstances and behavior. To respond to the need for nourishment and comfort at a time when eating may feel difficult, I want to offer a liquid meal that is simple to make and easy to drink.

Green smoothies are a fast and simple way to increase your intake of fruit and greens. The recipe for green smoothies is based on three core ingredients:

- *Fruits, such as bananas, mangos & berries*
- *Leafy greens, which provide vitamins, minerals, and fiber*
- *Something creamy: plant-based milk or yogurt*

Optional add-ins include protein powders, superfood powders, and/or nut and seed butters.

Prep Time: 5 minutes
Cook Time: 0
Yield: 2–3 servings

Tools:

- Blender
- Measuring cups and spoons

Ingredients:

- 3 cups (700ml) oat or almond milk
- 1 cup (140g) frozen berry mix
- 3 frozen bananas
- 1–2 cups (a couple of handfuls) chopped dark leafy greens, fresh or frozen[3] (kale, romaine lettuce, or spinach)

Optional additions:

- 2 tbsp cocoa powder
- 2 tbsp nut butter
- 2 tbsp ground flaxseed

---

3. I learned this tip to use frozen greens from Dawn Lisa Angerame.

Instructions:

1. Place all ingredients in a blender.
2. Pulse to break up any big chunks of frozen ingredients, then blend smooth.
3. Enjoy immediately.

From the Jewish Food Hero Kitchen

THE MOTHER OF MAR BAR RAVINA /
אימיה דמר בריה דרבינא

STORY

The mother of Mar bar Ravina is recalled as a committed and active mother. Mentions of her revolve around the caring actions she performs for her son.

The Talmud records how the mother of Mar bar Ravina would bring her son wheat that had been protected from water: kosher-for-Passover. It is also noted that she would prepare seven clean changes of clothes for him for each week to protect him from lice. Her actions were designed to support her son's ability to focus and excel as a Torah scholar.

PASSAGES

Talmud.b.Pesachim.40a–40b and *Talmud.b.Eruvin.65a*

CONTEXT

Both stories about the mother of Mar bar Ravina are intended to provide a real-life illustration during a legal discussion. In both stories, we see a mother caring for her child within the confines of Jewish law. The stories that record this mother's actions illustrate the ways in which Jewish learning and knowledge was present in the home and lived by real people. The mother of Mar bar Ravina is being held up as an example of what good mothers do for their children.

Perhaps the rabbis thought of the things that the mother of Mar bar Ravina did as "women's work": feeding and clothing the men in the *beit midrash*. Perhaps the rabbis who recorded it may have had these experiences with their own mothers, and are giving us a window into their day-to-day experience.

The mother of Mar bar Ravina's actions might be understood as going beyond typical maternal care for a child's health and physical comfort as complete ends in themselves. Her efforts can also be understood as doing everything possible to enable her son to concentrate and apply himself to his studies.[1] Her caretaking comes from a place of love for her son, but also from an understanding of Jewish law and the importance of her child excelling in Jewish studies.

AGGADAH

It seems as if the stereotype of "Jewish mother" could have been fashioned by my example. I feed and clothe my son, even when he is clearly old enough to take care of himself. Even as he sits in the study hall, I bring him what he needs so that he can focus on the most important things. I hear what people say about me.

But here's what most people miss: How learned I am. I support my sons' and daughters' learning precisely because I also learn from books, and from the men and women around me.

I'm not the only one silently entering the *beit midrash*, attending to the details while my child learns. There is a web of women all around, moving in the shadows and in the quiet of dusk. It is women, with our own Torah, who are the cornerstone of the learning community. We ensure that people are fed and clothed so that the wheels of Torah knowledge can continue to turn. It is a web of women whose stories are mostly told between the lines.

PROMPTS

- What is something you are interested in learning? What obstacles get in the way of that learning?
- In what ways do your seemingly menial or mindless daily responsibilities and tasks enable other people to achieve significant achievements?
- How would you update the "Jewish mother" stereotype?

Rabbi Rebecca Rosenthal is the Director of Youth and Family Education at Central Synagogue in NYC, where she lives with her husband and three children.

---

1.   Hauptman, Judith, *The Talmud's Women in Law and Narrative* (Nashim: A Journal of Jewish Women's Studies & Gender Issues, No. 28, Feminist Interpretations of the Talmud, Spring 2015) 35.

SLOW-COOKED CARAMELIZED ORANGES

The Mother of Mar bar Ravina was a devoted mother and a learned woman. I imagine her as a woman who would study whenever she had a free moment.

This recipe is one of my grandmother's, and she says that she learned this recipe from her mother, who learned it from her mother, etc. My grandmother used to make it when she lived in Morocco during Mimouna, a party on the last night of Pesach where you invite friends to eat chametz with you.

This is a simple but fancy dessert. It requires little preparation and two hours of hands-off cooking time.

The sugar levels can be adjusted to suit anybody's preference. Add lemon zest to get a fragrant, slightly bitter flavor, or leave it out to quickly satisfy a sweet tooth!

Prep Time: 5 minutes
Cook Time: 2 hours + 40 minutes
Yield: 4 servings

Tools:

- Grater
- Measuring cups and spoons
- Pot

Ingredients:

- 4 large oranges
- 2 cups (400g) sugar
  (or less to taste)
- 1 lemon

Instructions:

1. Put the oranges in the pot and cover with water completely. Then take the oranges out of the pot while you bring the water to a boil.
2. While water is boiling, grate about 1 teaspoon of skin off each orange.
3. Throw out grated skin and place the oranges in boiling water for 10 minutes.
4. Take the oranges out of the water and let them cool for 20 minutes.
5. Cut each orange into quarters.
6. Add 2 cups sugar and 6 cups water to a pot.
7. Place the oranges back in the pot and cook on low for 2 hours.
8. Garnish with lemon zest.

Esther Cabot *is a student at Ramaz Upper School in New York City. She enjoys creating dishes inspired by her family and friends' favorite foods.*

NEFATA / נפאתה

STORY

A woman named Nefata was given a *get*, but the witnesses wrote the wrong name, they wrote Tefata. A debate follows regarding whether the current witnesses are allowed to write a new and correct bill or not.

PASSAGES

Talmud b. Gittin 63b

CONTEXT

This story is used to teach a halachic ruling. That if a bill of divorce is written incorrectly, the witnesses who are writing it are allowed to write a correct one.

The rabbis recorded Nefata's name as an example of a case. Her personal story does not come into account.

AGGADAH

My name is Nefata. You hear my name. You hear about the misspelling. You hear the debate of the rabbis. The debate that made me wait even longer for my divorce.

At least I have a name?

I should be grateful, as I know that there are so many women who came before and after me, who have no name. There are even women who are the reason for halachic rulings and they are known as "a woman" or "the wife of" or the "daughter of" or the "sister of."

I should be grateful that I am my own person. I am Nefata.

But I am nothing more than a name. You do not know my personality. What my favorite color was. What my favorite food and drink was. What I did with my day. You don't know any names of my family. I am just Nefata.

You don't get to hear my anger and frustration. How could they get my name wrong? What type of name is Tefata anyways? And that doesn't even sound like my name! They had such a small task, and they messed it up.

Perhaps that is why my name is remembered in these books. Maybe it is a reminder to pay attention to what you are doing. Maybe it is a reminder to notice the woman in front of you, as you are signing a document that is changing her life – forever. Maybe it is a reminder that this document is something that has to do with another human's life and wellbeing – it is not just a piece of parchment and ink. It is with this document that a woman goes from attached (or at worst chained) to free. There is a person there.

And don't get me started on Rav Yitzchak ben Marta or Rav for that matter – how could they think that my husband, or any husband for that matter, would want someone to write the WRONG *get*?! I know that law is law, but sometimes within law you need to have some common sense.

You don't hear my story. About my marriage. If I have children. If I was happy. If my husband was a nice person. You don't even get to learn his name.

You get my name. You get a halachic ruling. I hope the ruling made in my name helps others receive their *get* in a timely manner. I am Nefata.

PROMPTS

- Would you rather: have a name but no backstory or have a backstory and no name? And why?
- Do you think that Nefata's name made a difference in the story? Why or why not?
- Why do you think the rabbis made a point of having her name?

Rabbi Eryn London *is a rabbi, chaplain, and Jewish educator living in London, UK.*

RED WINE BRAISED MUSHROOM AND BARLEY STUFFED CABBAGE HOLISHKES

We often mark big life changes with food. This recipe marks this moment for Nefata: offering comfort if she did not wish to separate, and celebration if she shared the desire to end the marriage.

Prep Time: 1 hour
Cook Time: 45 minutes
Yield: 12–16 rolls, serves 4–6

Tools:

- Cutting board
- Heat-proof baking dish with a lid
- Kitchen scale
- Large pot
- Measuring cups and spoons
- Medium mixing bowl
- Medium saucepan
- Sharp knife

Ingredients:

- 1 large napa cabbage, separated into whole leaves

For the stuffing:

- ⅓ cup (55g) barley
- 1½ tbsp olive oil
- 1 large carrot, diced small
- 12 oz (340g) mushrooms, sliced
- 1 medium onion, diced small
- 3 cloves garlic, minced
- Salt & ground black pepper, to taste
- ½ cup (120ml) red wine
- 4 cups (950ml) vegetable broth
- 3–4 sprigs thyme, fresh
- 1 bay leaf

For the sauce:

- 1½ cups (350ml) tomato sauce (homemade or canned)
- 2 tbsp tomato paste
- ½ cup (120ml vegetable broth)
- 2 tbsp apple cider vinegar
- 2 tbsp Silan (date syrup)
- ½ tsp salt, or to taste
- ¼ tsp ground black pepper
- ¼ tsp ground cinnamon
- ½ tsp ground coriander

To garnish:

- Parsley, stemmed and chopped

Instructions:

Make the stuffing:

1. Preheat the oven to 350° F (180 °C). Place the barley on a cookie sheet and toast in the oven for 6 minutes, then set aside.
2. Heat the olive oil in a medium saucepan over medium heat. Add the carrot, mushrooms, and onion and saute, stirring occasionally, until vegetables start to brown, about 8–10 minutes.
3. Add garlic, salt and pepper to taste, and saute for about 1 minute until fragrant.
4. Deglaze the pan with the red wine, scraping up any browned bits that may be clinging to the bottom.
5. Add half of the vegetable stock, thyme sprigs, bay leaf, and toasted barley and bring to a simmer, stirring occasionally.
6. Add additional broth as the barley starts to swell and absorb the liquid, repeating as necessary until the barley is almost fully cooked and the liquid has been absorbed.
7. Remove the thyme stems and bay leaf and set aside to cool before stuffing the cabbage.

Make the sauce:

1. Whisk together the tomato paste and broth in a medium mixing bowl. Add the remaining sauce ingredients and whisk to combine.
2. Set aside until ready to assemble.

Prepare the cabbage:

1. Bring a large pot of salted water to a boil.
2. Meanwhile, separate the cabbage into individual leaves and rinse to remove any dirt. Large, medium, and small leaves all work well in this recipe, but reserve the smallest leaves in the very center of the head for another use.
3. Prepare a large bowl of ice water.
4. Blanch the cabbage in the boiling water, in batches if necessary, for about 2 minutes per batch.
5. Shock the cabbage in the ice water bath to stop the cooking and help keep a bright green color.
6. Once chilled, drain the cabbage until ready to assemble.

To assemble and serve:

1. Lightly oil a large, heat-proof casserole dish.

2. Preheat the oven to 350° F (180 °C).

3. Line up your cabbage leaves for stuffing on a clean work surface. Pair together and slightly overlap smaller leaves.

4. Pat the cabbage leaves dry to remove any excess remaining water.

5. Center about 2 tablespoons of stuffing at the base of each leaf or pair of leaves. Leave at least ¼ inch on each side of the stuffing so it doesn't fall out.

6. Roll the cabbage up into tight rolls. Don't worry about tucking in the sides of the cabbage.

7. Place the rolls in your prepared pan and cover with the sauce. Alternatively, the prepared rolls and sauce may be refrigerated separately to bake at a later point. If preparing ahead of time, add an additional 20–25 minutes to the baking time.

8. Cover with foil or a tight-fitting lid and bake for 45 minutes.

9. Remove from the oven and let rest for 10 minutes.

10. Uncover, garnish with parsley, and serve.

Megan B. Tucker, *from LA, has a BA in Religious Studies, and graduated from the Culinary Institute of America. She created Mort & Betty's Vegan Jewish Deli.*

THE POTENTIAL BRIDE AND THE HAIRDRESSER[1] / האָרוסה ומעצבת השיער

STORY

Our story features a potential bride (i.e., fiancée) and a female hairdresser. They appear suddenly in a series of passages about what happens in an engagement when a man misrepresents the proposal by exaggerating the value of gifts he gives to his fiancée, or if he aggrandizes or diminishes his lineage. It's clear that when men mislead women, their engagement is invalidated.

The fiancée in this story learns that her fiancé has a woman – either a grown daughter or a maidservant – in his household who works as a hairdresser. Either of these women could theoretically be beneficial to a new wife, who could delegate tasks that she found distasteful or beneath her to the hairdresser. The groom thinks that offering something of greater value than promised seals the deal for his marriage.

The fiancée sees the risk involved, and immediately declares "[It is] not satisfactory for me." She assumes that hairdressers have a habit of talking. She does not want a woman in her household who might spread gossip about her, her husband, or their relationship throughout the town.

PASSAGES

Talmud.b.Kiddushin.49a

CONTEXT

The Talmud has a negative view of people who lie, so it is no surprise that in a passage about men who misrepresent the value of betrothal gifts, we learn that if the gift is of lesser value than promised, the betrothal is void.

---

1. These two figures are not mentioned directly in the text. The Talmud often writes inferentially – assuming the reader knows a lot from the context. So we have given these women titles in modern Hebrew as opposed to the usual Aramaic/Mishnaic Hebrew used in the other narratives.

On the surface and in the context of the other examples, this story is about a man's obligation to tell the truth to his intended bride. Yet on a much deeper level it deals with the relationship between the two women in question. One lives with her father/master, the other is about to enter into their household as a newcomer with senior status to the other.

We find ourselves in a world where women are subservient to men, and yet still can wield power, especially over other women. The Sages of the Talmud undoubtedly understood household power issues, and brought the female hairdresser into the text to illustrate how difficult these issues could be. In the end, the fiancée's opinion about the misrepresentation of lineage prevails. Despite the potential groom's opinion that the hairdresser is a benefit, the bride's perspective takes precedence. Even in an ancient patriarchal society, women were given a voice, especially when it came to accepting the overtures of a potential husband.

AGGADAH

The fiancée was reluctant to visit her suitor's home and meet his favorite maidservant. She had heard about this hairdresser – so talented and popular that women vied to have her braid their hair for Shabbat. She would weave beads and flowers and protection amulets into their hair, tucking the beautiful trinkets carefully into the shining plaits. The idea of moving into the hairdresser's household was more daunting to her than the prospect of marrying a man she barely knew. Everyone knew her; she knew everyone. It seemed impossible that a husband and wife would have any privacy, any secrets.

She wondered if there was a way to get rid of her…it might be difficult. She had been told that this woman was more than a mere servant-girl; she was a distant cousin of the groom whom he had taken in several years ago. Now it seemed as if she ran the entire household.

The hairdresser had seen the bride-to-be strolling through town with her mother and sisters, laughing and whispering together. An only daughter who had never known her mother, she would watch the women with envy.

The day they met was bright, but inside the home there was a gloom that hung over all who entered. The fiancée walked through the rooms slowly, inspecting each, not meeting the servants' eyes that followed her every move. Finally she came to the hairdresser's room. It

seemed that every surface was covered with the tools of her trade – bowls overflowing with beads and ribbons and trinkets in every color of the rainbow. It was beautiful.

Looking shyly at the hairdresser, the fiancée said, "You know so many people in our town." It was a statement more than a question, and as she barely nodded she thought she heard her new mistress murmur, "You must know so much."

The hairdresser paused before replying. "Did you know," she asked, "that there is a midrash about God and Mother Eve?"[2] The bride-to-be shook her head, so she continued, "God built her from Father Adam's side. But there are places where plaiting braids is called building, and it is told that God braided Eve's hair before bringing her to Adam." She paused again, and added quietly, "Braiding a woman's hair is a sacred task. A holy task. *Keddushat isha*, holiness of the woman."

The future bride nodded. As she let out a great breath of relief the gloom lifted, and the two women smiled.

PROMPTS

- How can we shed preconceived notions about one another based on race, religion, occupation, or social status?
- In a competitive world, how do we deal with feelings of intimidation and inferiority?
- Gossip is expressly prohibited in our tradition. We often forget that this includes praising someone when they're not present, as well as saying unkind things. Why do you think praise is prohibited?

Rabbi Jennifer Singer *serves a congregation in Sarasota, Florida. Ordained at age 59, she was previously a major gifts fundraiser and a writer.*

2.   Talmud.b.Eruvin.18a.

CREAMY CELERIAC PURÉE WITH FRIZZLED LEEKS

The story of the fiancée and the hairdresser is replete with themes of the unexpected – the bride is assumed to want a maidservant, but sees the servant as a liability; the servant is assumed to resent the fiancée. The aggadah opens to us the possibility that the two women's doubts could be healed – by each other. This dish too is unexpected, taking a humble ingredient, celeriac root, and transforming it into something luxurious. It is also comforting, like the potential relationship between the women.

You'll need two celeriacs for the purée. The finished purée is nutty and creamy and contrasts with the crispy frizzled leeks, listed among the beloved foods of the Jews in Numbers 1:15.

Prep Time: 15 minutes

Cook Time: 20 minutes

Yield: 4–5 servings

Tools:

- Cutting board
- Immersion blender, food processor, or food mill
- Sharp knife
- Spatula

Ingredients:

- 2 celeriac heads, about 2 lbs / 1 kg
- 1 large or 2 medium leeks, white and tender green parts only
- 1 tbsp all-purpose flour, or any other flour, such as garbanzo bean flour
- 1–2 tbsp olive oil, divided
- 1 tsp kosher salt, or to taste

Instructions:

1. Trim and peel the celeriac so that the smooth, white interior of the root remains without the fuzzy brown covering. Dice into cubes.

2. Place the cubed celeriac into a pot and fill with water to cover. Bring to a boil over medium heat, then reduce to a simmer and cook until fork-tender, about 20 minutes.

3. Meanwhile, make the frizzled leeks: trim the leeks and clean them well. Slice the tender part of the leek in half lengthwise, then slice into half-moon rings. Toss well in flour. Heat a small amount of olive oil in a skillet and fry the leeks until crispy, 3–4 minutes. Set aside.

4. When the celeriac is softened, drain well and return to the pot. Purée with the salt and 1 tablespoon olive oil, if desired, using an immersion blender, or transfer to a food processor or food mill and process to a smooth purée.

5. Season to taste and serve the purée topped with the frizzled leeks.

Tamar Marvin *is a student at Yeshivat Maharat, an educator, a PhD in Jewish Studies, and parent of three food critics. She blogs at 24six.*

THE PROSTITUTE FROM A CITY OVERSEAS / זונה בכרכי הים

STORY

A man, who was known to be diligent in the mitzvah of wearing ritual fringes (*tzitzit*), arranged a meeting with a prostitute in a city overseas, pre-paying her four hundred gold coins. She had six silver beds and one gold one arranged for him, stacked up with ladders in between. She sat naked on the gold bed, on the very top. He entered the room and climbed up the ladders to sit naked facing her. As he did this, his four ritual fringes slapped him across his face. He dropped down to sit on the ground; so did she. She asked him what defect he saw in her.

He answered that he had never seen a woman more beautiful than her, but then explained that the mitzvah of the fringes reminds us that God is the one who rewards and punishes human behavior, and that his four fringes appeared to him like witnesses who would testify against him if he transgressed by sleeping with a prostitute. The prostitute requested his contact information, including the name of his teacher and *beit midrash*, and he wrote it down and gave it to her before he left to return home.

She divided all her property into thirds, giving one third to pay off the government, one third to the poor, and keeping the last third, including the beds of silver and gold, for herself.

She traveled to the *beit midrash* of Rabbi Hiyya and asked him to help her convert to Judaism. Rabbi Hiyya inquired if this was because she was hoping to marry one of his students. She handed him the note with the student's name, and he gave her permission to marry, saying, "Go and take possession of your purchase." She arranged the same beds that she had arranged before, but this time they were permitted rather than prohibited. The Talmud notes that this was the reward that the man reaped in this world, and as for the world to come – we cannot know how much the reward will be.

PASSAGES

Talmud B. Avodah Zarah 17a

CONTEXT

This story is told in the context of a long discussion about the mitzvah of wearing *tzitzit*, or ritual fringes, which touches on themes related to being commanded in mitzvot, including gender.

Right before the story, it is written:

> It **is taught** in a *baraita* that **Rabbi Natan says: There is no mitzva,** however **minor, that is written in the Torah, for which there is no reward given in this world; and in the World-to-Come I do not know how much** reward is given. **Go and learn from** the following incident concerning **the mitzva of ritual fringes.**

Bringing an encounter with a non-Jewish prostitute as an example further links the mitzvah of fringes to its biblical passage in Numbers, which uses the word *zonim*, a word that shares the same root as the word for prostitute (*zonah*).

The non-Jewish, female, foreign prostitute must have been of low status in the eyes of the rabbis. Yet they share her story as that of a woman who is inspired to change everything. Leaving her profession and her religion, she seeks a righteous way of life in becoming and then marrying a Jew. If she can make this kind of monumental change, certainly a Jewish man who is from birth commanded in the mitzvot can also remember to follow them.

AGGADAH

Judaism is full of physical ritual objects that remind us of something important. This reminder is sometimes called a *zecher*. For example, the mezuzah that we touch and kiss on our way into a Jewish home reminds us to love God. A *shviti* – which is an artistic drawing of the four-letter name of God – reminds us to keep God in front of us always. The *tzitzit*, or fringes, on the four corners of our prayer shawl, or that we wear on a garment under our clothes, remind us of the *mitzvot* – that is, what we do as Jews.

In this section of the Talmud we find a long discussion about *tzitzit*. We learn that they are made of wool, tied in a special way, and ideally contain white string, with one string dyed sky-blue, or *tekhelet*, from a dye made with a special snail. The color was so true to the deep blue of the sky that it reminded people of the sapphires on which God's Throne of Glory rests, and therefore also directed the wearer's mind toward God (Talmud b. Menachot 43b). We learn how to affix *tzitzit* to the four corners of a garment, and there is a discussion about when to say the blessing over them, and who should say it. Wearing the *tzitzit* is primarily a *mitzvah* performed by men, but we also learn that: "Rav Yehuda would affix white and sky-blue strings to the garment [*pirzuma*] of his wife. And every morning he would recite the blessing: To wrap ourselves in garments with ritual fringes." (Talmud b. Menachot 43a)

The story of the prostitute explores the power of these *tzitzit* to remind us to follow God's commandments. When the fringes hit the man in his face, he remembered not to follow after every whim of his desire. In this case, they may help the man see the prostitute as a real human being, one of God's creations, rather than a transactional object. Likewise, the prostitute is so impressed that these fringes can reverse the man's actions that she is compelled to leave her entire way of life to pursue Judaism. Perhaps she also feels the deep love that is inherent in being seen for the human being she really is, and that is why she seeks out this particular man for marriage.

I like to imagine that like Rabbi Yehudah's wife, the former prostitute also took on the mitzvah of wearing *tzitzit* once she had become Jewish and married the man who came to visit her. I hear him reciting for both of them: "…to wrap ourselves in garments with ritual fringes."

PROMPTS

- What symbol, physical or otherwise, in your own life reminds you to live up to a higher standard and follow a higher calling?
- What can help us see beyond someone's social status, occupation, or identity to their character and humanity? How do we notice and release our automatic assumptions and judgments?
- With all the reversals in this story, what can we learn about the fluidity of gender roles, today and in ancient times? What makes us able to break out of those roles that we have inherited and are socialized in?

Danielle Stillman *is the campus Rabbi at Middlebury College in Vermont. She lives nearby with her family where they like to play outdoors.*

SWEET BEET LOAF CAKE

When you think of beets, your first thought is probably not a cake – just like the Prostitute from the City Overseas who changed her entire life, the outcome of her story and this loaf cake is a surprise for everyone.

Prep Time: 10 minutes
Cook Time: 45 minutes
Yield: 2 loaves

Tools:

- Mixing bowl
- Spoon
- Two loaf tins

Ingredients:

- 1 medium beet grated
- ¾ cup (150g) caster sugar
- ¾ cup (150g) vegetable oil
- ¾ cup (180g) applesauce
- Juice of half a lemon (2 tbsp / 20ml)
- 2 scant cups (280g) all-purpose flour
- ½ tsp baking soda
- 1 tbsp baking powder

Instructions:

1. Preheat a fan/convection oven to 160° F (320° C).
2. Peel the beet and grate it into a mixing bowl.
3. Add the sugar, oil, applesauce, and lemon juice and mix well.
4. Sift the dry ingredients into the bowl.
5. Mix to a unified batter, being careful not to overmix.
6. Pour the cake batter into two greased and/or lined loaf tins.
7. Bake for 45 minutes.
8. Cool to room temperature before slicing and serving.

Renana Spiegel Levkovich *is a web developer and she has a food blog and passion for food photography. She lives in Israel with her family.*

STORY

Queen Helena of Adiabene is known to us through the Mishnah, Talmud, and the writings of Josephus. Her family ruled over Adiabene, an area near the northern end of the Tigris River that had been part of the Assyrian, Persian, and Parthian Empires. She and two of her sons, Monbaz and Izates, converted to Judaism. The Mishnah and Talmud give us three separate examples of Helena's Jewish practice:

Helena donated two golden objects to the Temple in Jerusalem, a lamp and a tablet on which were written the verses pertaining to the *sotah* (a woman suspected of adultery) (Num. 5:19–22), to be used as part of her ordeal (Mishnah Yoma 3:10; also discussed in Talmud.b.Gittin 60a).

Helena took a Nazirite vow when her son returned safely from war. This vow would have involved not eating grapes, drinking wine or any alcoholic beverage; not coming into contact with a corpse; and not cutting her hair (Numbers 6:1–8). The original vow was for seven years, but it was extended for a total of seven or fourteen additional years when she came to the Land of Israel (Mishnah Nazir 3:6).

Helena built a large sukkah. The legality of its dimensions was the subject of Talmudic dispute (Talmud.b.Sukkah 2b-3a).

PASSAGES

Mishnah Yoma 3:10, Mishnah Nazir 3:6, Talmud.b.Sukkah 2b-3a, Talmud.b.Gittin 60a

CONTEXT

Cumulatively, these three examples of Queen Helena's Jewish practices paint the picture of a pious Jew-by-choice. The Nazir episode and the Sukkah episode both suggest that her practice sometimes may have reflected a limited knowledge or misunderstanding of rabbinic law,[1] but she is not condemned for it. Rather, she is described as following the rules of the Sages – and the Sages do not say anything against her. Interestingly, whereas the earlier, Mishnaic texts emphasize Queen Helena's own religious agency, the later, Talmudic texts – especially in Sukkah – consider her actions entirely in relation to rabbinic law and practice. This story, of Queen Helena of Adiabene as a woman of high standing and foreign origins who was a follower of rabbinic law, would have reinforced the norms that the rabbis were trying to establish.

Queen Helena's gender seems especially relevant vis-a-vis her donation of the golden tablet with the text of the admonition to be read to the *sotah* (the wayward wife). It is possible that this story was brought forward as an example of a "good" woman (Helena) being part of a system condemning a "bad" woman (the wayward wife).[2] However, the story can also be read differently, as in the modern midrash, below.

AGGADAH

In my adopted city, Jerusalem, there is a saying: "Whoever sees a suspected wife in all her disgrace, will keep themselves from wine."[3] I never took it seriously. Why should one woman's downfall keep another from her cups? But then one day, I went to Nicanor's Gate, to celebrate with a friend who had given birth and was to have the purification ritual that day. Before it was her turn, however, a different ritual took place: that of the *sotah*, a woman whose husband had accused her of adultery. Her hair covering was removed; even her clothes were torn; and she was made to drink a concoction which included the dissolved words of a curse, and dirt from the Temple floor. I saw her there, crying and protesting innocence, and I thought to myself: *I would do anything to avoid that fate.*

I have always tried to live in such a way that I am beyond reproach. As a female ruler, and a Jew who is a convert, I often feel others' eyes on me. If I fall short in any way, there will be many waiting to rejoice. Even when I built a beautiful sukkah and invited the rabbis as my guests, I could see them making measurements with their eyes, trying to see if I had

1. See discussion in Dr. Malka Zeiger Simkovich, "Queen Helena of Adiabene and Her Sons in Midrash and History," https://www.thetorah.com/article/queen-helena-of-adiabene-and-her-sons-in-midrash-and-history.
2. Lisa Grushcow, *Writing the Wayward Wife: Rabbinic Interpretations of Sotah* (Leiden and Boston: Brill, 2006), 104–5.
3. Talmud.b.Sotah 2a.

made a mistake. Perhaps that is why seeing that woman frightened me so – all women are vulnerable when the rules are made only by men.

And so, I swore to be different. When my son and I gave donations to the Temple, I insisted on donating a golden tablet, with the words of the *sotah*'s curse inscribed on it, for use by the priests – showing that I, Queen Helena, had nothing in common with a woman who would fall so low. But I wanted to go further, and I remembered that saying. I had seen a suspected wife in her disgrace; and so, I would keep myself from wine and other intoxicants. I would never find myself in a situation in which I might lose control. Everyone thought my Nazirite vow was taken because my son went off to war. But it had much more to do with a war I was waging within.

Soon the seven years of my vow became fourteen, and then twenty-one. It was meant to be a temporary vow, but I didn't want to let it go. I was afraid of what might happen.

Something did happen, but not what I expected. One of my sons had a daughter. I had seven sons, and everyone called me blessed, but I had always yearned for a daughter. And now, I had a granddaughter. I held her in my arms and I gazed down at her face, and I thought to myself: Is there anything she could do that would be so terrible, that I could not forgive her? Is there any mistake that she could make, that I would want her to suffer like the woman I saw that day? Would I even want her to experience all the restrictions that I myself had chosen to take on?

That very day, just before the festival of Sukkot, I ended my Nazirite vow. I went to the Temple and made the offering. I eagerly anticipated going home, for a long-awaited cup of wine. But first, I stopped by Nicanor's Gate, and I asked for the tablet I had donated. I told them I wanted to modify it, to add to the design. I brought the tablet to an engraver I knew, and I asked her to add three letters, so subtly that you would only see them if you knew to look. The letters were Hebrew, but they came from a legend which originated in my homeland; the story of one of my ancestors, who asked for a saying to make a sad man happy, and a happy man sad. *Gimel, zayin, yud – gam zeh ya'avor* – "this too shall pass."

I could not overturn the rules. But when the next woman came forward for the *sotah*'s ordeal, I wanted her to know that the moment she was in would not last forever. The moment we were *all* in would not last forever. The God of Israel, the God I had chosen, was neither male nor female, and favored neither women nor men. This God was a God of expansiveness and possibility, a God who cared for the vulnerable, a God of change and hope.

I went home. I sat in my beautiful sukkah, savoring my cup of wine. I held my baby granddaughter. And I started to tell her stories.

PROMPTS

- Are there times when, like Queen Helena, we are afraid to be associated with others who share aspects of our identity? How might we move from being enemies to allies?
- It has been said that "all theology is autobiography." How does Queen Helena's life shape her theology? Can we find moments in our own life stories that have shaped our beliefs about God?
- Queen Helena is concerned about proving herself as an outsider, but she also brings a unique perspective. How can we move from tolerating or including others to actively valuing their presence?

Rabbi Dr. Lisa J. Grushcow *is rabbi of the Reform synagogue in Montréal, and has a doctorate in Talmud. Her children won't eulogize her cooking.*

GRAPE AND LEMON SQUARES

Queen Helena of Adiabene took a Nazirite vow to thank God for returning her son safely from war. This dish would be the perfect treat for the end of Queen Helena's vow.

Whole grapes bursting with juicy goodness take on an entirely new depth of flavor once they're baked to perfection, enveloped in a creamy vanilla and lemon filling, and brought together with a hearty crust.

Prep Time: 15 minutes
Cook Time: 1 hour
Yield: 9–16 servings

Tools:

- Medium mixing bowl
- Sheet parchment paper
- Square baking dish, 9″×9″ (22cm×22cm)

Ingredients:

For the crust:

- 1 cup (90g) quick oats (regular or gluten-free)
- 1½ cups (170g) almond flour
- ¾ tsp salt
- ¼ cup (60ml) water

For the filling:

- 1 cup (235ml) unsweetened applesauce
- 2½ tbsp freshly squeezed lemon juice (or juice from about 1 lemon)
- ¼ tsp salt
- 2 tsp vanilla extract
- ¼ cup (40g) whole wheat flour (or gluten-free alternative)
- 1½ lbs (about 650g) red grapes

Instructions:

1. Preheat the oven to 350° F (175 °C) and line a baking dish with parchment paper.

2. In a medium bowl, thoroughly combine the dry crust ingredients, then add the water, stirring quickly with your fingers to combine for about 20 seconds until you have a soft, crumbly dough.

3. Press ¾ of the dough evenly into the bottom of the parchment-paper-lined dish.

4. Place all filling ingredients except the grapes in the empty dough bowl, and combine thoroughly.

5. Mix in the grapes, then pour the whole mixture as evenly as possible onto the crust. Make an effort to keep the tops of the exposed grapes as clean as you are able to for a more aesthetic end product. Add the remaining dry crust crumbles, sprinkling it over the top.

6. Bake for 1 hour or until the crumble on top is slightly browned and the liquid is bubbling.

7. Allow to cool completely so that it can firm up a little before slicing into squares.

8. Can be kept for a day or two on the counter, or several days in the refrigerator.

Shana Balkin *is the recipe developer, writer, and photographer behind Salad Therapy. Shana and her family live in Houston, Texas.*

STORY

A Chaldean astrologer[1] tells Rabbi Akiva that his daughter will die by snake bite on her wedding day. Knowing this prediction, she feels worried. On her wedding night, she sticks a sharp hair clip into her wall for a moment. In the morning, she pulls it out to discover a snake, dead, stuck to the pin through its eye.

Her father asks her: What did you do to deserve being saved from the snake's bite? And she tells him: Last night, at my wedding feast, a poor person came to the door. Everyone was so busy feasting that they didn't notice him. So I took the food that you, Father, had given to me, and I gave it to him.

Her father declares: You performed a mitzvah last night. And he goes into the city, telling this story, declaring that giving charity doesn't only prevent tragic, unnatural deaths, but also any death.

PASSAGES

Talmud.b.Shabbat.156b

CONTEXT

This story illustrates a tension between the belief in predestination and Jewish ideas about free will. The talmudic rabbis accepted that astrology was real, but debated whether Jewish people were immune to its influence.[2]

Rabbi Akiva's daughter's story needed to have a message that was inclusive of all Jews. In this sense, it fits the idea that all Jews are not under the influence of astrology.

If the story had depicted a rabbi escaping his astrologically determined death by snake bite, a reader might assume the rabbi's survival was due to his special status. Instead, this

---

1. An ancient semitic people/tribe.
2. Jacobs, Louis (1995), *The Jewish Religion: A Companion*. Oxford University Press.

story is about a woman, a person of lower status, who is nevertheless more powerful than destiny. Her prior knowledge of the potential for danger enables her to cleverly save herself.

This story teaches that anyone can save themself through their own actions, that high status is not necessary to make one's own fate.

AGGADAH

This story of Rabbi Akiva's daughter uplifts women by giving Rabbi Akiva's daughter autonomy that astrology and patriarchal social norms try to take away from her.

When the astrologer tells Rabbi Akiva the prediction, instead of his daughter, the implication is that he is responsible for her fate. Rabbi Akiva simply assumes that nothing can change her fate. But his daughter is already subverting it by worrying and planning for herself.

Rabbi Akiva's daughter takes two independent actions in this story. First, she gives the wedding meal from her father to a poor person who knocked on the door during the wedding feast. Second, she takes her hair pin and sticks it into a wall, killing the snake. Even though her action of giving charity appears inconsequential to the astrological prediction, it's clear from the way the story is told that this very act in fact contributes to her averting her own death. This illustrates the power small actions have to fight what is overwhelming and beyond our control. What's hard for Rabbi Akiva's daughter is learning about her own fate and having the courage to try to change something, but the changes themselves are simple.

By contrast, there is nothing recorded about Rabbi Akiva taking actions to protect his daughter from her fated death. His faith in the system overrides his concern for his own child.

Therefore, we must apply this today similarly, especially in the area of education. Girls and women, no matter the subject or setting, must recognize that their intuitions can be used to both question and challenge what they are being taught about the world and about themselves. Asking questions like "why" and "from where is this derived" is just as much their right as it is the talmudic scholars'. Furthermore, women should go so far as to ask how the material is applicable and how they can act on it.

Education can be hierarchical and status-based. Experts have more authority than individuals about what their experiences mean. Teachers can tell students whether their questions are worth asking. Often, students are taught how things are, but not why they are that way or how they can be changed. Rabbi Akiva's daughter shows the value of changing these norms and fighting back for one's own perspective to be recognized.

PROMPTS

- Rabbi Akiva declares that charity saves someone from any death, not only an unnatural death. What does that mean about giving charity?
- Does Rabbi Akiva's daughter only give charity to save her life? How does this alter the meaning of the story?
- What does it mean to be part of a people that is not subject to destiny? How does that change the way we should behave?

Sarah Farbiarz and **Susie Nakash** graduated from Abraham Joshua Heschel high school in 2022. They like to sing and play guitar together.

SAFFRON COUSCOUS WITH BELUGA LENTILS AND POMEGRANATE

Rabbi Akiva's daughter's prophesied death by snake bite was averted by virtue of her kind treatment of poor people. This dish combines the yellow, black, and red colors of a poisonous snake and celebrates her much deserved good fortune.

Prep Time: 30 minutes

Cook Time: 30 minutes

Yield: 6 servings

Tools:

- Cutting board
- Large bowl
- Measuring cups and spoons
- Medium pot with lid
- Medium saucepan
- Sharp knife

Ingredients:

For couscous:

- 1 cup (150g) Israeli couscous
- 1½ cups (225ml) low-sodium vegetable broth
- 1 tbsp olive oil
- ½ tsp saffron strands (or 1 tsp turmeric)

For lentils:

- ½ cup (100g) beluga lentils (small black lentils)
- 1½ cups (355ml) water or vegetable broth
- 1 tbsp olive oil
- Pinch of salt
- Pinch of pepper

For pomegranate:

- Either one large pomegranate or a container of pomegranate seeds

Instructions:

1. In a medium pot, bring vegetable broth, olive oil, and saffron to a boil.
2. Pour in couscous, cover, and continue simmering on medium/low heat for 8–10 minutes, until broth is absorbed. Remove from heat after and set aside.
3. In a medium saucepan, combine beluga lentils with water or vegetable broth, bring to a boil, and simmer while stirring occasionally for 15–20 minutes until lentils are tender but not mushy.
4. Add salt, pepper, and olive oil to the lentils. Stir and set aside.
5. Combine the couscous and lentils in a large serving bowl.
6. Slice the pomegranate in half and, holding it cut side down above the serving bowl, hit the rounded side with the back of a wooden spoon to send the pomegranate seeds tumbling on top of the rice.
7. Gently stir the seeds through the couscous lentil mix, and serve.

Chelsea Feuchs *is a rabbinical student at Hebrew Union College. Chelsea enjoys teaching as an opportunity to center conversations about gender in the Jewish community.*

RABBI ELAZAR BEN AZARYAH'S
WIFE / ביתהו דרבי אלעזר בן עזריה

STORY

The wife of Rabbi Elazar ben Azaryah appears in the Talmud when she is consulted by her husband after he is asked to become head of the yeshiva.

It all started when Rabban Gamliel, the leader of the Sanhedrin, publicly embarrassed Rabbi Yehoshua. The rabbis were so upset that they removed Rabban Gamliel from his post, and began looking for a new leader. After considering and rejecting Rabbi Yehoshua and Rabbi Akiva, they settle on Rabbi Elazar ben Azaryah, a descendant of Ezra.[1]

They selected Rabbi Elazar ben Azaryah because his wisdom would enable him to refute any potential challenge from Rabban Gamliel, and because he was wealthy enough to cover costs and taxes.

Rabbi Elazar ben Azaryah's first and only response to being offered the position is that he must consult with his household before making the decision. He consults his wife, who raises two concerns: First, the rabbis could turn on him as they did on Rabban Gamliel. He replies that although this was possible one should take advantage of an opportunity regardless of how long it may last. Second, she points out that he has no white hair and is not old enough to lead the rabbis. At this moment a miracle happens and, even though he is only eighteen years old, Rabbi Elazar ben Azaryah's hair turns white.

After the discussion with his wife, he decides to accept the position and makes the Yeshiva open to anyone who wants to learn, in stark contrast to Rabban Gamliel's selective style. Hundreds of benches were added and even Rabban Gamliel came to study, harboring no ill will.

---

1. Rabbi Yehoshua was rejected for his role in Rabban Gamliel's removal as that might upset Rabban Gamliel. Rabbi Akiva was rejected because he was descended from converts and Rabban Gamliel's resentment might affect him without protection from a strong lineage.

PASSAGES

Talmud.b.Berakhot.27b–28a

CONTEXT

This story tells us about Rabbi Elazar ben Azaryah, his wife, and their relationship. This story also answers questions readers might have about the choice of Nasi and the selection process, all within a casual domestic setting.

The story shows Rabbi Elazar ben Azaryah's decision-making process and how he addresses the concerns around him becoming *Nasi*. His qualifications are confirmed within a marital discussion and he is able to accept the role.

Perhaps incidentally, by sharing this story of a wise man consulting with his wife, readers might feel that the Sages considered their wives to be trusted advisors. The conversation between this couple highlights the natural back-and-forth nature of conversation between peers, common in rabbinic discussion. This familiar pattern sits comfortably in the Talmud as it brings a woman's voice into a big decision.

AGGADAH

The story of Rabbi Elazar ben Azaryah's wife implies a crucial message: women's perspectives strengthen the decision-making process. They should be partners in decisions; their feedback should be valued and sought.

The text doesn't indicate that women are consulted in the process of selecting a new *Nasi*. The other rabbis go directly to Rabbi Elazar ben Azaryah and ask him to take on this role. It is only when Rabbi Elazar ben Azaryah takes initiative and asks his wife for guidance that a woman is included in the decision-making process. Her inclusion is fundamental: he consults her as an essential step in considering the position, and only decides when the issues she raises have been satisfactorily dealt with.

She highlights two concerns: how he may be treated by others, and how his experience will be perceived. These issues are visible to her, rather than to him, thanks to her female perspective: women's actions in relation to others and their physical appearances are dis-

proportionately scrutinized, making women more highly attuned to issues of treatment in interpersonal relationships, and of other people's value judgments of them.

The fact that Rabbi Elazar ben Azaryah's wife's concerns are recorded as her own shows both that Rabbi Elazar ben Azaryah had not previously considered them and that the Sages deemed them valid. Rabbi Elazar ben Azaryah's wife's perspective and input contribute to a more informed and well-rounded decision-making process.

In modern times, we understand the value of including women in decision-making from the boardroom to the kitchen table – theoretically, at least. Today a diverse group of women's voices are still all too often ignored. The responsibility to amplify women's voices falls on men who have traditionally been included in leadership, as well as women who are new to that sphere. This recorded story about Rabbi Elazar ben Azaryah's wife teaches us that not only do individuals benefit from consulting the women close to them, but our religious and civic institutions are strengthened by women's input, whether it is recorded or not.

PROMPTS

- What are the elements of an effective partnership in intimate relationships? What have you seen that inspires you in other relationships?
- In what ways are women encouraged to be a part of big conversations? In what ways are they discouraged?
- Does consultation always mean inclusion? How can we ensure that voices and perspectives are actually allowed to be influential forces, rather than just given token airspace?

Talia Levin is a student at Barnard College and the Jewish Theological Seminary. She hopes to pursue a career in social justice or counseling.

CORN LATKES WITH MANGO SALSA

Rabbi Elazar b. Azaryah broke the mold by consulting his wife and including her in the decision-making process. Here, I offer a new take on this traditional favorite: using corn instead of potato to make latkes.

This recipe is quick and easy to prepare from fresh ingredients using simple equipment. When you bite into the latkes, you not only experience a wonderful flavor, but there is also a pleasant light crunch of the corn kernels. When mangoes are not available, make the salsa with peaches, nectarines, or for something different, fresh tomatoes.

Prep Time: 20 minutes
Cook Time: 20 minutes
Yield: 12–15 small latkes

Tools:

- Large mixing bowl
- Measuring cups and spoons
- Whisk

Ingredients:

For the corn latkes:

- 4 tbsp cornmeal
- 4 tbsp plain flour
- ½ cup (120ml) non-dairy milk
- 15 oz (420g) fresh corn kernels (approximately 3–4 corn ears)
- 2 finely chopped green chili peppers (or to taste)
- 2 tbsp finely chopped red onion
- 3 tbsp finely chopped red pepper (capsicum)
- 2 tbsp finely chopped coriander or parsley
- ¼ tsp black pepper
- Salt to taste
- Oil (canola/vegetable/olive) as needed

For the mango salsa:

- 2 firm but ripe mangoes, peeled, deseeded, and chopped into ½ inch (1 cm) cubes
- ½ cucumber, finely chopped
- 1 finely chopped small red onion
- 2 tbsp finely chopped coriander or parsley
- 1 finely chopped jalapeño or small green chili pepper (or to taste)
- 3 tbsp finely chopped red pepper (capsicum)
- 1 tbsp lime juice (or to taste)
- Salt to taste
- 2 or 3 pinches of sugar

Garnish:

- Extra chopped coriander or parsley

Instructions:

Make the corn latkes:

1. Combine all ingredients in a large mixing bowl and whisk until thoroughly mixed.
2. Heat 2 tablespoons oil in a nonstick skillet over medium-high heat.
3. Scoop a tablespoon of the batter into the hot pan and gently flatten with the back of a spoon. Depending on the size of the pan, you can fry 3 or 4 at a time. Avoid overcrowding the pan.
4. Cook until golden brown on both sides, approximately 2 minutes per side.
5. Remove from the pan and place on a paper towel to remove any excess oil.
6. Repeat until all of the batter is gone.

Make the mango salsa:

1. In a stainless steel or glass bowl, thoroughly mix all of the salsa ingredients together.
2. Let sit for at least 10 minutes so that the flavors can all meld together.
3. Garnish with coriander or parsley.
4. Serve alongside or on top of the crisp corn latkes.

Esther Daniels *was born in Bombay, India. She credits her mother with transmitting creativity with food. She lives in Melbourne and creates innovative kosher recipes.*

RABBI HAMA BAR BISA'S WIFE /
ביתהו דרבי חמא בר ביסא

STORY

"Is there a father who stands before his son?" Rabbi Hama bar Bisa's wife greeted her husband with these words after twelve years of separation. She didn't tell him how much she missed him, or how nice it was to have him home. Instead, with a sharp question, she pointed out a consequence of his absence.

After many years of studying away from his family, Rabbi Hama decided to return home. Nearing his house, Rabbi Hama thought of his colleague Rabbi Chananya who had startled his own wife to death by returning from a long absence unannounced. To avoid sending his own wife to an early grave, Rabbi Hama decided to wait in the study hall while someone informed his wife of his return. Rabbi Hama was surely pleased with himself for being a "thoughtful" husband in comparison with Rabbi Chananya.

A young scholar in the study hall impressed Rabbi Hama with his sharp, incisive mind and deep knowledge of Torah. The interaction saddened Rabbi Hama, for he realized that if he had remained with his family, his own son could have been as smart as this scholar; not realizing, however, that this scholar, Rabbi Oshaya, was his son, Rabbi Hama returned home. Rabbi Oshaya walked shortly behind him. Upon arriving home, Rabbi Hama assumed that the scholar followed him in order to ask him a question – so Rabbi Hama stood up in order to honor the learned man. Rabbi Hama's wife, watching this entire scene unfold, shattered Rabbi Hama's pride by rhetorically asking, "Is there a father who stands before his son?" In being absent from his son's upbringing, Rabbi Hama unknowingly forfeited the honor that children owe their parents. Rather than a son deferring to the greatness of his father, the father deferred to his son as the superior, laying bare the utter inversion of their relationship.

PASSAGE

Talmud b. Ketubot 62b

CONTEXT

This Talmudic story is set among a series of anecdotes that critique men who leave their families to study Torah. Rabbi Hama knew that neglecting one's family for many years could have detrimental effects, such as it did to Rabbi Chananya's family. His wife's final words at the end of the narrative underscore the fact that his behavior was irredeemable. The Talmud includes this story to warn its students that for all its merits, Torah study should never preclude fulfillment of duties to family.

When some husbands would abandon their families in order to study, it was the wives and mothers who picked up the slack. The strength of the rebuke that Rabbi Hama's wife offers shows the immorality of abandoning one's family for Torah study, while lauding the power of women who single-handedly maintain their households and hold their husbands accountable.

AGGADAH

In some Jewish communities, husbands still leave their homes for extended periods of Torah study, leaving their wives to do the work that is incumbent on both of them to complete. In other communities, economic realities, military enlistment, and/or professional ambition can pull or force one parent or both to work countless hours, travel around the world, or live at distance. The drive for success and self-fulfillment can become excessive or self-centered, and overshadow the responsibility we have to our family members. Whatever the circumstances causing the separation, those left behind can feel abandoned. Geographic distance creates emotional distance, and reconnecting when reunited can be hard work.

This story is a testament to the quiet labor and heroism of those left behind who keep everything functioning in another's absence. It is an empowering call for none of us to be comfortable with one-sided arrangements where the burden to run a family or raise children falls on one person in the family.

Rabbi Hama's wife welcomes her husband home with words which point out the severe consequences of his extended absence of twelve years. He does not even recognize his own son.

Her words were few, but forceful and wise, and her message was powerful. Rabbi Hama's wife teaches us that nothing is done properly if its fulfillment involves abandoning our loved ones and our responsibilities to them.

In our historical moment of rampant individualism and hyper focus on personal achievement and productivity, Rabbi Hama's wife's voice resounds with urgent moral clarity. Will we join her and make the call a chorus?

PROMPTS

- In what ways do we allow "higher" pursuits to pull us away from our family responsibilities? How and what could we prioritize?
- Is balance possible when we want to pursue individual ambitions and cultivate meaningful interpersonal relationships with friends, family, and/or community members? Does something always have to give?
- How can we stand up for ourselves when our needs aren't being met?

Pammy Brenner *received degrees in Yiddish Studies at Barnard College and the University of Oxford. She studied Torah at Migdal Oz and the Drisha Institute.*

VEGAN LULLABYE BREAD

I see Rav Hama bar Bisa's wife as a dedicated, hardworking single parent and loving mother who has raised an intelligent and loyal son.

I made this recipe for her because it reminds me of the lullabye Rozhinkes mit Mandlen. Rav Hama bar Bisa's wife might benefit from something sweet and soothing to eat.

Lullabye Bread is my name for German Hefezopf bread. It's similar to challah and is usually braided, but the dough is richer and more like brioche. It always includes raisins and is topped with almonds or crystal sugar. Although the classic recipe calls for butter, eggs, and milk, I have found it just as tender and delicious when made with plant-based ingredients such as almond milk and coconut oil.

Prep Time: about 3½ hours
Cook Time: 30–35 minutes
Yield: 1 loaf

Tools:

- Baking sheet
- Bowl
- Electric mixer (preferably with kneading hook)
- Kitchen scale
- Measuring cups and spoons
- Parchment paper
- Paring knife
- Saucepan
- Small bowl
- Small whisk
- Wooden spoon

Ingredients:

- 1 cup (240ml) unsweetened almond milk (or other non-dairy milk)
- 3 inch piece of cinnamon stick, broken in half
- 2 long strips of lemon peel
- ¼ cup (60ml) coconut oil
- ⅓ cup (67g) sugar
- 2¼ tsp active dry yeast
- Pinch of sugar
- ¼ cup (60ml) water
- 1 tbsp egg replacer
- 3½ to 4 cups (470–540g) bread flour or all-purpose flour
- 1 tsp salt
- 2 tbsp water
- ½ cup (80g) raisins
- 1 tbsp honey or maple syrup
- 1–2 tsp almond milk
- 2–3 tbsp chopped almonds

Instructions:

1. Lightly grease a baking sheet or line it with parchment paper.

2. Pour the almond milk into a saucepan. Add the cinnamon stick, lemon peel, coconut oil, and sugar and cook over medium heat, stirring to dissolve the sugar and melt the coconut oil, until the mixture comes to a boil. Set aside to cool to lukewarm (about 105° F / 40° C).

3. In a small bowl, combine the yeast, pinch of sugar, and ¼ cup water and whisk to dissolve the yeast. Let rest for about 5 minutes or until thick bubbles form.

4. Place 3½ cups flour and the salt in the bowl of an electric mixer. (If mixing the dough by hand, simply add a few extra minutes to each step.)

5. Remove the cinnamon stick pieces and lemon peel from the warm milk mixture and pour the liquid into the mixer bowl.

6. Add the yeast mixture and stir to combine.

7. Mix the egg replacer and 2 tablespoons water with a whisk, rest for one minute, and add to the dough. Mix the dough with a dough hook for about 2–3 minutes.

8. Add the raisins and mix for another 2–3 minutes, or until the dough is smooth. If the dough is sticky, add more flour as needed.

9. Cover the bowl and let rise in a warm place for about 2 hours or until doubled in size.

10. Punch the dough down and cut it into 3 equal pieces. Working on a floured surface, roll the pieces to make strands of about 12 inches (30cm) long. Braid the strands and place them on the baking sheet.

11. Mix the honey and a teaspoon of almond milk together and brush on top of the braid. Add an extra teaspoon of milk if necessary to make a smooth liquid.

12. Sprinkle with almonds. Let rise again for about 40–45 minutes.

13. Preheat the oven to 350° F. Bake for 30–35 minutes or until puffed and golden brown.

14. Let cool before slicing with a serrated knife.

Ronnie Fein, cooking teacher/demonstrator/food writer, has authored four cookbooks including Hip Kosher *and* The Modern Kosher Kitchen.

RABBI YEHUDA HANASI'S MAIDSERVANT / אמתיה דרבי

STORY

Rabbi Yehuda HaNasi's maidservant was a domestic worker in the home of Rabbi Yehuda HaNasi, also known as Rabbi Judah the Prince. He was the head of the Sanhedrin[1] in the mid-second century CE. He is also credited as the editor, or redactor, of the Mishnah. He is simply referred to as Rebbi in the Gemara.

The thread between the many mentions of her in the Talmud is her wit, sharp logic, and compassion.

The Talmud records that Rabbi Yehuda HaNasi's maidservant possessed expertise in language and that, because she lived in Rabbi Yehuda HaNasi's house, the rabbis assumed that she heard the most proper Hebrew spoken at that time.[2] The rabbis overheard her speaking in her daily life and from this they gained understanding about specific words.

The Talmud also highlights her linguistic prowess and her talent in crafting clever euphemisms[3] to describe domestic realities she saw. When the wine jug was empty she said, "the ladle used for drawing wine from the jug is already knocking against the bottom of the jug."[4]

One instance shows her being advised by Rebbi to show mercy to Hashem's creations when she tries to sweep some weasels out of the house.[5] She learns from this and in time issues a ruling that holds compassion and mercy at its center.

She once saw a man hitting his adult son and she recommended he be excommunicated. She uses a verse from Leviticus to substantiate her view. The rabbis, in deference to her, uphold the ruling.[6]

---

1. Jewish Court.
2. Talmud.b.Megillah.18a.
3. Talmud.b.Eruvin.53b.
4. Talmud.b.Eruvin.53b.
5. Talmud.b.Bava Metziah.85a.
6. Talmud.b.Moed Katan.17a.

Finally, she emerges as a central figure in the narrative of Rebbi's death. Seeing her master struggle in pain, mercy compels her to distract the rabbis from their prayers, enabling Rebbi to break free from his physical body and for his soul to depart.[7]

PASSAGES[8]

Talmud.b.Megillah.18a

CONTEXT

As a member of Rebbi's household, the maidservant would have lived and worked close to the center of Jewish power and politics in Israel – the Galilean town of Beit Shearim, and later Tzippori, close to the Sea of Galilee.

She would have seen and heard Rabbi Yehuda HaNasi and his fellow colleagues salvage Jewish law as they practiced from the ruins of the Temple and the shadows cast by the might of the Roman Empire.

Her depth of knowledge and her intelligent interactions serve to reflect her master's brilliance, since it was he she learned directly from. At times she serves as a foil for Rebbi and the rabbis as she voices an opposing perspective.

Her interactions with the rabbis also demonstrate their tentative engagement with women who, by virtue of their wit and intelligence, "earned" their place in the continuing Talmudic conversation.

AGGADAH

While I had worked in other wealthy households, Rebbi's house was rich in other ways. At first I was struck by the abundance of words, the profusion of languages – Greek, Latin, Hebrew, and Aramaic – that flowed from his table like wine. Animated conversations tumbled out of rooms and mingled in the corridors. After some time, I also came to see that Rebbi's house was imbued with kindness and compassion. There were subtle, yet thoughtful

---

7. Talmud.b.Ketubot 104a.
8. See also: Talmud.b. Eruvin 53b, Talmud.b. Bava Metziah.85a, Talmud.b.Moed Katan.17a, Talmud.b.Moed Katan.17a, Talmud.b.Ketubot 104a.

gestures he directed not only to his students and visiting scholars, but to us his servants – the lowliest and overlooked.

At first all I heard were sounds wafting over my head like music. Then I formed an affinity for certain words – I took note of how they rhymed and rolled off the tongue – words like "*halogelogot*" and "*salseleha*." Slowly I sculpted the words into sentences and then they morphed on their own into ideas and arguments. I followed them and wove the threads of these arguments around me to create my own tapestry of understanding. I became a student from afar, one ear in the study hall while my hands and body attended to the house.

I felt sure that Rebbi noticed and so I became the beneficiary of his largesse. He made sure the doors and windows to his study hall were always open so I could hear the student discussions. And, eventually, so they could hear me. This subtle gesture of kindness opened the door to an ongoing conversation between me and the scholars.

One day the rabbis were struggling with the meaning of "*halogelogot*." The next day, inspecting the garden in full view of their window, I loudly asked the gardener: "How long will you go on scattering your '*halogelogot*?'" Looking, the students saw the gardener holding purslane (a type of succulent), and they understood.

They pored over the Book of Proverbs all morning, trying to work out the meaning of the word "*salseleha*." That afternoon I walked by and asked a student who had particularly long locks of hair, "how long will you '*mesalsel*' your hair?" Then they understood the verse in Proverbs:[9] "Turn wisdom around and around and it will exalt you."

Wisdom wafted around me like the steam from the cauldrons on the kitchen fires. Just as I sampled the food from the pots, I delighted in the morsels of knowledge I gleaned. I breathed it in, understood and spoke it out loud. And over time, my voice was heard by his students and other scholars.

I also learned from Rebbi's subtle ways of showing kindness and mercy to others. His example guided my arguments with the scholars. While they also argued for compassion,

9.　Proverbs 4:3.

perhaps because my place was on the outside or on the sidelines looking in, I had a different perspective on who was suffering and in need of kindness.

At the end of my master's life, I stood apart from the scholars once more. From their place below, they begged for God to show mercy and keep him alive. From my view above, I realized that it is we who needed to show mercy to Rebbi and let him go. It was ultimately through my subtle act of kindness – the shattering of a jug – that prayers gave way to a second of silence and he was released from this world.

PROMPTS

- What relationship dynamics do we typically associate with domestic workers and their employers? Which side of the relationship do we imagine ourselves occupying?
- This story shows us a woman using and developing her intellectual capacity while working in a domestic role. What does this seeming contrast tell us about the value we attribute to learning and professional pursuits versus domestic work?
- Perhaps you enjoy words like Rabbi Yehuda HaNasi's maidservant did, or maybe you speak more than one language. What kind of doors are opened by linguistic ability?

Rabbanit Judith Levitan *is a lawyer and educator. She lives in Sydney, Australia, where she represents the community at interfaith events, runs tefilah services, and teaches.*

PURSLANE, POMEGRANATE, AND TOFU BOUREKAS

I imagine Rabbi Yehuda HaNasi's maidservant to have been a capable cook, who served the family, students, and high-profile visitors.

I was intrigued by the story of her identifying purslane when the rabbis could not understand the word.

Purslane is a type of succulent eaten widely across warm climates across the world. It can often be found in Asian or Arabic grocers. It can be replaced with spinach, as in this recipe. If you do source purslane, use half the quantity, chop it to a similar size to the onions, and saute it with them, without wilting it down.

Prep Time: 15 minutes
Cook Time: 40 minutes
Yield: 11–12

Tools:

- Cutting board
- Large baking sheet
- Lemon juicer
- Large knife
- Large mixing bowl
- Large saute or frying pan with a lid
- Weighing scales/cups
- Parchment paper
- Pastry brush

Ingredients:

- 1 tbsp olive oil
- 14 oz (400g) fresh spinach leaves or 7 oz (200g) fresh purslane, washed
- 1 onion, peeled and finely diced
- ½ tsp salt
- 1½–2 tbsp sumac
- 1 tbsp lemon juice
- 3 tsp pomegranate molasses
- 1.8 oz (50g) firm tofu, diced into tiny cubes of ¼ inch (½ cm)
- 1 11 oz (320g) packet of ready-rolled vegan puff pastry
- Extra olive oil to stick and glaze the bourekas
- 1–2 tbsp sesame seeds

Instructions:

1. Heat the oil in a saute pan over medium heat. Add the onions and gently sweat, stirring from time to time until they are soft but not browned. Add the spinach and cover with the lid until it has wilted down. Remove the lid and cook a little longer until the water released has cooked off.

2. Turn into a sieve to drain off any further water. Press down to squeeze out any remaining moisture, then tip into a bowl.

3. Stir in the sumac, salt, lemon juice, and pomegranate molasses. Add the cubed tofu. Taste and adjust as necessary. If preparing ahead of time, this mix will keep in the refrigerator for two days.

4. Preheat oven to 350° F (180° C) and line a large oven tray with baking parchment, or lightly oil.

5. Unroll the pastry and cut into 3½ inch (9 cm) squares.

6. Lightly brush the edges of each square with olive oil and spoon a scant tablespoon of filling into the middle. Fold over one corner to the other to make a triangular parcel. Be careful not to overfill, and make sure you push out any extra air pockets. Use any pastry offcuts to make mini parcels.

7. Brush lightly with oil and sprinkle with sesame or nigella seeds. Bake for 25–30 minutes until golden brown.

8. Cool a little before eating – best eaten warm. They will keep for a couple of days in the refrigerator, but warm them for 10 minutes in a hot oven to crisp up the pastry before eating.

Victoria Prever *is the food editor at the* Jewish Chronicle *newspaper. She also works as a cookery teacher, food consultant, and freelance food writer.*

RABBI YOHANAN'S SISTER / REISH
LAKISH'S WIFE / אחתיה דרבי יוחנן

STORY

We first meet Rabbi Yohanan's sister in the context of his first encounter with Reish Lakish:

Once, Reish Lakish, then a bandit, saw Rabbi Yohanan swimming in a river, so he jumped in and pulled him out. Rabbi Yohanan said to him, "Your strength should be for the Torah."

Reish Lakish replied, "Your beauty is for women." So Rabbi Yohanan said, "My sister is even more beautiful than me. Come with me, and I'll give her to you in marriage."

Reish Lakish went with Rabbi Yohanan. Rabbi Yohanan taught him Torah and Mishnah and Talmud and made him a great man.

One day, they had an argument in the Beit Midrash regarding when weapons acquire the ability to become impure. Rabbi Yohanan said, from the time they are fired in a furnace. Reish Lakish said, from the time they are scoured with water after they have been fired.

"Well," Rabbi Yohanan said, "a bandit would know their weapons."

"What was it worth, coming here with you? Here they call me 'master,' and when I was a bandit, they called me 'master.'"

"I have brought you into the presence of God," Rabbi Yohanan replied.

The argument upset Rabbi Yohanan. It upset Reish Lakish. It upset him so much that he became ill. So Rabbi Yohanan's sister, now Reish Lakish's wife, came to her brother to entreat him to pray for her husband. "Think of my children," she said.

"God cares for orphans," Rabbi Yohanan replied, quoting Jeremiah.

"Think of me, I will be a widow," she said.

"God cares for widows," Rabbi Yohanan said, finishing the verse from Jeremiah, and did not pray for Reish Lakish.

So Reish Lakish died.

The rabbis sent Elazar ben Padat to go comfort Rabbi Yohanan over the death of Reish Lakish, for he had a sharp mind, but Rabbi Yohanan would not be comforted. He went out into the street, rending his clothing and weeping, crying, "Where are you, son of Lakish? Where are you?" until he lost his mind.

Seeing this, the rabbis prayed to God to take his soul, and Rabbi Yohanan died.

PASSAGES

Talmud b. Bava Metzia 84a

CONTEXT

In this story Rabbi Yohanan's sister stands in for Rabbi Yohanan himself – Reish Lakish is taken by Rabbi Yohanan's beauty, but, at his urging, marries his sister instead. And even when she is not standing in for her brother – when she comes to beg for her husband's life – she is still defined by him. The text calls her not Reish Lakish's wife, but Rabbi Yohanan's sister. She herself seems to realize that in approaching her brother, she must do so in her role as his sister, and not the wife of his friend. She doesn't mention Reish Lakish, but instead focuses on Rabbi Yohanan's blood relatives – the innocent bystanders, so to speak – and the people that Rabbi Yohanan should be taking into account – her children (his nieces and nephews) and herself (his sister). Her identity, in this story, revolves around her brother.

However, Rabbi Yohanan's sister also belongs to a long line of women from Jewish tradition who take the initiative to stand up for their husbands/brothers/children when they are in danger. Her actions echo those of Rachel, Michal, Avigayil, and Batsheva, among others, though her foremothers are more successful than she. In this way she is a sort of archetype. She doesn't have a name, but we know her from other stories – only Rabbi Yohanan is not King David, or King Saul, or even Lavan. Where those men were moved by the women in their stories, Rabbi Yohanan remains stubbornly unsympathetic to his sister's plea.

Beyond the homoeroticism of the story of Rabbi Yohanan and Reish Lakish, it also serves as an example of the machismo of the male halachic world. These are two of the most important figures in the Talmud. They are representative of the halachic system. And though Reish Lakish has left the hyper-violent world of banditry behind, his relationship with his Torah partner is still combative and challenging. He and Rabbi Yohanan butt heads and speak cruelly to each other. Both of them dismiss the importance of the other in their lives.

And then there is Rabbi Yohanan's sister, refusing only to be a proxy, to remind the men, and the reader, that when Torah arguments spill over into real life, the implications can be life and death, and that what is at stake is not only the lives of the men themselves, but the lives of the people around them. Rabbi Yohanan's sister demands empathy but gets none. If she is a proxy for her brother, it is that she is what he is not – she is more beautiful, more empathetic, and more merciful, and so takes her place within the honored tradition of her foremothers.

AGGADAH

I knew better than to say his name when I came to you, my brother, begging for his life. Think of the blood of your blood, the last of the beautiful of Jerusalem. Think of me, your sister, offered and given to a bandit because you could not give of yourself.

Oh, but you made him into a great man. You turned his weapons into words and fashioned all that fluid strength into something in your own image – sharp and sure and unmoving and wise. You were always so, looking for something to hit that wouldn't break against you, flirting with the evil eye until he pulled you, dripping, from the river and you pulled him into our lives.

You two were flint and stone, striking against each until you both burst into flames.

This is the fate of women – we must gird ourselves with what little we have – our children, our wits, our empathy – and walk into fires not of our own making. I must gather myself, as so many of my foremothers have done.

You say – God cares for the orphans; He cares for the widow I will be – but does He care for brotherless sisters? And if He cares, should you not care too?

271

All your talking, all your Torah, round and round, thrust and parry – what does it amount to? Knife, sword, or sickle – what does it matter when it becomes itself – whether sparking from the fire, or scoured in water? A knife is still a knife. It can still kill, and it did.

I took your place for him, when I became his wife, now you take my place, roaming through the streets like a restless widow, weeping and tearing your clothes.

So I remain alone – a mother to orphans, wife to no one, and sister to no brother.

So tell me, does God care for brotherless sisters?

PROMPTS

- Do you have siblings? How is your relationship with them different from other relationships in your life?
- Many stories in Tanakh involve women confronting men for the sake of people they love. What does this say about the Tanakh's approach to women and their role in society? How does the story of Rabbi Yohanan's sister fit into/depart from the "Tanakh" model?

Tiki Krakowski *works as a freelance translator, editor, and writer. She lives in Jerusalem with a most excellent roommate, and her neurotic dog, River.*

FERMENTED LEMON SPREAD

When life gives you lemons, pickle them! Pickling is about making the best of what you've got. If Rabbi Yohanan's sister/Reish Lakish's wife came into my home, I would help her see the lemons in her life and guide her to make the best of what she has.

Pickling is a great way to preserve seasonal fruits and veggies all year long. It makes the vitamins and minerals in fruit easier for your body to absorb. Best of all, pickled lemons are probiotic. Kumquat lemons are best for this recipe because of their thin peel, but any organic lemon will do.

Add this pickled lemon spread to tahini, dressings, marinades, soups, and stews.

Prep Time: 20 minutes
Fermenting Time: Approximately 3 weeks
Yield: 1 jar

Tools:

- Cutting board
- Sharp knife
- Teaspoon
- Glass jar with airtight seal

Ingredients:

- 15 lemons
- 3 tbsp salt
- 1 tbsp paprika (optional)

Instructions:

1. Wash the lemons thoroughly. If using store-bought lemons, scrape off waxes from the peel, or briefly submerge the lemons in a bowl of boiling water to melt the wax away.

2. Cut off the tips and slit the lemons almost in half lengthwise, but don't cut all the way through. Leave the two halves still attached at the base. Then make another slit, as if you were cutting the lemons into quarters, but again not all the way through.

3. Sprinkle ½ teaspoon of salt into the slits of the lemons.

4. Put the salted lemons in the jar and press down.

5. Seal the jar and let the pickles ferment for 3 weeks at room temp.

6. During the first week of fermentation, it is important to release built-up pressure from the jar. Open the jar, press the lemons down to submerge them in the juices, then close the jar. Repeat this every day for the first week.

7. After three weeks of fermentation, the lemons should be ready. The peels should be soft, the juices thick, and they should taste and smell like a citrus vinegar.

8. Once the lemons are ready, they can be blended into a sauce with paprika.

Nava Ratzon is a clinical nutritionist, and fermentation freak. She lives on her farm with her husband, baby girl, and some chickens and pickles.

STORY

Our section opens with two women who prepare mustard, offer it to rabbis, and have it rejected. First, Abaye (who is a Rabbi but is usually mentioned without the title) declines to consume some "mustard" prepared by his foster mother, Em. Then we meet another character, Rav Hiyya bar Ashi, who also refuses mustard prepared by the wife of his teacher, Rabbi Ze'eira.

Rabbi Ze'eira's wife is surprised by Rav Hiyya's refusal and an interrogation ensues. She reminds him that when she made mustard for his Rabbi he enjoyed it – why, then, is Rav Hiyya refusing her mustard?

In an attempt to resolve the contradiction, Rava bar Shabba offers a possible explanation: the preparation method, which included stirring with garlic, meant it was permissible to eat.

PASSAGES

Talmud b. Shabbat 140a

CONTEXT

Rabbi Ze'eira's name, written זעירא in Babylonian Jewish Aramaic, literally means "seed." This passage is about mustard – not the yellow deli sauce we think of today, but a condiment made by crushing brown or white mustard seeds and dissolving them in vinegar, wine, or water. The reference to mustard here in the Tractate Shabbat is a legal debate on the effect of the process and timing of the preparation on the permissibility of consumption.

The discussion leading up to this passage states a series of opinions about mustard preparation, including that on Shabbat one may prepare mustard by dissolving seeds in a jar of liquid, but not by crushing the seeds, as well as the opposite opinion, that crushing is permitted, but dissolving is prohibited. Eventually, the rabbis mention the concept of making it with a *shinui* on Shabbat, literally meaning a "change" in the method, as compared to *darko b'chol* – a different way than on a weekday. The *shinui* can just be done in a manner that is similar to the way the action is done during the week, but weirdly, or inefficiently.

Since many Shabbat prohibitions are more lenient when it comes to food preparation, it is sensible that Rabbi Ze'eira's wife would be perplexed by the dismissal of her spicy sauce. However, the Talmud nevertheless is subtly critical of her failure to consider their methods of preparation. Inherent in this story is that the women are preparing food for the household and not spending their days discussing the laws of Shabbat; therefore, they are less knowledgeable of the Shabbat laws than the rabbis who are refusing their dressing.

AGGADAH

Rabbi Ze'eira's wife spent all week planning the dish she would bring to the community Shabbat lunch: a rainbow of chopped and lightly sauteed vegetables, supplemented with the fresh herbs she dried last August. As usual, she designed it dairy-free and nut-free, anticipating that these choices would lead to the largest number of people being able to enjoy it.

What brought these freshly harvested vegetables together was her homemade dressing. All of her neighbors and friends could agree: Rabbi Ze'eira's wife's unique dressings could make any person fall in love with any vegetable. Never trying to upstage any one ingredient over another, she always seemed to know the right combination of oil, vinegar, and spices to unite leaves, fruits, roots, and seeds.

Just as she was whipping up yet another ephemeral concoction, a small paper bag at the back of her pantry caught her eye. Pausing her blender, she reached back and opened the folded corners, barely able to recognize the tiny brownish black specks at the bottom of the bag. These were wild garlic mustard seeds, harvested from dried-out stalks while hiking in late fall. They would be the perfect addition to this summer salad medley. With her usual eyeballing technique, she tossed the entire bag of seeds into the blender.

As Rabbi Ze'eira's wife tried to fall asleep on Erev Shabbat her offering was already sitting in her refrigerator, ready to be carried down the block in a sustainably sourced mahogany bowl with matching serving utensils.

It was almost the summer solstice and everyone was excited to enjoy the community Shabbat lunch in the courtyard. Rabbi Ze'eira's wife placed her mahogany bowl on the buffet table alongside processed foods, packaged hummus, a few casseroles, a bowl containing mostly iceberg lettuce, and fizzy bottled sodas.

As soon as *Kiddush* and *Motzi* were recited, one by one people began to fill their plates.

By the time she made it to the front of the buffet line, there were no bagels in sight and barely any side dishes on the buffet. Except…there was her mahogany bowl – still full, both utensils cemented in their original position. No one was sampling her dish. It was as if it was invisible! Each person skipping over the myriad colors and flavors, and instead choosing pale tuna, egg salad, and cola. What could be causing this oversight of her skill and effort?

Feeling humiliated, she wanted to interrogate each diner – what was drawing them away from her dish, but toward the others? She decided to ask Rabbi Zahav, because she knew she would tell her the truth.

"Your dish," said Rabbi Zahav, taking an extra breath, "appears to be covered with tiny insects!"

"Oh!" gasped Rabbi Ze'eira's wife. "Those aren't insects, they are seeds from wild garlic mustard!"

"How about we try this," said Rabbi Zahav. "I'm going to give it a toss – that should integrate the seeds into the dish. Would you mind if I used these garlic stalks instead of your mahogany serving spoons?" She placed a large portion of salad on her plate, making a point to show it off to everyone and eat it in plain sight. Almost instantly, the buffet was swarming with folks, eager to dig into Rabbi Ze'eira's wife's dish.

PROMPTS

- Consider the relationship between your values and your ego. How do you balance living your truth and inspiring others with coming through as authentic and open-minded? Is a dish you cook ever "yours" – even if you've designed the recipe or grown the ingredients?

- When someone else prepares food for you that you either know or fear doesn't meet your values, what are some ways you naturally respond or react?

- What are your priorities: sourcing of ingredients, method and location of preparation, food miles? How can modern Jews, with varying levels of Shabbat and kosher observance, balance the value of sharing food in the community with their personal preferences?

Sarah Chandler *aka Kohenet Shamirah is a Jewish educator, ritualist, activist, and poet, serving as the director of Romemu Yeshiva and CEO of Shamir Collective.*

MUSTARD, MISO, AND MAPLE DRESSING

Rabbi Ze'eira's wife made a mustard recipe that was refused. This mustard, miso, and maple syrup dressing is sure to delight.

Xanthan gum is the secret ingredient in oil-free salad dressings. It thickens and emulsifies liquid dressing so that it sticks to the leafy greens or vegetables. This dressing can be stored refrigerated for 5 days in a glass jar.

You can adapt this recipe to your own taste:

- *Sweet to spicy: Alter the mustard variety.*
- *Sourness: Add more white or apple cider vinegar.*
- *Creamy: Swap out the tahini, xanthan gum, and water for 1 cup of unsweetened plant-based coconut or soy yogurt to get a creamier thick dressing for coleslaw or cucumber salad (if serving the same day).*
- *Thicken or make it thinner: Reduce the water to ½ cup to thicken this dressing.*

Prep Time: 5 minutes
Yield: makes approximately 1½ cups (350ml)

Tools:

- Blender or whisk
- Glass bowl
- Measuring cups and spoons/kitchen scale
- Glass jar to store

Ingredients:

- ¼ cup white miso paste
- ¼ cup fresh lemon juice
- 1 tsp apple cider vinegar or white vinegar
- 1–2 tbsp Dijon mustard
- 2 tbsp maple syrup
- 1 tbsp tahini
- 1–3 cloves garlic, minced
- A pinch of citrus zest from lemon, lime, or orange
- 1 cup water
- ½ tsp xanthan gum powder

Instructions:

1. Place all ingredients in the blender or in a glass bowl.

2. Blend or whisk until smooth.

3. Pour into a glass jar with a lid. Place in the refrigerator for a few hours before serving so the xanthan gum can thicken up.

From the Jewish Food Hero Kitchen

RACHEL, THE WIFE OF RABBI AKIVA /
רחל, אשת רבי עקיבא

STORY

The story of Rachel, the wife of Rabbi Akiva, is told in two different places in the Talmud, and also in the minor tractate, Avot de-Rabbi Nathan. There are meaningful differences and contradictions in the various versions of her story. However, in all versions, Rachel sacrifices her social standing, the promise of her inheritance, and twenty-four years of living with her husband. She does so in order that Akiva – seen by others as an ignoramus, but in whom Rachel saw a momentous spark – could spend long years studying Torah. Ultimately this leads to him becoming the legendary Rabbi Akiva from whom all our Oral Tradition follows.

In the versions brought in the Babylonian Talmud, Rabbi Akiva returns from the study hall after having been away from his wife for twelve years. He overhears a neighbor – in one version described as an old man, in another as a wicked person – taunting her. This character berates Rachel for choosing the man who had effectively abandoned her to go study Torah. She was, after all, the daughter of a very wealthy man who'd disowned her when she'd married Akiva the simpleton.

Rachel answers her mockers with intransigence: "If he would listen to me, he would sit and study for another twelve years." Rabbi Akiva hears this and turns around to heed her wishes: he goes off for another twelve years, returning to their home followed by 24,000 students.

Rachel goes out to meet her husband, and is again mocked by her neighbors, as well as by Rabbi Akiva's students, but she pays no heed. She falls at his feet as his students, not knowing who she is, try to push her away.

Her husband honors her with words that could hold no higher meaning to himself and his students: "Leave her. Both my Torah knowledge and yours are hers."

It is widely agreed among the sources that Rachel is richly rewarded for her years of sacrifice. In some versions, her father gives her and Rabbi Akiva half of his wealth and other forms of inheritance. In another version, Rabbi Akiva brings her "a gold tiara engraved with a depiction of the city of Jerusalem." This is a gift that, in their extreme poverty, he had once told her he would give her if only he could.

PASSAGES[1]

Ketubot 62b–63a

CONTEXT

Rachel has long been held as an ideal example of a woman who makes sacrifices for her husband and is rewarded richly for it. Rachel's story differs poignantly from a series of other stories which precede it in the Talmud. These stories feature husbands leaving their families for extended periods of time in order to study Torah. Loss or tragedy ensues.

The rabbis who included these stories appear to berate, or at least warn, men who leave their wives for long periods of time in order to study. But there is a difference between abandoning one's wife, and being physically absent but keeping one's wife present in one's heart and regard.

Rachel is rewarded with wealth, her husband's great success, and most movingly, with her husband's devotion in love. The marriage of Rachel and Rebbe Avika is a true love story: a story of love, of commitment, and of perseverance.

Rachel is a symbol of what sacrifice can bring when the one who sacrifices holds perfect faith in that sacrifice.

AGGADAH

Rachel. She knows something deep inside. She knows it and the men in her life do not. Not only the men in her life; no one else knows.

I see her. I watch her. She holds on to her truth. She won't – *she can't* – let it go. No matter how deep her suffering, how aching her shame.

---

1. Rachel appears in Talmud.b.Ketubot. 62b–63a, Talmud.b. Nedarim 50a, Avot de-Rabbi Nathan, Talmud.b.Shabbat 59b.

The women on our street taunt her. I don't, but I don't defend her either. I'm too weak. Nothing like Rachel.

She remains steadfast. She sends him off again. She sees much further. She told me so once. For the most part, almost always, Rachel keeps to herself. I am her neighbor, but we barely speak. But one day the words came pouring out of her, like a closely guarded sheep that slipped away. She said to me, as we washed our dresses by the river, "he will be a great teacher one day."

How did she know that? He knew nothing when she met him. Nothing. He, a grown man, he went to *cheder* with my little boy.

Her wisdom and her strength are much greater than anyone else's here, even Akiva's. This much *I* know. But she doesn't use them for her own glory.

Yes, Rachel is the wisest one. Wiser than Akiva, I'd say.

She sacrifices, yes, but I can see she doesn't bemoan this sacrifice as others would. She knows something, knows what the reward will be. No one ever calls Rachel a prophet, but I think she is.

PROMPTS

- Where in your life do you sacrifice for the sake of others?
- Can you identify places where you are whole with that sacrifice? Places you are less than whole?
- Do you consider self-sacrifice a value you'd like to hold?
- Which of your own needs and desires will you not sacrifice?

Leah Hartman is a creative writer, a copywriter & brand voice specialist, and a literary translator. Leah lives in Jerusalem with her husband and seven children.

SMOKY EGGPLANT SALAD WITH HERBS, TAHINI, AND POMEGRANATE

This recipe perfectly fits Rachel's story, as it takes a simple vegetable and elevates it by pairing it with tahini and pomegranate. Similarly, Rachel chose her "simpleton" husband and was ultimately rewarded, elevating their lives together.

This eggplant salad has been a staple recipe of mine for years. It has converted many from eggplant dislikers to eggplant lovers, and the flavors pair well with many Mediterranean dishes.

Prep Time: 10 minutes

Cook Time: 15 minutes

Yield: approximately 2 servings

Tools:

- Cutting board
- Frying pan
- Knife
- Measuring cups and spoons

Ingredients:

- 1 medium eggplant
- 4 garlic cloves, minced
- ¼ red bell pepper, minced
- 1 tbsp olive oil
- 1 tsp smoked paprika
- 1 tsp liquid smoke
- Juice from 1 lemon
- 2 tsp tahini
- 2 tsp fresh basil
- 2 tsp fresh parsley
- 2 tsp fresh chives
- 1 tsp sesame seeds
- ½ cup pomegranate seeds (about half an average pomegranate)
- Salt and pepper to taste

Instructions:

1. Slice the eggplant into small cubes and set aside.

2. Mince the garlic and bell pepper while heating up the olive oil in a pan.

3. Add the garlic and bell pepper to the hot oil, and saute on medium heat.

4. When they become fragrant, add the eggplant, salt, pepper, and paprika and cook for about 5–7 minutes until soft.

5. Add the liquid smoke, lemon juice, tahini, basil, parsley, and chives. Cook for another 3–5 minutes, until the eggplant is fork-tender.

6. Top with pomegranate seeds and herbs.

Bailey Cohen *is a personal chef near Washington, DC. She is passionate about plant-based cuisine and enjoys integrating many whole plant foods into dishes.*

RAV ADDA BAR MATTANA'S WIFE / ביתהו דרב אדא בר מתנא

STORY

The wife of Rav Adda bar Mattana makes a lasting impression with one sentence in the Talmud. Her husband was a fourth-century *Amora* and disciple of Rava. Her story starts with the pithy statement, "in him who makes himself cruel to his sons and other members of his household like a raven for the sake of Torah."

The rabbis illustrate this truth with a story. As Rav Adda bar Mattana prepares to leave for the house of study, his wife asks him how she should provide food for their children in his absence. He answers her with a question, "Are all of the reeds in the marsh already gone?" He implies that if the family has finished their food supply, he has no more money to offer and she should cobble together additional meals from reeds gathered from the marsh.

PASSAGES

Talmud b. Eruvin 22a

CONTEXT

This short story, with only two lines of dialogue, reminds us that study of Torah must not make us cruel in life.

The story comes immediately after a description of the raven-like qualities of those who are dedicated to Torah; one who gets up early to study, stays late in the evening, and fasts and deprives himself. Rava then raises this example of Rav Adda bar Mattana, comparing him to a raven who behaves cruelly to his family. In this way, the Sages use this story to highlight the limits of the mitzvah of studying Torah. The study of Torah, which the rabbis see as the highest of mitzvot, doesn't exist in a vacuum of our human, social, familial responsibilities. A person has gone too far if in their dedication to study he neglects his family.

Rav Adda bar Mattana's wife's simple question to her husband illustrates the human and familial cost of holy behavior. The argument has more force spoken by Rav Adda bar Mattana's wife than it would if it were stated hypothetically by one of the rabbis: in his absence, his wife is fully responsible for feeding their children.

AGGADAH

"I have that big client meeting tonight, so I won't be home till late and have to be in the office again tomorrow by 7 am."

"We're out of food. You told me you were grocery shopping today and cooking dinner tonight."

"Isn't there some peanut butter in the cabinet?"

The roles in this Talmudic story still resonate in many relationship dynamics today. We can easily imagine these types of conversations taking place between couples of any genders, siblings, or a parent and an eldest child. In any relationship involving a distribution of responsibility, one party's dedication to the fulfillment of their own needs can have dire consequences when the impact on others' needs is not considered.

Rav Adda bar Mattana's wife makes sure her husband leaves aware of how his commitment to study burdens his wife. When he goes to study, he will have a vivid mental image of his family at home without food.

No longer a victim of his abandonment, we might envision his wife standing in the doorway insisting he go to town and collect more suitable sustenance for his children than marsh reeds. With the courage she demonstrated in standing up to her husband, perhaps she might collaborate with other rabbis' wives to change the way that Torah study negatively affects family life.

With one question to her husband, Rav Adda bar Mattana's wife has illustrated for Talmud readers that our personal devotions must be balanced with our shared responsibilities, as well as demonstrating the force of one well-placed question.

PROMPTS

- Where in your own life is the dynamic between Rav Adda bar Mattana's wife and her husband mirrored?
- How do you envision Rav Adda bar Mattana's wife responding in the Talmud? How might she respond today?
- Are there ever times when you need, or choose, to behave like a raven, at the expense of family or relationships?

Rebecca Kaufman *is a rabbinical student at HUC and student rabbi at Congregation Beth Jacob in El Centro, CA. She lives with her husband, Tavir.*

AGUAJÍ (GREEN PLANTAINS SOUP)

This vegan recipe is a great way to honor Rav Adda bar Mattana's wife's sense of self-sufficiency. She managed to care for and feed her family, even with minimum resources.

The key ingredient in this recipe is green plantains (not green bananas). Humble in appearance but very versatile, green plantains are rich in complex carbohydrates, so the final result is a nutritious and filling meal.

Prep Time: 10 minutes
Cook Time: 50 minutes
Yield: 4 servings

Tools:

- Grater
- Immersion blender, conventional blender, or food processor
- Soup pot

Ingredients:

- 2 tbsp (30ml) extra virgin olive oil
- 2 small white onions, chopped
- 5 fresh garlic cloves, minced
- 2 tsp dried oregano
- 2 dried bay leaves
- 3 green plantains (450g total – approximately 150g each)
- 8 cups (1900ml) water
- ¼ cup (10g) fresh cilantro or parsley, chopped
- ¼ tsp salt and black pepper (or to taste)

Instructions:

1. In a soup pot add the extra virgin olive oil and saute the onions, the roughly chopped garlic, oregano, and dried bay leaves on medium-low heat, until everything is fragrant and the garlic is lightly golden.

2. Peel the green plantains. Cut one of them into 6 to 8 pieces and add to the sauteed vegetables, together with the water and cilantro leaves.

3. Cook on medium-low until the plantain pieces are cooked through.

4. Meanwhile, finely grate the other two plantains. Add ¼ teaspoon each of salt and black pepper, shape into balls, and set aside.

5. Remove the bay leaves from the cooked plantain mix and blend the remaining vegetables with an immersion blender.

6. Lower the heat, add the plantain balls to the soup, and simmer until they are cooked through.

7. Serve hot, with an optional garnish of fresh tomato relish, avocado, and a drizzle of extra virgin olive oil.

Hannah Abreu is the chef behind "Kasheribbean," a blog where she showcases her culinary traditions and fusion ideas as a Dominican Sephardic Jewess.

STORY

"Rav Hisda's daughter is different." This declaration appears in Talmud b. Chagigah 5a, in a discussion of the precautions men must take in their interactions with women. Husbands ought not send particular cuts of meat to their wives on Shabbat eve, for fear that they might rush in their food preparations and not handle the prohibited meat appropriately. But not Rav Hisda's daughter. She was considered an expert, a knowledgeable authority who could be trusted to know the details of Jewish law, especially in the kitchen, and follow them diligently even in complicated cases.

Rav Hisda, a well-known Rabbi of priestly and impoverished lineage, lived in Kafri, in southern Babylonia, in the second half of the third century and the first decades of the fourth century. Together with his wife, the daughter of Hanan bar Raba, he raised many children, among them a daughter who married Rami bar Hama and, after her first husband's death, married Rava. This woman is known in the Talmud as "Rav Hisda's daughter."

Rav Hisda's daughter appears numerous times in rabbinic sources, and in each case she is presented as an exceptional person. In one passage, she appears as a precocious young girl sitting on her father's lap, correctly prophesying the future. Another passage depicts her as the devoted daughter of an important Rabbi, concerned about her father's health and sleeping habits. Elsewhere, she is depicted as the wife of the head of the yeshiva, going to extraordinary lengths to protect her husband from demons, especially those found in the bathroom. Other tractates describe her successfully advocating on behalf of women who came to her husband's court, or explicating the details of rabbinic law with her husband, on behalf of other women. In Ketubbot 39b, her husband cites her in a halachic discussion with his colleague Abaye, and in Talmud b. Yevamot 34b Rava warns her that his colleagues are gossiping about her. In a particularly dramatic story, she jealously drives a rival rabbi's wife out of town when she fears that woman might seduce her own husband.

The narrative of her death is quite shocking. The text describes that, within thirty days of delivering a baby, she immersed in a ritual bath without her husband present, caught cold, and died, her bier trailing her husband to the Babylonian city of Pumpedita.

In each Talmudic reference, the text presents Rav Hisda's daughter as a woman with close familial relationships to powerful rabbinic figures, not least her father, Rav Hisda, and her second husband, Rava, and, moreover, as a halachic authority in her own right, someone with integrity, charm, devotion, and smarts. Someone who ought to be trusted and respected. Especially in the court and the kitchen.

PASSAGES[1]

Talmud b. Chagigah 5a

CONTEXT

Rav Hisda's daughter was the daughter of an important Rabbi. As a member of a rabbinic family, she learned rabbinic traditions from her male relatives and had direct access to them, thereby able to insert her knowledge and opinions into the halachic process in ways that women from non-rabbinic households or those of lower social class might not have had access to. This context helps us understand the significance of the stories about Rav Hisda's daughter in which she displays halachic knowledge about meat consumption, and also intervenes in conversations with her husband that relate to his work as a communal figure in the courthouse.

In a recent article titled "The Talmud's Women in Law and Narrative," Judith Hauptman argues that women in rabbinic households in antiquity learned a considerable amount of halacha, performed religious rituals that necessitated a high degree of facility with that halacha, and used their knowledge to implement new rules or tweak existing ones based on their experiences.[2] In other words, though rabbinic texts often caution against women's study of halacha and give the impression that the entirety of rabbinic law was produced by men, many women indeed studied, enacted, contributed, and transmitted rabbinic traditions. Hauptman argues, in this article and in a companion article titled "A New View

---

1. See also, Talmud b. Bava Batra 12b, Talmud b. Eruvin 65a, Talmud b. Berakhot 62a, Talmud b. Ketubbot 85a, Talmud b. Chullin 44b, Ketubbot 39b, Talmud b. Yevamot 34b, Talmud b. Ketubbot 65a, Talmud b. Shabbat 129a, as well as Berakhot 56a, in which Rav Hisda's daughter's death also becomes a plot point.
2. Judith Hauptman, "The Talmud's Women in Law and Narrative," *Nashim: A Journal of Jewish Women's Studies & Gender Issues* 28 (2015): 30–50.

of Women and Torah Study in the Talmudic Period" (2010), that many of the stories that depict women participating in the development of halacha happened in contexts related to food preparation – whether baking matzah, removing a portion of dough (*hafrashat halah*) before baking bread, preparing an *eruv tavshilin* before a holiday to make cooking permissible, preparing mustard on the Sabbath, trimming vegetables for the post-Yom Kippur meal, eating before *Kiddush* on Friday nights, or using an oven on a holiday.[3]

AGGADAH

Rabbis' daughters represent a special class of women in rabbinic texts.

Evoking Gloria Anzaldua's scholarship about identity in the borderlands, Wendy Zierler writes, in an article about depictions of rabbis' daughters in nineteenth-century Jewish literature, that "throughout Jewish history, the rabbi's daughter has occupied a 'borderland' between traditional Jewish gender divisions... As a borderland figure, the rabbi's daughter enjoys a privileged exposure to the world of Jewish scholarship and ritual leadership, presenting an alternative to the traditional binary divisions of Jewish gender roles."[4]

Studying depictions of rabbis' daughters specifically in the Talmud, Dvora Weisberg notes that such women are often depicted as knowledgeable women, but also sometimes regarded with suspicion because of their power to wield knowledge of Torah and rabbinic halacha in ways that undermine the rabbis.[5] In certain instances, their status as insiders is celebrated, and in others it is feared or marked as being especially dangerous. Their close proximity to rabbinic figures might also have impacted their opinions about rabbinic culture – though in complicated and perhaps counterintuitive ways. Their characters are sometimes evoked in rabbinic sources to lend authority to a particular rabbinic precept, and at other times to undermine or nuance it.[6]

---

3. Judith Hauptman, "A New View of Women and Torah Study in the Talmudic Period," *Jewish Studies: An Internet Journal* 9 (2010): 249–292.

4. Wendy Zierler, "The Rabbi's Daughter In and Out of the Kitchen: Feminist Literary Negotiations," *Nashim: A Journal of Jewish Women's Studies and Gender Issues* 5 (2002), 83–104, quote on 84.

5. Dvora Weisberg, "Desirable But Dangerous: Rabbis' Daughters in the Babylonian Talmud," *Hebrew Union College Annual* 75 (2004): 121–161.

6. Rav Hisda's daughter has also captured the imagination of academics, memoirists, and fiction writers, mentioned for example in Ilana Kurshan's *If All the Seas Were Ink: A Memoir* (St. Martin's Press, 2017); appears in

Rav Hisda's daughter does not only weigh in on matters of rabbinic practice or law, however. She also exerts agency over her personal life. In Talmud b. Bava Batra 12b, when her father asks her whom she would like to marry, she answers unexpectedly, that she wishes to marry both of the men offered to her. And, decades later, when she is told that she won't be able to bear children with her second husband because more than ten years have passed since the death of her first husband, she again answers assertively that she intended to remarry for the entirety of her widowhood, and therefore such a rabbinic precept does not apply to her – she even speaks up to assure the men in the room that her womb hasn't closed up (Talmud b. Yevamot 34b).

Rabbis seem to have frequently married their colleagues' daughters, as is the case with Rav Hisda's daughter, and so rabbis' daughters also often became rabbis' wives, and soon enough rabbis' mothers, too. In all of these cases, it's worth noting that the point of reference in rabbinic sources is usually the Rabbi himself, and the ways in which his relative relates to him or his ideas.

What was Rav Hisda's daughter's name? We don't know, because the Talmud didn't think that was essential information to preserve. But what's in a name anyway? In the sources, she is remembered not by name but in relation to others, usually her father and husband – but she is not always defined by these relationships. Even without a known name, she exerts some degree of power and agency over her own choices, and also on behalf of others. When reading Talmudic passages about her or other rabbinic women like her, we can ask: why did the text choose to include this story in its corpus, how and to what ends is it employing her character, and what values do the narratives about her promote?

Ruth Calderon's *A Bride for One Night: Talmudic Tales* (Jewish Publication Society, 2014); and features as the protagonist in Maggie Anton's work of historical fiction, *Rav Hisda's Daughter* (Penguin, 2012).

PROMPTS

- What does your name mean, and how is it significant to you?
- Have you ever been in a position to give someone else a name? If so, how did it feel to make such an important decision on behalf of someone else?
- If you were asked to call yourself in relation to someone else, rather than using your personal name, how would you hope to be called? (e.g., "Daughter of…" or "Friend of…" or "Advocate for…" and so on)
- What are spaces and places in which you are most "in your comfort zone," and which make you uncomfortable or less confident – and what does that say about you?

Sarit Kattan Gribetz *teaches Jewish Studies at Fordham University, and studies at Yeshivat Maharat. She co-authored this piece with her daughters,* **Sophie** *and* **Daniela**.

ROASTED SWEET POTATOES WITH TAMARIND AND CRISPY SHALLOTS

The texts about Rav Hisda's daughter reveal her many facets: a loyal daughter, a jealous lover, and a learned woman. This recipe is an offering to celebrate Rav Hisda's daughter in all her complexity.

This dish is tangy from the tamarind, and sweet and earthy from the potatoes and coriander. It's layered with spice from the chili, crunch from the fried shallots, and garnished with fresh herbs and lime.

You can find tamarind in the form of a compressed block or from shelled pods at Asian grocery stores or online. Makrut lime leaf is optional, but it adds a beautiful aroma to the dish.

Most of this recipe can be prepped a few days before serving.

Prep Time: 1½ hours
Cook Time: 45 minutes
Yield: 4–6 servings

Tools:

- Large bowl
- Large pot
- Frying pan
- Baking sheet
- Sieve

Ingredients:

For the fried shallots:

- 5 oz (135g) shallots (about 5 cloves)
- ¾ cup (180ml) vegetable oil
- Small pinch of salt

For the tamarind sauce:

- 2.6 oz (75g) tamarind pulp from a compressed block or from shelled pods
- ⅓ cup (80ml) boiling water
- 3 tbsp (2 oz / 56g) shaved palm sugar or brown sugar
- 1 tbsp sugar or maple syrup, to taste
- ½ tbsp sambal oelek (or sriracha), to taste

- 2 tsp sweet soy sauce
- Juice of half a lime, plus wedges for serving
- Pinch of salt

For the roasted sweet potatoes:

- 3 lbs (1.4 kg) sweet potatoes (about 6 potatoes), skin on
- 8 tbsp reserved shallot oil, divided
- 2 tsp ground coriander
- 1 tsp ground cumin
- ½ tsp fennel or anise seeds, crushed
- Black pepper
- Flaky sea salt
- Handful of cilantro leaves
- 3 green onions, thinly sliced
- 1 red chili pepper, thinly sliced
- 2 kaffir lime leaves, thinly sliced, optional

Instructions:

Method for the fried shallots and shallot oil:

1. Slice the shallots thinly with a mandoline. Heat oil with a small pinch of salt in a wok or pot over medium-low heat. Test to see if oil is hot enough by dropping in a shallot slice; it should sizzle and bubble.
2. Add all the shallots and stir gently. The shallots will bubble and turn lighter in color in around 3 minutes or so. Continue stirring until the edges become lightly golden.
3. Increase to high heat and continue stirring until shallots start to become golden, about 5–7 more minutes. Keep a close eye on the shallots as they can brown quickly.
4. Immediately strain shallots through a fine mesh sieve and reserve the oil in a bowl to use later to roast the potatoes. Transfer shallots to a plate lined with paper towels and let cool completely. They will continue to crisp up and turn golden as they cool. The shallots can be stored at room temperature for 5 days. (Recrisp in a 200° F / 93° C oven if needed.)

Method for the tamarind sauce:

1. Separate tamarind pulp into small chunks and place in a small heatproof bowl. Pour ⅓ cup (80ml) boiling water to cover the tamarind. Cover and let sit for 30 minutes. Break up the pulp occasionally to help soften the tamarind.
2. Strain tamarind mixture through a fine mesh sieve into a bowl. Use your hands and press down firmly to extract as much paste as possible. Some pulp will stick to the underside of the sieve; scrape this into the bowl as well. You should end up with around 4 tablespoons of thick paste. Discard fibers and seeds. The paste can be made ahead of time and stored in the fridge.
3. Add tamarind paste, shaved palm sugar, sugar or maple syrup, sambal oelek, soy sauce, and pinch of salt into a small pot.
4. Heat gently until it just reaches a simmer; do not boil. Stir often and continue heating over very low heat until sugar is melted.
5. Add lime juice. Taste and adjust with more sugar, maple syrup, or salt to balance the sweet and sour. Add more sambal oelek if you want it to be spicier.
6. Use the sauce immediately or store in the fridge for up to a week, where the flavors will mellow.

Method for the roasted sweet potatoes:

1. Fill a large pot with lightly salted water and bring to a boil.

2. Quarter and cut sweet potatoes into 2–3-inch wedges, placing the cut potatoes in a bowl with water to keep from oxidizing.

3. Add the cut sweet potatoes to the boiling water for 5 minutes. Drain and rinse with cold water. This can be done a day ahead.

4. Preheat the oven to 400° F / 205° C. Add 6 tablespoons of the reserved shallot oil to a sheet pan, being careful not to overcrowd. Use two pans if necessary. Place the oiled pan in a preheated oven until smoking hot, around 5–7 min.

5. Toss sweet potatoes with 2 more tablespoons of shallot oil, pepper, and spices. Spread on the hot baking sheet (you should hear a nice sizzle when the potato hits the pan). Arrange in a single layer with no wedges touching.

6. Roast in the oven until the underside of the potatoes is browned, about 15–20 minutes. Turn and continue roasting until the outsides are charred, about 10–15 more minutes.

Assemble:

Transfer roasted sweet potatoes to a large bowl. Toss gently with tamarind sauce and flaky sea salt just before serving. Garnish with fried shallots, cilantro leaves, thinly sliced green onions and chili peppers, and kaffir lime leaves if using. Serve alongside lime wedges.

Lauren Monaco Grossman *is a graphic designer and home cook, baker, and ice cream maker. She enjoys expressing her multiracial identity through the food on her table.*

STORY

Rav Rehumi's wife lived alone for most of the year. Her husband was a devoted student of Rava, the famous fourth-generation *Amora*, and lived in Mehoza at the school. At that time, the vocations of many men forced them to reside away from home and family. It was Rav Rehumi's custom to return home to his wife and family once a year, on Erev Yom Kippur.

One year, on the eve of Yom Kippur, Rav Rehumi became absorbed in his studies and did not go home. Meanwhile, his wife was at home, excitedly anticipating her husband's imminent arrival. Waiting for him, Rav Rehumi's wife repeatedly said to herself, "now he's coming," confident that he would arrive according to their custom.

He did not arrive, and his wife became increasingly distressed and started to cry. Meanwhile, Rav Rehumi was sitting on the roof of the *beit midrash*. In the exact moment that a single tear fell from Rav Rehumi's wife's lashes, the roof upon which Rav Rehumi was sitting crumbled. He fell to the ground and died on impact.

PASSAGES

Talmud b. Ketubot 62b

CONTEXT

Though the Talmud maintains that studying Torah is a crucial aspect of a Jewish life, this story reinforces that it should not replace or supersede familial commitment.

Throughout the Talmud there is a frequent suggestion that verbal wrongdoing is more severe than monetary wrongdoing. This story posits that verbal wrongdoing does not have to be deceptive but rather can involve causing emotional pain or sadness. This story serves as a warning to future Talmud scholars not to ignore promises to their families in the misguided belief that doing so for the sake of Torah learning is justified.

Rav Rehumi's wife's story is part of a larger discussion about how often husbands of different vocations must return home from their jobs to have sex with their wives. This story serves to discredit Rav Adda bar Ahava's opinion that Torah scholars are allowed to leave their wives for two to three years without permission. Rav Rehumi's annual visit is explicitly timed: on Yom Kippur, a day when sexual relations are forbidden. The story also forefronts the emotional journey of Rav Rehumi's wife – from excited anticipation, to distress, to crying. This emphasizes the importance the Talmud places on men satisfying their wives' diverse needs: not only conjugal but also emotional.

Rav Rehumi's failure to value his wife causes her emotional distress of such magnitude that it literally kills him.

AGGADAH

Bleary-eyed she saw the time: 6:30 AM. She willed herself out of bed, and made her way downstairs to the coffeepot awaiting her. As she came to life over her steaming mug and the morning news, she grew excited. Every year on Erev Yom Kippur, her husband returned home from his overseas job studying Torah. Sure, the random texts and quick FaceTimes were nice, but he was always so busy, and Erev Yom Kippur was the one day that they really got to spend time together. She missed his laugh, cooking the pre-fast meal together, the way he massaged her shoulders. She missed being a family.

She was well taken care of, to be sure. Living with her parents most of the time, she was constantly surrounded by people who loved her and kept her busy: family movie nights, friends inviting her to study groups and dinners, long hours at work. But she always felt a lingering sense of loss, one that was only remedied when her husband was home. She understood why he needed to leave, and she appreciated that he didn't force her to come with him, allowing her to pursue her own professional goals. But she couldn't help but miss his presence. Still on her first cup of coffee, she texted him a short message saying how excited she was and asking for his ETA. When he didn't respond right away, she sighed and decided to do a last-minute cleaning of the apartment that they owned together, which remained empty most of the year. She took her time sweeping and dusting and scrubbing, one ear straining for the ding of a message. When lunchtime came, she called him, but it went straight to voicemail. Netflix distracted her for a bit as she sorted through old bills, just trying to keep herself busy. She jumped every time the phone beeped, but it was just her friends, her mother, or a text reminding her of a sale at the local supermarket.

Yom Kippur was fast approaching, and she was getting more and more nervous that he wouldn't make it in time or that perhaps he was hurt. Why wasn't he answering? She tried calling the airline, but they said that he hadn't shown up for the flight. Panicked, she called his *beit midrash*…and found out that he had decided not to return home. Hearing this made her heart drop.

Was 364 days a year not enough to devote to his studies? On their one day together, how could he get so immersed in his learning that he did not even bother to let his wife know of his change of plans? Didn't her anxious texts mean anything to him? She asked to speak to him, the displeasure surely seeping into her voice, but the school secretary said he was refusing to come to the phone. Tears of frustration and anger brimmed in her eyes; after all she had done, he couldn't even be bothered to speak to her and explain. How humiliating to be ghosted by her own husband on Erev Yom Kippur.

As she blinked, one tear slowly rolled down her face. In that exact instant, the roof, on which her husband was taking a break and lounging, collapsed. He fell to the ground and died.

PROMPTS

- Rava warns: "A person must always be careful about mistreatment of his wife. Since her tears are easily elicited, punishment for her mistreatment is immediate." Should Rava's warning apply to all tears, regardless of gender? Are male and female vulnerability valued / managed / treated differently in intimate relationships?
- Does mandating scheduled "together time" between spouses or parents and children create emotional connection?
- Historically, women have subsumed their own desires, both emotionally and professionally, for the sake of their husbands' careers. How do you see this paradigm play out in your family of origin? How does this paradigm play out in your own life now, and what are the implications for you?

Rachel Vidomlanski *is a graduate of SAR High School (2021). Following a gap year in Israel, she plans to study cognitive neuroscience at Brown University.*

SALTY PEANUT SPAGHETTI SQUASH

The most poignant moment of Rav Rehumi's wife's story is when she cries. Thinking of the saltiness of tears, I decided to create a salty peanut spaghetti squash recipe to honor her story.

Prep Time: 30 minutes
Cook Time: 1 hour 15 minutes
Yield: 8 servings

Tools:

- Cookie sheet
- Saucepan
- Cutting board
- Colander

Ingredients:

- 1 spaghetti squash
- 1 large head broccoli
- 1 large white onion
- 1 tbsp (15ml) olive oil
- 1 tsp (5ml) minced garlic
- ¼ tsp (1ml) ginger
- ½ cup (120ml) natural peanut butter
- 1 tsp (15ml) lime juice
- 2 tbsp (30ml) maple syrup
- 1 tbsp (15ml) rice vinegar
- ¼ cup (60ml) soy sauce
- 1½ cups (350ml) broth

For toppings:

- sesame seeds
- scallions

Instructions:

1. Preheat the oven to 400° F (200° C) and microwave the whole spaghetti squash for 5 minutes to soften.
2. Cut the spaghetti squash in half, take out the seeds, and place it facedown on a baking sheet lined with parchment paper. Bake for 1 hour.
3. Cut broccoli into small florets and chop the onion.
4. Heat a pan with oil and add in onion, broccoli, garlic, and ginger.
5. Cook for a few minutes until the broccoli softens a bit.
6. Microwave the peanut butter for 30 seconds to soften.
7. Mix peanut butter, lime juice, syrup, vinegar, and soy sauce in a small bowl.
8. Add in ½ the broth to the broccoli and let it evaporate, then add the rest of the broth.
9. Once all the water has evaporated, remove from heat.
10. Mix in the sauce and spaghetti squash.
11. Plate and top with sesame seeds and scallions.

Serena Olshin is a student at Ramaz school in New York. She loves to play basketball and can often be found with a book in hand.

STORY

Rav's wife appears in a perplexing vignette. Her husband, Rav, is one of the most prominent scholars of his day, the rare *Amora* who has the privilege of disagreeing with a *Tanna*. He is so famous he's known just as Rav (Rabbi): an immediately recognizable, one-named personage, like Cher, or Pele, or Batman.

One day Rav's uncle, Rabbi Chiya, makes a sideways remark about Rav's wife to her husband, saying the Holy One should protect him from something worse even than death. Rav goes out, contemplates, and recalls the verse from Kohelet (Ecclesiastes): "And I find woman more bitter than death."[1]

It turns out that Rav's wife vexes her husband. When he asks for lentils, she cooks peas, and when he asks for peas, she cooks lentils. Their son Chiya, named after his uncle, tries to play peacemaker and acts as the go-between. If Rav tells Chiya he wants peas, Chiya tells his mother that Abba (Rav's first name, which coincidentally also means father) wants lentils. If Rav tells Chiya he wants lentils, Chiya tells his mother that Abba wants peas.

Rav softens and thinks that his wife has finally gotten in tune with him. He remarks to Chiya about the improvement, and Chiya confesses that he has been switching the orders when he conveys them to his mother. Much as Rav admires his son's cleverness and wishes he'd thought of employing the same stratagem, he scolds Chiya for lying on his behalf. Quoting the prophet Jeremiah, Rav warns his son of the dangers of dishonesty, saying, "They have taught their tongue to speak lies, they are worn out from wrongdoing."[2]

PASSAGES

Talmud b. Yevamot 63a

---

1. Ecclesiastes 7:26 (The Hebrew Bible, translated by Robert Alter).
2. Jeremiah 9:2 (The Hebrew Bible, translated by Robert Alter).

CONTEXT

The story of Rav's wife and family comes in a Talmudic passage dealing with daily interactions: how to navigate business dealings and marital relationships, both choosing a spouse and living with them. It interrogates issues of communication between spouses, the role of children in their parents' relationships, the limits of honesty.

Later in the story we learn that Rabbi Chiya, the very one who implies that Rav's wife is so difficult, makes a point of bringing gifts to *his* wife, "just because." Rav asks why, considering that Rabbi Chiya is as annoyed with his wife as Rav is with his. Rabbi Chiya responds: isn't it enough that she keeps the house and raises the children and keeps me on the straight and narrow? The rabbis acknowledge in this passage that while women may do things that their husbands find disagreeable, the value they bring to the home far outweighs the occasional aggravation and should be given its proper appreciation.

AGGADAH

Rav's Wife in the Kitchen: A Re-Imagining in Three Parts

Part I.

> He says he wants peas, but I'm making lentils. I don't even care. He orders me about, then eats so quickly he doesn't even taste the food. Peas? Lentils? What difference does it make? He travels so much now, he is barely home. It's quiet here. I'm in the mood for lentils and they will be heavenly with the cumin and sesame I bought in the market today. If he sits long enough to enjoy them, it will be a miracle. And if he doesn't sit with me, why should I bother to make what he wants?

Part II.

> Chiya, my sweet boy, has taken to telling me what Abba wants to eat. Fine, fine. I like to talk with my boy and spend time with him in the kitchen. It gets lonesome in here. Since Chiya started cooking with me, suddenly Abba likes the food. He sits and enjoys. We all three sit together, talking and laughing. Now Abba compliments the food, and never complains because he wanted lentils and I served peas.

Part III.

My Chiya is growing up, and no longer cooks with me. Soon he will find a wife of his own and leave me. My kitchen is less lonely now, though. Abba comes in to tell me what he wants. He doesn't bark orders at me anymore, just asks sweetly. Sometimes he sneaks in when the food is almost ready and sticks a spoon in to taste. I don't shoo him away.

PROMPTS

- How does the way someone asks for something influence your interest in doing what they ask?
- When do children (or third parties in general) have wisdom to offer that helps us see our own relationships more clearly?
- When is a lie worth its own dishonesty?
- Who are the people that vex you? What would you change about their approach to you, if you could?

Naomi Gurt Lind *is a Hebrew College rabbinical student, writer, singer, crossword puzzle enthusiast, bread baker, and the mother of two genius children.*

JACHNUN – YEMENITE SWEET SLOW-COOKED BUTTERY PASTRY ROLLS

Rav's wife, like many women, is intricate and delicate – just like jachnun.

Jachnun is a pastry bread from Yemenite Jewish origin, and consists of a thinly rolled pastry dough spread with butter and baked at a low heat overnight for about 12 hours.

The purpose of this is to be able to serve fresh warm bread on the morning of the Sabbath without having to prepare it or turn the oven on. When served with the traditional condiments – hard-boiled eggs, grated tomato, and schug, it is quite a rich dish and slightly sweet, so a little goes a long way.

Growing up in a Yemenite-Israeli home, one of the most memorable parts of my childhood was spending time in my grandmother's kitchen on Friday afternoons. I would watch her as she painstakingly rolled out layers of dough by hand, pieced them together in a circular fashion, and placed them in her specially crafted tin pots, which she left baking in the oven overnight – the aroma would wake us up and we would run down to the kitchen to enjoy as a family on Saturday mornings!

Prep Time: 30 minutes

Cook Time: 10–12 hours

Yield: 12 servings at approx. 150 grams each

Tools:

- Parchment paper
- Baking tray
- 9"×13" cake pan
- Kitchen scale (optional)
- Large bowl to transfer dough into
- Plastic wrap
- Rolling pin (optional)

Ingredients:

- 8 cups (960g) flour
- 2 tbsp sugar
- 1½ tbsp salt
- 2 tbsp honey
- 1 tbsp baking powder
- ¼ cup (60ml) oil
- 2¾ cups (650ml) warm water
- 1–2 cups unsalted margarine softened at room temperature

Instructions:

1. Place the flour, sugar, salt, honey, baking powder, and oil in a large mixing bowl.

2. Add the water and stir until the dough is sticky. Knead until all water is absorbed and the dough becomes smooth and soft to the touch.

3. Transfer dough to a greased bowl and cover with plastic wrap. Allow to rest for 1 hour at room temperature.

4. Oil a large baking tray. Break off a baseball-size dough ball with your fingers. Each dough ball should weigh approximately 150 grams. Tuck the edges under to make a ball, and place on the oiled tray smooth side up. Repeat with the remaining pieces of dough to make 12 dough balls.

5. Loosely cover the dough balls with plastic wrap and let rest at room temperature for 3 hours.

6. Place a long piece of parchment paper across the bottom of a 9″×13″ cake pan. Heavily grease the work surface with margarine or oil and set a ball of dough on top.

7. Push and use your hands to stretch the dough into a paper-thin large circle, as far as you can without tearing the dough. Place a dollop of margarine (equivalent to 1 tablespoon) on top of the dough and spread lightly and evenly.

8. Fold the top side down to the center, then fold the bottom to meet the edge of the other folded edge in the middle. Take your fingers and, starting with either the right or the left side, gently roll into a cylinder.

9. Line the baking tray with parchment paper and place rolled jachnun on top in a linear fashion. Repeat the same folding and rolling technique with the remaining dough balls and place in the cake pan.

10. Cover the cake pan tightly with heavy aluminum foil (a double layer of foil is ideal).

11. Place in the oven to bake overnight (10–12 hours) at 205°–215° F (100° C).

12. Place the cooked jachnun on a platter and serve. It's traditionally eaten with grated tomatoes, Yemenite schug (spicy cilantro dip), and hard-boiled eggs.

Doreet Jehassi is the owner of the Ma'lawah Bar in California, specializing in Yemenite breads, soups, and condiments. She is the mother of three children.

RAV YOSEF'S WIFE / ביתהו דרב יוסף

STORY

Rav Yosef's wife is featured in three Talmudic stories that are all concerned with clarifying applications of Jewish law.

In Tractate Beitzah 29b,[1] her actions are used as evidence in a debate about whether it is permissible to sift flour a second time during a holiday. In the anecdote, she is sifting flour on the reverse side of a sieve as a precaution against breaking this potential prohibition[2]; her husband tells her he wants "good quality bread," implying that she can just sift the flour the normal way.

In Tractate Kiddushin 81a, the rabbis discuss rules established to keep men and women who are not married from being alone. Here we learn that Rav Yosef's wife has a platonic friendship with Rav Beivai. This information provides critical context; it explains why Rav Yosef takes extra precautions to ensure that the two are not alone together when Rav Beivai visits Rav Yosef's home.[3]

The most notable story about Rav Yosef's wife is in Tractate Shabbat, where we encounter her lighting Shabbat candles.[4] Normally, she lights the Shabbat candles late. Her husband advises her against this, sharing a verse from Exodus 13:22[5] that references the pillars of cloud and fire that guided the Israelites through the wilderness. Just as the daytime pillar of cloud made a transition to the nighttime pillar of cloud while it was still light out, so too, the candles must be lit earlier. After hearing this, Rav Yosef's wife thinks that she must light the candles extremely early. Too early, in fact. An elder clarifies that there is some flexibility, but she should not light the candles too early or too late.

---

1. Talmud.b.Beitzah.29b.
2. Sifting flour in an upside-down sieve is a "*shinui*," or a way of performing a forbidden activity to avoid culpability. See: Shulchan Aruch. Orah Hayim. 506:2.
3. Talmud.b.Kiddushin.81a.
4. Talmud.b.Shabbat.23b.
5. Exodus 13:22; The pillar of cloud by day and the pillar of fire by night did not depart from before the people.

PASSAGES

Talmud b. Shabbat 23b, Tractate Beitzah 29b, Tractate Kiddushin 81a

CONTEXT

The story of Rav Yosef's wife occurs following a conversation about the rewards merited by various mitzvot. Lighting Shabbat candles merits a particularly great reward; according to Rav Huna, a person who regularly lights Shabbat candles will be rewarded with scholarly sons. After citing evidence of this principle the Gemara reports the story of Rav Yosef's wife.

The anecdote is told in story form. It is not indirectly reported by another Rabbi but is located directly in the text, beginning with the words, "The wife of Rav Yosef…" We don't get a *beit midrash*-based debate about candle-lighting timing but a real-life demonstration. Rav Yosef brings Torah beyond the *beit midrash* and to his wife. He does not explicitly say, "Light the candles earlier." Rav Yosef's wife deduces as much, and is later corrected when she starts lighting the candles too early.

The story of Rav Yosef's wife does more than just teach us about when to light Shabbat candles. After all, if that was the Gemara's only goal, the text could simply specify a candle-lighting time and move on. Taking us into the house of Rav Yosef and his wife accomplishes something much greater. By zooming out of the *beit midrash*, the Gemara demonstrates that the Torah of the *beit midrash* can be practically applied by everyone, not just the rabbis. Additionally, it is through Rav Yosef's explanation to his wife that we learn a possible answer to an implicit question in the text – Why does lighting Shabbat candles take such precedence, and merit such great reward? When we light Shabbat candles, we are not only kindling a powerful light, but we are emulating God as a guide through darkness.

AGGADAH

On Friday afternoons, I am always rushed to finish weekday tasks before candle lighting. There is inevitably something left to do and I feel aggravated that I haven't done everything perfectly. When I first read this story, I was immensely frustrated with Rav Yosef and this "elder." Doesn't her husband know how hard she works? Who is this random elder and what gives him the right to give unsolicited advice?

But what if Rav Yosef wasn't criticizing her, but rather was concerned that his wife was overdoing it, trying to make sure everything was perfect before rushing into Shabbat? The "elder" in the text is male, but what if we imagine her as Rav Yosef's wife's own mother?

Every woman (and every person) deserves a name. With an ode to kindling light, I have named Rav Yosef's wife Leora, literally "light unto me," and her mother "Orly," literally "You are my light." I imagine their conversation going something like this:

Leora: (disgruntled) Shavua tov, Mom.

Orly: Not so tov by the way you sound…What's wrong?

Leora: Uch, how can you always tell something is wrong?! Yosef told me off for lighting the Shabbos candles too late and it was all I could think about for the entirety of Shabbos! I barely manage to light the candles on time, and now he wants me to light them before it even gets dark?! There is no way I can pull that off! We'll end up with raw chicken for dinner or the kids won't have clean clothes to change into or I'll get fired for leaving work early or…

Orly: Whoa whoa whoa. Slow down. All this from some stupid comment about the candles?

Leora: Well, no, not exactly…I mean, the whole week has been a mess. The oven broke and then Keren left her teddy at day care and… (Leora starts to cry).

Orly: Oy, *bubaleh*…it sounds like you have a lot going on. Listen. No one said you had to be superwoman.

Leora: Yes, but…

Orly: Enough of this "I'm not good enough." Was there something to eat for Shabbos dinner? Were the kids wearing something? Did you manage to light candles before sunset?

Leora: Yes, and yes. And…barely. It was a close call.

Orly: Okay, so you light the candles a little earlier next week. We're not talking 4 hours earlier. Maybe 10 minutes earlier. I think Yosef wants you to relax a little more. He just has a…

meshugenah way of expressing it. Make one less side dish. Put him in charge of pre-Shabbos bath time. And you'll actually get to go into Shabbos without feeling like a headless chicken.

Leora: Okay....

Orly: *Bubaleh*, lighting Shabbos candles is a powerful act. You can give yourself that gift, you know. It's a magical moment. Find a way to savor it. Superwoman doesn't have time for Shabbos candles. But you do.

Leora: Thank you, Ema. You always help illuminate what's important.

Orly: Keep shining bright. I love you.

PROMPTS

- What is your relationship with candle lighting? How do you feel about this ritual?
- Who are the people who have influenced your Jewish identity or practice? What did they say or do that had an impact?
- The elder in this story advocates for a "just right" approach – not too early and not too late. What are areas in your life where a "happy medium" is important?
- When you feel imprisoned by your expectations, who helps you regain balance?

Heather Renetzky is a Hebrew College rabbinical student. She graduated from Macalester College and believes in the healing power of homemade babka.

SWEET POTATO AND GOLDEN BEET CHOLENT

Rav Yosef's wife is best known for her early Shabbos candle lighting. Cholent, a traditional Shabbat meal made with beans and barley, requires a commitment to begin cooking in advance, making it a perfect dish for Rav Yosef's wife. This sweet potato and golden beet version is particularly well-suited because it uses warm and bright vegetables that reflect the colors of a flame.

This cholent celebrates vegetables as hearty and beautiful on their own, to be cut open and served at the end of a luxurious 12-hour simmer. Thanks to this slow cook time, the flavors are bold and umami-rich.

If you prefer not to use beets, try parsnips, carrots, or portobello mushrooms.

Prep Time: 30 minutes
Cook Time: 12 hours
Yield: 6 servings

Tools:

- Cutting board
- Measuring cups and spoons
- Sharp knife
- Slow-cooker or Dutch oven
- Vegetable peeler

Ingredients:

- 1 sweet onion
- 5 small golden beets
- 2 large sweet potatoes
- 3 large yellow waxy potatoes
- ¾ cup (130g) barley
- ½ cup (90g) navy beans
- ½ cup (90g) small red beans (e.g., aduki – not kidney)
- 7 cups (5 liters) low-sodium "beef" stock
- ¼ cup barbecue sauce
- 3–4 cloves garlic
- 2 tsp smoked paprika
- 2 tbsp nutritional yeast
- 1 tbsp sugar
- Pepper to taste
- Optional: 1 tbsp (15ml) refined coconut oil or canola

Instructions:

1. Prepare vegetables: peel and cut onion in half, remove skins from beets with a vegetable peeler or paring knife, mince garlic, and wash potatoes. (Leave potatoes whole and unpeeled.) Rinse barley and beans and place in the slow-cooker or Dutch oven with the vegetables.

2. Fill the dish with enough stock to cover the vegetables, along with barbecue sauce, nutritional yeast, garlic cloves, spices, and oil (if using).

3. Cook at 250° F (120° C) in the oven or in a slow-cooker, turning the vegetables at the 6-hour halfway point, tasting, and adding either water or stock if needed.

4. Remove from heat at the 12-hour mark and slice the vegetables before serving.

Rachel Hershkovitz lives in Seattle and works at PETA as a media writer. Her mother, Elisheva, was the inspiration for Rachel to go vegan.

RAVINA'S MOTHER / אמא של רבינא

STORY

Ravina's mother appears twice in the Talmud. In both instances, her son brings up her name to clarify that she transmitted his father's particular observance of Jewish law and customs to him.

Ravina's mother's words are first mentioned during discussion on breaking bread after the *HaMotzi* blessing. The prevailing opinion is that bread should only be broken after the completion of the blessing. However, Ravina states that, according to his mother, his father would conclude the *HaMotzi* blessing as he broke off a piece from the whole bread loaf.[1]

The Sages debate the day on which it is permitted to eat new grain after Passover; Ravina recounts that his mother told him that his father would not eat new grain until the evening following 17 Nisan.[2]

PASSAGES

Talmud.b.Berachot.39b, Talmud.b.Menachot.68b

CONTEXT

Scholars assume that Ravina's mother transmitted practices to her son out of necessity, since her husband, Rav Huna, had died when their son was still young. These stories show a son preserving the opinions of his father on matters where he disagreed with the majority view thanks to the teachings he learned from his mother.

The influence of Ravina's mother[3] may appear to be slight, but undoubtedly she possessed a keen understanding of halacha. She was aware that her husband's customs differed from common practice, and shared them with her son so that they were preserved.

---

1. Talmud.b.Berachot.39b.
2. Talmud.b.Menachot.68b.
3. The Talmud records opinions from two individuals with the name Ravina; the elder Ravina was the uncle to the younger one, and was sufficiently trustworthy that he was charged with selling the wine inherited by his

Ravina could not state that these opinions were in his father's name because he had not learned them from him directly. However, he could share that his mother – an authoritative source – had taught them to him, which allowed them to be preserved in the tradition.

AGGADAH

Even as a young girl, she had enjoyed learning the minutiae of the many laws that ordered her life. One of the reasons she married Rav Huna was because she saw that he was a person who would give detailed explanations for everything.

During their married life, their days were filled with discussions about the classes he had taught that day in the *beit midrash*. He would share the disputes and arguments that he had heard that day; from this, she learned the art of establishing or refuting a claim.

The loss of her husband also meant the loss of opportunities for her own contributions to have some influence in the world of Jewish learning.

This wasn't what I envisioned, she thought as she stood next to the burial plot for her now-deceased husband. Her joy at seeing her son mimicking his father was now permanently enshrined in the past. There would be no more new learning from him now.

It pained her that her son would know nothing of his father. He had been a respected scholar, a beloved teacher, and a treasured friend. She knew that his presence would continue to be felt in the world because of his many contributions in the *beit midrash*. But she also understood that he had held certain particular views which might disappear.

She vowed that she would not let that happen. And she knew that there was still one way to preserve his legacy for their son: she would take her husband's place as her son's teacher.

When you see the words "Ravina's mother" in the Talmud, you will think of her: mother, widow, and teacher.

---

orphaned nephew (Talmud.b.Ketubot.100b). The Ravina most likely to be sharing his mother's words on his father's practices, then, is the younger one. His father is identified as Rav Huna.

PROMPTS

- What spaces exist for transmitting tradition beyond those dedicated explicitly to teaching?
- How do different members of a household learn from each other?
- In what ways do you preserve memories and habits of deceased loved ones?
- Do you have any traditions that differ from conventional Jewish practice? Did you learn these traditions from your family or did you create them yourself?

Zoë Lang *works at Maimonides School in Brookline, MA. She enjoys teaching a weekly parshah shiur and attending as many Talmud shiurim as she can.*

CREAMY COCONUT, RED LENTIL, AND APPLE SOUP

Ravina's mother, a widow, was busy during the day teaching her son Jewish law. This soup would have been nutritious and simple for her to make as a weekday dinner meal.

Lentils are a good source of fiber, protein, iron, and are low in calories. Coconut milk gives this soup a delicious creamy texture and rich flavor. This soup is delicious, easy to pull together, and perfect for batch cooking.

Prep Time: 20 minutes

Cook Time: 35 minutes

Yield: 6 servings

Tools:

- Chopping board
- Chef knife
- Deep saucepan with lid
- Liquidiser / stick blender
- Serrated knife
- Vegetable peeler

Ingredients:

- 1 tbsp vegetable oil
- Pinch cayenne pepper
- ½ tsp ground cumin
- 2 tsp ground turmeric
- 2 large onions, peeled and finely chopped
- 2 garlic cloves, peeled and finely chopped
- 1½ inches (3 cm) fresh ginger, peeled and finely chopped
- 1 large apple, cored and medium diced (skin on)
- 10 oz (300g) red lentils
- 14 oz (200–400ml) tin coconut milk, according to taste
- 5 cups (1.2 liters) water
- Juice of 1 lime
- Salt and freshly ground pepper, to taste

Optional garnishes:

- Toasted coconut flakes
- Sprigs of coriander leaves
- Apple crisps (slivers of skin-on apple, baked at 150° C / 300° F for 40 minutes or until golden and crispy)
- Lime zest

Instructions:

1. Heat oil in a large saucepan over medium-high and add the cayenne, cumin, and turmeric. Stir until fragrant, about 1 minute.
2. Add onions, garlic, and ginger and cook, stirring, until softened, about 8–10 minutes.
3. Add apple and lentils and stir to coat in the spice mix.
4. Stir in coconut milk and water and bring to a boil.
5. Reduce the heat and simmer, stirring occasionally, until lentils are completely soft, 20–25 minutes.
6. Add lime juice and season with salt and pepper.
7. Ladle into serving bowls and top with preferred garnish.

Denise Phillips *is the author of seven kosher cookbooks blending traditional and modern Jewish cooking.*

SERACH BAT ASHER / סרח בת אשר

STORY

Serach[1] is the daughter of Asher and the granddaughter of Jacob. She first appears in the list of the Israelites who went down to Egypt.[2] Her name appears again in the census taken in preparation for conquering the Land of Israel.[3] This is significant because women are rarely mentioned by name in the Torah's male-centered lists and narratives. Even more startling, these references indicate that Serach was alive both during the time of Jacob and during the Exodus – a span of 400 years.

Serach's longevity is said to stem from a blessing bestowed upon her by Jacob. Concerned that the news that Joseph was indeed alive would shock and kill their father, Jacob's sons turned to Serach. She broke the news to Jacob gently playing the harp and singing, "Joseph, my uncle is alive and rules the land of Egypt." In gratitude, Jacob blessed her, saying, "my daughter, may death never prevail against you forever, for you have revived my spirit."[4]

A crucial episode of Serach's story is found in the Talmud.[5] As the Israelites prepared to leave Egypt, Moses sought to fulfill the oath sworn to Joseph, to carry his bones with them. Unable to find Joseph's coffin, Moses turned to Serach, who remained from Joseph's generation 400 years earlier. She told Moses, "The Egyptians fashioned a metal casket for him and sunk it in the Nile to bless its waters." So Moses stood on the bank of the Nile and called out, "Joseph, Joseph, the time has come for the oath that God swore to our father Abraham, that he will redeem His children…do not delay your redemption, because we are delayed on your account." Joseph's coffin immediately rose from the water and the Exodus from Egypt was able to go forward.

1. Talmud.b.Sotah.13a. Also in Torah: Genesis 46:17 and Numbers 26:46. Several additional midrashim.
2. Genesis 46:17.
3. Numbers 26:46.
4. Sefer HaYashar, Book of Genesis, Vayigash 9.
5. Talmud.b.Sotah.13a.

Serach's story continues on – the midrash identifies her with the Wise Woman of Abel-beth-maaacah of King David's time[6] and she appears in rabbinic times to solve a disagreement in the Beit Midrash.[7]

One tradition teaches that Serach never died but rather, like Elijah, entered Gan Eden alive. However, Jewish folklore says that Serach went into the Babylonian Exile with the Israelites, never returning to Eretz Yisrael, and ultimately settled in Isfahan in what is today Iran. She is said to have died in a fire in 1133 CE and to have been buried in the Jewish cemetery in a tomb that bore the inscription, "Serach bat Asher, the daughter of our Patriarch Jacob."[8]

PASSAGES

Sotah 13a:14

CONTEXT

The Talmudic story of Serach bat Asher appears in a discussion of the burials of Jacob and Joseph, noting that Moses himself participated by finding and transporting Joseph's coffin. This raises the question: How did Moses know where to find Joseph's coffin? Serach, who is acknowledged as having been alive at the time of Joseph's death, reveals the location to Moses.

Though the mentions of Serach bat Asher in the Torah may have originally been rather insignificant, she has proved irresistible to the Jewish textual and folkloric imagination. Because of her longevity, Serach is a witness to history and she is called on time and time again to answer the unanswerable. Whether or not the initial mentions of Serach were meant to indicate she was in some way special, the figure that emerges from across Jewish texts is a unique and significant one.

---

6. Bereshit Rabbah 94, also see Rashi on II Samuel 20:16–22.
7. Pesikta de-Rav Kahana 11:13.
8. Tradition locates Serach's grave in a cemetery in Lenjan, near Isfahan. It is an important place of pilgrimage for Persian Jews. See Houman Sarshar, *Esther's Children* (Philadelphia: The Center for Iranian Jewish Oral History and The Jewish Publication Society, 2002) 367–371.

AGGADAH

Women may recognize the emotional labor we too often carry in the story of Serach bat Asher. It is Serach, with her empathy and kindness, whom Jacob's sons ask to break the news to their elderly father that Joseph is alive. Four hundred years later, Moses counts on Serach to remember where Joseph is buried – how often are women asked where the car keys are or which refrigerator shelf the leftover meatloaf is on?

In other texts, Serach appears at crucial times to solve a crisis or settle a dispute. Through her steely determination she saves her entire town from a siege by David's general Yoav. In Rabbinic times, Serach appears at the Beit Midrash and participates in the discussion. She disputes Rabbi Yohanan's description of the parting of Sea of Reeds, and in the end, her explanation is the preferred one. Eventually, she goes into exile with her people and makes a home there. Never returning to the land of Israel, she becomes a nurturer of a permanent diaspora.

But Serach is more than an empathetic, coffin-finding, question-answering problem solver. She emerges from the text as a multifaceted personality – empathetic and emotionally intelligent, sagacious, determined, and even ruthless. She is a symbol of women's wisdom. She knows things that only she knows and has seen things no living soul has. No one else can provide what she does, and through her unique knowledge she is a catalyst for the Divine plan.

A witness to enslavement and redemption, war and exile, rabbinic debates, and a flourishing diaspora, Serach is an embodiment of communal memory. What would she think of the past millennium of Jewish history? What would she tell us about going forward? What would she make us promise to always remember?

PROMPTS

- Why do you think Serach bat Asher is mentioned in the lists of names in Genesis and Numbers?

- Do you think women possess a special kind of wisdom? If so, what are its distinguishing features?

- Do you think women serve as repositories of communal memory? In general? Of Jewish memory, specifically?

- Do you think extreme longevity like that of Serach would be a blessing or a curse?

Rabbi Martha Bergadine is the Education and Programming Director at the United Jewish Congregation of Hong Kong. Rabbi Bergadine was ordained by the Hebrew Union College.

NUT AND BEET STUFFED DATES AND PRUNES

Serach bat Asher was a repository of communal memory. This recipe is all about memory for me and reminds me of my family, childhood, and Sephardi Henna parties before religious weddings.

Like Serach bat Asher, I am transported in time when I make and eat these treats. My mother used to make stuffed dates and prunes, and I hope that my daughters will keep this tradition alive.

This recipe is easy to make, colorful, healthy, and contains no added sugar.

This dish is sweet but not too sweet; the beetroot powder provides a tang that balances the sweet smoothness of the nuts.

Prep Time: 30 minutes
Cook Time: 0
Yield: 36 stuffed fruits, 12–18 servings

Tools:

- Kitchen scale
- Sharp knife
- Cutting board
- Plate
- Serving plate
- Rolling pin
- Mini sieve or tea leaf infuser

Ingredients:

- 12 pitted medjool dates
- 24 pitted dried prunes
- 6 oz (150g) shelled walnuts
- 4 oz (100g) shelled pistachios
- Beetroot powder

Instructions:

1. Cut the dates in half lengthwise and stuff each with ½ and ¼ a walnut.

2. Use your thumb to form a deep compression in the middle of the dried prunes, without piercing them.

3. Stuff each prune with a few pistachios.

4. Lay the stuffed fruits on a serving plate.

5. Using a rolling pin, crush the remaining pistachios and walnuts. Sprinkle over the stuffed fruits.

6. Use a small sieve or tea leaf infuser to gently sprinkle beetroot powder over the stuffed fruits on the serving plate.

7. Serve with fresh mint tea, or store in the refrigerator for up to one week.

Fabienne Viner-Luzzato *is French-born, with Tunisian and Italian origins. She and her husband live in London, where she runs a cookery school. They have three children.*

SHLOMTZION / SALOME
ALEXANDRA / שלומציון אלכסנדרה

STORY

Shlomtzion was the last Queen of Judea. She was married to King Yannai (Alexander Jannaeus) and was sister to the Sage Shimon ben Shatach. She became Queen after Yannai's death. She ruled alone and was the last ruler to lead the Jewish people independently, before the Romans installed puppet kings.

Three stories praising Shlomtzion in the Talmud are as follows:

The first story takes place during a meal that King Yannai and his wife eat together. At the end of the meal, King Yannai remarks that there were no men with whom to recite the Grace after Meals blessing. He said to Shlomtzion: "Who will provide us with a man to recite the blessing on our behalf?" Knowing that the absence was a direct result of her husband having executed all the Sages, she answers carefully. First, she demands his promise that, if she brings a man to say the blessing, her husband will not cause him harm. Her request fulfilled, she brings her brother, the Sage Shimon ben Shatach, to say the blessing.

The second story occurs when Shlomtzion plans a wedding feast for her son. During her preparations, all the vessels become impure. This means that anyone who touches these vessels will need to immerse in a ritual bath before being allowed to visit the Temple. To fix the situation she breaks them all into small pieces and gives them to a metalsmith to weld together anew. Unfortunately, the Sages rule that even though the vessels had been broken down and rebuilt, they were still considered impure.

Finally, a more metaphorical tale is set during the times of Rabbi Shimon ben Shetach and Queen Shlomtzion. The story goes that monsoon rains fell heavily for one whole week. Crops blossomed and bloomed, wheat grew plentifully, barley and lentils became extraordinary in size and quality. The Sages tied, dried, and stored seeds of these bounteous crops, so that future generations could see that righteousness causes agricultural bounty.

PASSAGES[1]

Sifra.Bekhukotai.1:1[2]

CONTEXT

Shlomtzion lived during the time when the Pharisees and the Saduccees were vying for control. The Talmudic Sages were followers of the Pharisees, so they portrayed her husband Yannai in an extremely negative light in their writings.

Shlomtzion was highly regarded by both her husband and her brother, and her actions were considered worthy of being included in Talmudic debates on points of Jewish law.[3]

The story of the blessings after the meal was told in the Talmud in order to discuss a point of law regarding the Grace after Meals. Shlomtzion's presence in the story is purely tangential from the Talmudic perspective.

However, there is a clear contrast within this story between the characters of King Yannai and his wife, Shlomtzion. Yannai is portrayed as a stupid man, who rid his kingdom of all its sages and then couldn't figure out how to say Grace after Meals without their help. Shlomtzion, on the other hand, is portrayed as a sensible and smart woman. She knows that her brother is still alive and can make the blessing for the king, but before she mentions this, she exhorts a promise from her husband that he won't harm him. Her brother, Rabbi Shimon ben Shatach, treats her with the same respect that her husband Yannai demonstrates.

The story about Shlomtzion breaking and rebuilding vessels is told in order to make a point of Jewish law, in this case regarding the feasibility of recycling old impure vessels in order to make them pure. Shlomtzion attempted to find a legal loophole in order to avoid having to go through the lengthy process of purifying her vessels, but her own brother ruled that this was impossible and so her actions were decreed ineffective. It is worth noting that the

---

1. See also, Talmud.b.Brachot.48a, Talmud.b.Shabbat.16b.
2. Translation by Rabbi Shraga Silverstein, Sefaria.
3. It is worth noting that Josephus Flavius mentioned many other details of her life and portrayed her much more negatively.

Talmud doesn't shy away from the possibility that a point of Jewish law can be learned from the actions of a pious woman such as Shlomtzion.

The story of the monsoon rains, which also appears in the Babylonian Talmud[4] without mention of Shlomtzion, implies that Shlomtzion and her brother Rabbi Shimon ben Shatach were righteous leaders who led the nation to behave in a righteous manner. The Sages were extremely impressed that the rain came exactly on time, and they preserved the beautiful crops to demonstrate what crops can look like when Jewish people follow the laws of the Torah.

AGGADAH

Year 67 BCE, Jerusalem

I may be the Queen of Judea, but my life has not been easy to live. I have no peace of mind.

I buried two husbands, and my second husband abandoned the righteous path that I was raised in. My brother and I have worked hard to reset the path of Israel after his death, and we succeeded, if God's blessing of our crops is proof of success. I have had the great privilege of having my actions taken seriously by the Sages and discussed in the context of Jewish law in the highest courts in our land.

I can see the end of an era looming and something else entirely blooming. I can see that the Roman Empire is creeping in, and that my sons are power-hungry and eager to fight among themselves. Sadly, their actions and gaze reveal that they have no respect for me. I hear rumors that my son Aristobulus is hatching a plan to seize the throne from me – his own mother! – and I fear that I do not possess the spiritual and physical strength to resist him.

How did I get here? What did I do wrong? These questions are gnawing at my heart as my own lifeforce wanes. Perhaps every mother whose children stray too far from their moral upbringing asks herself this in the dead of the night. I tell myself that I did not have the power to choose my husbands, and perhaps with men such as these by my side, I had no

---

4. Talmud.b.Taanit.23a.

hope of raising righteous sons and daughters. Perhaps the influences of the outside world were too strong, the pull of Roman culture too tempting for my children to withstand.

When I leave this world, what legacy will I leave? Will it be one of failure, as the ruler who was unable to preserve Israel's independence? Or will I be remembered as a pious female leader? Maybe my ultimate legacy will depend on who is doing the telling.

I beg of history that she not judge me solely by my husbands or by my children's lives. May history not judge me solely by the collapse of the Israelite kingdom or the events that will surely lead to the destruction of our Holy Temple. Look instead at the way I lived my life: my valiant attempts to keep the Romans out of the Land of Israel and my fierce loyalty to the independence of the Jewish people. Remember me for what was in my heart: my connection to God, and my unwavering dedication to keeping his Torah.

PROMPTS

- Is perceived power always true power? How can you bring power back into your life in places you feel you have lost it?
- Have you had to navigate complex family situations? What could you have done differently to produce other results?
- Who are your allies in life? Which friends/family members will support you, even when the rest of the world doesn't?

Hadassah Levy is a digital marketer who teaches and learns Torah at every opportunity. She lives in Eli, Israel, with her husband and four children.

BLACK-EYED PEA SOUP

A woman with strength and influence deserves a dish that is as bold and multifaceted as she is.

This soup is hearty and flavorful, with a stewed-tomato base and important cameos from smoked paprika, two kinds of pepper – the habanero and the jalapeño – and, of course, garlic. The recipe includes instructions for stewing fresh tomatoes, but canned tomatoes will absolutely do just fine. This dish is perfect anytime of year, with or without a savory cornbread and sauteed collard greens to complement its rich and distinct flavors.

Prep Time: 30 minutes
Cook Time: 60–90 minutes
Yield: 8 servings

Tools:

- Cutting board
- Large stockpot
- Large saucepan
- Measuring cups and spoons
- Sharp knife

Ingredients:

- 2 tbsp extra virgin olive oil
- 1 tbsp smoked paprika, plus more for oil
- 1 Vidalia or sweet onion, chopped
- 4 cloves garlic, minced
- 1 lb (450g) dried black-eyed peas (soaked 8 hours or overnight in salted water, rinsed, and drained)
- 8 large or 12 medium tomatoes, stewed as per recipe below (or two 14.5 oz / 400g cans of stewed or crushed tomatoes)
- 6 cups (1.42 liters) vegetable stock
- 2 bay leaves
- 2 habanero peppers
- 1 jalapeño pepper
- Handful flat-leaf parsley, chopped
- 1 tsp kosher salt
- ½ tsp fresh ground black pepper
- Scallions for garnish

For stewing tomatoes:

- 12 medium or 8 large tomatoes, peeled and roughly chopped
- 4 cloves garlic, minced
- 2 tbsp olive oil
- 1½ tsp kosher salt
- ½ tsp fresh ground black pepper
- ½ tsp sugar
- 1 tbsp fresh parsley
- ½ tsp crushed red pepper

Instructions:

For the stewing tomatoes:

1. Peel and chop tomatoes (blanch them in boiling water to make the skins easier to remove).
2. Heat olive oil to medium heat in a large saucepan, and sauté garlic until fragrant.
3. Add tomatoes, lower the heat, and stir for 5–7 minutes while the tomatoes render their juices.
4. Lower the heat to a simmer and continue to cook the tomatoes for 20–25 minutes, stirring frequently.
5. Add salt, pepper, crushed red pepper, and fresh parsley toward the end of cooking.

For the black-eyed pea soup:

1. Heat olive oil in a large stockpot with a few grinds of black pepper and a sprinkle of smoked paprika.
2. Add onion and garlic and saute until fragrant.
3. Add the soaked and rinsed black-eyed peas and stir until combined.
4. Add tomatoes, vegetable stock, bay leaves, sliced habaneros and jalapeño, smoked paprika, sugar, and salt and pepper to taste.
5. Bring the soup to a boil, then reduce the heat and simmer for about 45 minutes, or until the beans are tender.
6. Add parsley during the last few minutes of cooking.
7. Taste and adjust salt and pepper as necessary.
8. Ladle into bowls and garnish with sliced scallions.

__Ginna Green__ is partner and chief strategy officer at Uprise, a consulting practice. Ginna lives in South Carolina with her husband and four kids.

THE SOTAH WOMAN / האשה הסוטה

STORY

Tractate Sotah delves into the potentialities and eventualities of the case of a Sotah woman, a woman suspected of adultery that cannot be proven, as presented in the Bible, in the Book of Numbers, chapter 5.

Specifically, a woman whose husband suspected her of adultery, as determined by her having been observed in seclusion with a man who was not her husband, underwent the Sotah ordeal. The ordeal consisted of drinking bitter waters that had had the Name of God erased into them, as per the biblical text. It was trial by water, as it were, for if she were guilty, her belly would swell and her "thigh" (presumably her reproductive organs) would fundamentally explode, whereas if she were innocent, she returned to her husband with the blessing of God. She conceived, and experienced a very different kind of belly-swelling.

The Talmud details the procedure by which a woman undergoes the Sotah trial – beginning with the husband's suspicions. He warns his wife not to seclude herself with another man, a warning that should be unnecessary, given the laws against it, and the Talmud explains that she is also warned against speaking with the man. The warning comes, presumably, because she has already been observed in seclusion – but without two formal witnesses and a warning that this seclusion is a violation of Jewish law, the woman does not enter a status of Sotah, and she is permitted to return to her husband and the marital bed. Once her Sotah status is established, she and her husband are prohibited to one another, until or unless she is found to be innocent. The woman is brought to the Temple priests for the ordeal – to dishevel, and likely uncover, her hair, presumably to shame her – and they try hard to get her to confess to the suspected adultery. After all, if she were to confess, there would be no need for this dramatic and traumatic ordeal.

PASSAGES

Midrash Tanhuma, Naso 6 [1]

---

1. Midrash Tanhuma-Yelammedenu, Trans. Samuel A. Berman. Recovered from Sefaria: https://www.sefaria.org.il/ Midrash_Tanchuma?lang=bi.

CONTEXT

The case of a Sotah woman spurs the body of law on this complicated situation – a suspected, but unprovable, case of a woman's adulterous liaison (if, in fact, it happened). Tractate Sotah does not describe the ordeal from a historical perspective, perhaps to protect the privacy of any woman required to undergo the ordeal, but more likely because, according to the Talmud itself (Sotah 9:9), the whole process was stopped by Rabban Yochanan ben Zakkai some time before the destruction of the Temple.

Though the Talmud makes no direct mention of a specific woman who underwent the Sotah ordeal, the midrash does. Midrash Tanhuma is a work of aggadah that dates back to the fifth or eighth century CE. It recounts the story of two sisters, and how one was willing to accept the other's "adulteress" label to ensure her sister's "innocent" verdict, so that they would be able to move on with their lives. Unfortunately, that is not how events played out:

[There is] a story about two sisters who resembled each other. Now one was married in one city and the other was married in another city. The husband of one of them wanted to accuse her of infidelity and have her drink the bitter water in Jerusalem. She went to that city where her married sister was. Her sister said to her, "What was your reason for coming here?" She said to her, "My husband wants to have me drink [the bitter water]." Her sister said to her, "I will go in your place and drink it." She said to her, "Go." She put on her sister's clothes, went in her place, drank the bitter water, and was found clean. When she returned to her sister's house, she joyfully went out to meet her, then embraced and kissed her on the mouth. As soon as the one kissed the other, she smelled the bitter water and immediately died, in order to fulfill what is stated (in Ecclesiastes 8:8), "No human has control over the wind to contain the wind, nor is there control on the day of death [...]."

AGGADAH

A woman could not become a "Sotah" without her husband accusing her of infidelity. For a husband to accuse his wife of infidelity, a breakdown of trust between the couple presumably had already taken place, or the rumors flying about her infidelity would surely have been met with incredulity. When trust is strong between a married couple, even a whiff of impropriety is best handled by means of direct communication. The ordeal of the Sotah should only have been a last resort – when a given couple could not reconcile and the woman would not confess to this wrongdoing – to the extent that a Divine judgment was required to reveal her status (whether an adulteress or not). Presumably, the pregnancy that followed the innocent woman's ordeal is a Divine statement of support for the couple's home, and, presumably, they managed to eliminate whatever distance between them had led them to the point of the ordeal of the bitter waters.

This trust and unity of purpose describes the sisters' behavior toward each other. Both understood the risk they took, and the unaccused sister was willing to engage in the subterfuge for the sake of protecting her sister – without even knowing whether her sister was guilty. That is the knee-jerk trust that, when present between a couple, would obviate the need – ever – for a Sotah ritual. The sisters thus demonstrated the paradigm of trust between loving parties. Where they failed was in the lie.

The Sotah ritual, notes Ramban, is the only mitzvah that requires God's participation in the mitzvah of the ceremony itself – that is, the ceremony could not be completed without God's involvement, and judgment.[2] It was God who revealed whether the suspected woman was guilty of adultery or not at all. When the unaccused sister drank the water and was revealed to be innocent (of course), she nearly got away with making a mockery out of the process – her ordeal was a lie. But since God judged the ordeal, the lie could not stand. It should surprise nobody that the lie was put to rest when the accused sister came in contact with the Sotah water and immediately perished. The truth will out.

---

2. Cf. Ramban on Numbers 5:20.

PROMPTS:[3]

- The rabbis inform us that the Sotah ritual was rarely, if ever, enacted. Why do you think it was important for the rabbis to tell us this?

- In the text, God's involvement/judgment is required when there is a crisis involving adultery. Today, in cases of adultery, what role does God/religious leaders and community play when there is a breakdown in, and potential mending of, marital trust?

- The text says there were "two sisters who resembled each other"; in your opinion, do these sisters share mental/emotional/spiritual qualities as well?

- This public ritual is humiliating for the woman. What public rituals today are related to the judgment of women's sexuality? How can they humiliate married and single women?

Anne Gordon *is the deputy editor of Ops & Blogs at* The Times of Israel. *A veteran educator, she co-hosts the* Talking Talmud *and co-founded Chochmat Nashim.*

---

3.   Prompts by Kenden Alfond.

BLACK AND WHITE COOKIES

The ordeal of the bitter waters, the trial by water, was meant to show if the woman in question was innocent or guilty. This binary application of justice made me think of the iconic black and white cookie.

These black and white cookies look and taste incredible. The cookie has a cake-like texture and the glaze hardens just right, while still keeping the cookies soft. They come together in less than 30 minutes and require just a handful of pantry staples.

Prep Time: 10 minutes
Cook Time: 20 minutes
Yield: 18–20 cookies

Tools:

- Large mixing bowl
- Measuring cups and spoons
- Parchment paper
- Rimmed baking sheet
- Two small bowls

Ingredients:

For the cookies:

- ½ cup (120ml) unsweetened soy milk
- 1 tbsp (15ml) apple cider vinegar
- ¼ cup (60ml) sunflower oil (or melted coconut oil)
- ⅓ cup (70g) sugar
- 1 tsp vanilla extract
- 1 tsp lemon zest
- 1¼ cups (170g) all-purpose flour
- ½ tsp baking powder
- ½ tsp baking soda
- A pinch of salt

For the icing:

- 2 cups (250g) powdered sugar, divided
- 3 tbsp (45ml) unsweetened soy milk, divided
- 1½ tbsp (11g) unsweetened cocoa powder

Instructions:

1. Preheat the oven to 350° F (175° C) and line a large baking sheet with a piece of parchment paper.

2. Place soy milk and apple cider vinegar in a large mixing bowl and set aside for 2–3 minutes, or until the milk begins to curdle.

3. Add the oil, sugar, and vanilla extract to the bowl and whisk to combine.

4. Add in the lemon zest, flour, baking powder, baking soda, and salt. Gently fold the dry ingredients into the wet until the batter is smooth.

5. Pour 1–2 tablespoons of batter per cookie onto the baking sheet, making sure to allow enough space between them for spreading. You may need to work in batches or use two baking sheets.

6. Transfer to the oven to bake until set and lightly golden brown around the edges, around 12–15 minutes.

7. While the cookies are baking, make the glaze. Combine 1 cup of powdered sugar with 1½ tablespoons of soy milk in a small bowl and whisk until smooth.

8. In a separate smaller bowl, mix the remaining powdered sugar and milk with the cocoa powder.

9. Remove the baked cookies from the oven and let them cool completely.

10. Glaze half of the cookies with a thin layer of vanilla glaze and then glaze the other side with the chocolate glaze.

From the Jewish Food Hero Kitchen

THE TWO MIRIAMS /
מרים מגדלא שיער נשייא ומרים מגדלא דרדקי

STORY

Miriam Magdala (known as "Miriam, the Braider") and another Miriam (known as "Miriam, the Childminder") are involved in a case of mistaken identity, involving none other than the Angel of Death ("Death") himself.

Death, who would frequently spend time with Rav Beivai bar Abaye and share his experiences with him, tells of the time he sent one of his emissaries to fetch a Miriam Magdala, known as "Miriam, the Braider." Alas, when the emissary returned, he had mistakenly brought – in other words, killed – "Miriam, the Childminder" instead.

Death chides his agent for bringing the wrong woman, but when the emissary suggests that Death return the unlucky Miriam to life, Death says: "Not so fast. As long as this mistaken Miriam was already taken, she should remain among the dead."

Hearing of this egregious mix-up, Rav Beivai asks the emissary how he was able to take her if she was not supposed to die yet. The agent explains that the opportunity presented itself as Miriam the Childminder accidentally burned herself while tending to a fire. This breach in her luck was the small opening needed for her to be taken prematurely.

Rav Beivai and Death trade quotes about whether people can be taken before their predetermined times, and Death explains that he shepherds the souls of a generation until the predestined time for that generation passes, and only then does he turn them over to the angel Duma, keeper of the souls of the dead.

Rav Beivai inquires about what happens to the extra years of those who die prematurely, and Death says that he finds a young Torah scholar who does not react when others insult him and he gives him the extra years.

344

PASSAGES

Talmud b. Chagiga 4b–5a

CONTEXT

The eerie tale of the two Miriams in the Miriam Mix-Up is part of a series of vignettes which quote scriptural passages that were said to make different *Amoraim* cry. The Talmud says that Rav Yosef would cry when he would come to the verse, "but there are those swept away without justice."[1] This leads Rav Yosef to ask the deep and ever perplexing question: Is there anyone who departs this world before his or her time?

The Miriam Mix-Up is the anecdote brought to illustrate the possibility of untimely death, and an example of the Talmudic Sages grappling with some of the most complex theological challenges: How can bad things happen to good people? Can someone die before his or her time? What happens after we die? It was common for the Talmudic scholars to anthropomorphize concepts like Death.

There is also the belief that in general, death is meted out as a punishment or atonement for sin. This story can serve as a reminder that death is normally a restitution for errant ways, but at the same time, it is also an acknowledgement of the unfairness of life.

Perhaps the story uses women as the subjects of the mix-up as a way to garner sympathy, playing on the inclination of its readers at the time – men – to protect women. So the story of a woman dying young or without due cause might be more jarring and therefore more memorable.

AGGADAH

The two Miriams' first names are given because they are the impetus for the mix-up. Their respective professions are given as a means of distinguishing between the two women.

In truth, though, the Miriam Mix-Up presents the women as virtually interchangeable. Neither Death nor his emissary seem particularly troubled that they cut the wrong woman's

---

1.   Proverbs 13:23.

life short. While Death initially appears irked, in the end he appears to shrug it off instead of truly making restitution and returning the wronged Miriam back to the living.

Ultimately, in this story we do not learn much about the two Miriams themselves. Of Miriam the Braider, we only know that she did hair, but the story is silent about her age and what – if anything – she did to deserve death. Nor do we learn about what happens to her in the future, including how long her life was extended by her fortune in the mix-up.

Regarding Miriam the Childminder, we only know that she cared for children and that she died without justification. We do not know how old she was, any details about her family, or who she might be leaving behind. We only know that she has a bit of bad luck – her accidental burn – which metamorphosizes into a true tragedy. The details of the two women's lives are not given in this Gemara.

At the end of the story, Death attempts to assuage Rav Beivai's concerns with his reassurance that the years Miriam the Childminder lost were given over to a man, albeit a seemingly righteous one. While this idea is supposed to be a consolation for this Miriam's abbreviated life, it begs the question: Was there no righteous woman who could benefit from the windfall of Miriam the Childminder's misfortune? Not only does a woman lose her life unjustly and too soon, but there is a further affront as her lost time is said to be given to a man instead of a woman.

The sad story of the Miriam Mix-Up and its theological question of whether a person dies before their time still resonates today. Everybody knows somebody who seems to die before they should. Untimely bereavements can raise unsettling questions about justice, the meaning of life, and our own mortality. It is no surprise that we might want to blame an Angel of Death or his minions as we search for answers.

PROMPTS

- Is there such a thing as "dying before one's time"? Or should we believe that whatever happens was simply meant to be?
- The two Miriams become a blur of names. How has individuality been honored in your experiences of grief and remembrance?
- What promises, assurances, and comfort does Judaism offer about and around death and dying?

Jessica Levine Kupferberg *is a writer, poet, blogger, wife, mother, daf yomi learner, and former attorney. She made aliyah from Southern California in 2014.*

MINI FIRE-ROASTED STUFFED PEPPERS

This recipe came into my mind while reading the tale of the Two Miriams because Miriam the Childminder got burned by a fire that led to her untimely death.

The stuffing vegetables are lightly charred and then roasted. You can use any vegetable of your choice and any grain you like – for example couscous or quinoa.

To vary the flavor, you could change the curry powder for any spice or herb blend that you like.

Prep Time: 20 minutes

Cook Time: 50 minutes

Yield: 4–6 servings

Tools:

- Nonstick frying pan
- Spray bottle for olive oil

Ingredients:

- 1 cup (190g) medium grain white rice
- 1¼ cups (300ml) water
- 1 zucchini, diced
- 1 generous handful mushrooms, sliced
- 1 tsp extra virgin olive oil, separated into quarters
- 1 red onion
- 1 tsp and ½ tsp kosher salt, separated
- 1 tsp curry powder
- 1 tsp garlic powder
- Juice of half a lemon
- 6 medium or 10 mini capsicum

Instructions:

1. Wash the rice thoroughly and put it in a nonstick pan with the water and 1 tsp kosher salt. Cover and cook according to directions.

2. Dice the zucchini and onion and slice the mushrooms.

3. Remove the cooked rice from the heat, transfer to a bowl, and set aside.

4. Add ¼ tsp olive oil to a nonstick pan, along with the zucchini, mushrooms, and the rest of the salt. Cover with a lid and heat on high for 3 minutes. Mix, turn heat down to medium, re-cover, and allow to keep cooking.

5. After 6 minutes, add the red onion and ¼ tsp olive oil. Mix, reduce heat to medium, and cook uncovered for 3 minutes.

6. Preheat the oven to 350° F (180° C).

7. Add the garlic and curry powder to the pan of vegetables, mix, and turn heat down to low.

8. Add the rice back into the vegetable pan, along with ½ tsp olive oil. Gently mix to combine and add the lemon juice.

9. Remove the stalks and seeds from the capsicums. Spoon the rice and vegetable mixture into each one.

10. Place the capsicums on a tray and bake in the preheated oven for 25 minutes, until the edges are slightly charred and the capsicum is cooked.

Ellie Jedwab is a wife and mother living in Melbourne, Australia. She has developed 100+ recipes for cookbooks and enjoys part-time catering.

TWO SPIRITS SPEAKING WITH EACH OTHER / שתי רוחות שמספרות זו לזו

STORY

Folklore within folklore, the Talmud shifts from a discussion of proper burial practices to stories from beyond the grave. In this tale, the spirits of two young women are overheard by a pious and poor man. He is in the doghouse with his wife for giving too much to charity in an already difficult year. On the eve of Rosh Hashanah he sleeps in a cemetery, where he overhears the two ghosts.

The first spirit says to the other, "My companion, let us swim the air of eternity and listen behind the *pargod*, the heavenly curtain, to hear what Divine retribution will be loosed upon the world this year!" Her friend bemoans, "I cannot! For I am buried under a mat of reeds. But you go, and tell me what you hear." Her friend goes and reports on the coming blight, information which the pious man uses to save his and his wife's crops.

The following eve of Rosh Hashanah, the pious man again goes to sleep in the cemetery and the experience is repeated. This time, the man tells his wife the truth about where he got his agricultural predictions. This revelation leads the wife to confront the second ghost's mother, saying: "Go and I will show you, your daughter is buried under a mat of reeds!"

When the adventurous spirit asks her friend to roam the next year, she declines, "Let me rest, words between us have been heard by the living." The Talmud claims this legend as proof that the dead know what happens amongst the living – and, characteristically of the Talmud, immediately offers a counter-narrative: that someone else had just died and brought them the news.

PASSAGES

Talmud b. Berakhot 18b

CONTEXT

With its guidance on demons and dream interpretation, this story is, like most of the Talmud, no stranger to the supernatural. While ghosts and the *pargod* are found elsewhere in Talmudic lore, the mat of reeds במחצלת של קנים, *machtzelet shel kanim,* which holds the second ghost captive, is a more rare and curious subject. A helpful explanation is offered in the commentary *Ben Yehoyada.*[1]

He teaches that souls cannot separate from their body until it is fully decayed. While linen shrouds are ideal, because they cause faster decomposition, a poor family might only be able to afford a mat of reeds. But if that's the case here, why would the pious man's wife need to reveal this to the ghost's mother? *Ben Yehoyada* shares that she was indeed buried in a linen shroud by custom (and with financial help from the community). But *Amgoshi,* neighboring sorcerer priests, dug up her grave and took her shroud for witchcraft! By Providence, beside her grave was a mat of reeds. They wrapped her in it and returned her to the grave.[2]

So, remember! Reed mat burials hinder a spirit's transition and, ideally, a community should come together to ensure respectful burial regardless of financial circumstance.

I see this story as intentional aggadic balance to the more logistical halachic burial law discussions. Through these ghosts and their impact on the community, the storyteller illustrates complex emotions that surround death and burial.

AGGADAH[3]

Two pairs of women are at the center of this story, and the precise nature of the two relationships remains unclear. This is what I see in the connections between these women:

The first dyad is our ghostly gals, called רוחות, plural of *ruach* "wind, air, direction, mind, disposition, spirit, soul."[4] The relationship between the ghosts is open for interpretation. Are

---

1. Yosef Hayim, 1800s Sephardic Baghdad. I translated his teaching with fellow Queer Talmud Camp/SVARA-nik, Rabbi Bryan Mann.

2. https://www.sefaria.org/Berakhot.18b.7?lang=bi&p2=Ben_Yehoyada_on_Berakhot.18b.4&lang2=bi.

3. When I first taught this story as "Best Friends… FOREVER!" in a Halloween Talmud study, I baked *Ruchot Challot* to depict the story of the spirit girls. I staged the challah on the entry for "Ghost" in Geoffrey W. Dennis's "Encyclopedia of Jewish Myth, Magic, and Mysticism" (2007), complete with moon and headstone challahs.

4. Jastrow, M. (1903) רוח in: *A Dictionary of the Targumim, The Talmud Babli and Yerushalmi, and the Midrashic Literature,* pg. 1458. The word רוחות is often used to refer to demons or a class of demons, such as the *ruach ra/* evil spirit which came over King Saul (1 Samuel 16:14–16). I believe these characters are not demons, seeing as they were buried. In any case, the connection between souls and wind is fascinating.

they just friends or something more? In modern Hebrew at least, the word chaverta חברתה means "friend" as often as it means "girlfriend" in the romantic sense. In the Talmud the word *chaver* is used to mean everything from "fellow comrade" to "magical charmer" – the root meaning "to join" at its core. If we're looking for Lesbian Jewish Ghosts – which, be honest, who isn't? – I'd say we have found them! There's little to indicate that their relationship is why they are dead so young, but the Talmud does have an unfortunate history of "burying the gays."[5]

The second dyad is Mrs. Pious Man and Mrs. Ghost Girl's Mom. The Talmud records that they have a **quarrel** [*q'tata*]. What can we imagine their interaction looked like from the many definitions and connected meanings of this word?

קטטה Jastrow pg. 1347: quarrel, dispute, discord – from root קטט: cut, diminish; make fine/even the woof [weaving/weft] by beating; vex, annoy; to thin, to produce a fine (high) sound, to sing tenor or soprano.

My instinct is that the discord or drama in the conversation between these two women is the very fact that one reveals shocking news about the other's buried daughter. The Steinsaltz translation describes the news as being delivered "scornfully." While a reasonable guess, this tone is not exactly in the Talmud text. Imagine instead the reaction any mother might have to being told her daughter's grave has been ransacked by magicians.

My best hope is that the wife was trying to convince the mother that she should rebury her daughter so that she could adventure freely, like the wind, with her *soul mate*.

---

5. See Rabbi Yochanan & Resh Lakish BT Bava Metzia 84a.

PROMPTS

- Which ghost can you relate to most? Are you full of energy, trying to drag a friend out on an adventure? Or are you buried under a "mat" of work, exhaustion, or anxiety?
- The *pargod* is The Divine's record of the past and the future. If you could journey to the heavenly curtain, what would you want to learn? What mystery are you looking for the answers to?
- Why do we tell ghost stories? What makes a Jewish Ghost Story?

Olivia Devorah Tucker *(they/them, transfemme) is a "Queer Talmud Nerd," inspired by SVARA's Queer Talmud Camp. Olivia believes and teaches "All Challahs Are Beautiful!"*

VEGAN CARROT CAKE

The word "meren" in Yiddish holds two meanings: carrots and to increase. Symbolic of hopes for increased merits in the year ahead, many people choose to cook with carrots at Rosh Hashanah.6

As the poor man visited the graveyard on Erev Rosh Hashanah, it's nice to imagine that he brought these two female spirits a carrot cake to celebrate the holiday.

This plant-based carrot cake is moist and is naturally sweet with grated carrots, fresh orange juice, pineapples, and applesauce.

This carrot cake can be served at the end of any meal and would be lovely for Kiddush.

Prep Time: 10 minutes
Cook Time: 30 minutes
Yield: 8–10 servings

Tools:

- Box grater
- Food processor (optional)
- Kitchen scale
- Measuring cups and spoons

- Large mixing bowl
- Small mixing bowl
- Square or rectangular cake pan
- Wooden spoon or whisk

Ingredients:

Wet ingredients:

- 1½ cups grated carrots (organic carrots taste better if you can find them)
- ½ cup (83g) crushed canned pineapple slices or chunks
- ½ cup (120g) applesauce
- ¼ cup (60ml) freshly squeezed orange juice
- Juice of 1 lemon
- ½ cup (100g) caster sugar

Dry ingredients:

- 1½ cups (180g) spelt flour
- 1½ tsp baking powder
- ½ tsp baking soda
- ½ tsp ground cardamom
- ½ tsp ground nutmeg
- ½ tsp cinnamon
- ¼ tsp salt
- ½ cup raisins or currants

---

6. *Simanim: The Symbolic Foods of Rosh Hashanah.* PJ Library.

Instructions:

1. Preheat the oven to 350° F (175° C) and grease a round cake pan with a bit of coconut oil or some nonstick baking spray.

2. Grate the carrots in a food processor or with a hand grater and set aside.

3. In a large bowl or food processor, combine all the wet ingredients except the grated carrots. After all the ingredients are incorporated, add the grated carrots and stir to combine.

4. In a separate, smaller bowl, mix together spelt flour, baking powder, baking soda, cardamon, nutmeg, cinnamon, and salt.

5. Fold the dry ingredients into the wet, taking care not to overmix the batter.

6. Transfer the cake batter into the prepared baking pan and bake in the preheated oven for 25–30 minutes, or until a toothpick inserted into the center comes out clean.

7. Allow the cake to cool completely before slicing into small squares and serving.

From the Jewish Food Hero Kitchen

STORY

The story of Tzafenat bat Peniel[1] is a traumatic story of sexual violence that has been recorded in the Talmud.

Tzafenat was the daughter of the High Priest Peniel. People would gawk at her, and her beauty was spoken about and well known. During the time of the *churban* (the destruction of Jerusalem by the Romans), she was abducted. Her captor abused and raped her throughout the night. In the morning, he clothed her in seven layers and took her to be sold.

An extremely ugly man wished to buy her, but wanted to see what she looked like first. The captor assured him of her great beauty, but the ugly man insisted on seeing her first, and removed six of the layers of clothes. At this, Tzafenat herself tore the seventh and final layer, fell to the ground and rolled in the ashes, crying out to God in her agony: "Perhaps You can show no pity to us," she said to God, "but why do You show no pity for the holiness of Your mighty Name?"

In her plea to God, Tzafenat bat Peniel[2] uses the word "us" rather than "me." With this word choice, she links the sexual violence done to her with the tragedy of the destruction of Jerusalem. The Gemara then quotes the prophet Jeremiah, who witnessed the destruction of the First Temple, and whose words seem to echo Tzafenat's story. The Gemara notes that both Tzafenat and Jeremiah use the word "us" to define "the" terrible catastrophic events as having happened "to us" rather than "to me."[3]

Tzafenat bat Peniel's story ends with the words, "God Himself shares this pain, and His name is also disgraced."

---

1. Talmud.b.Gittin.58a.
2. Talmud.b.Gittin.58a.
3. Tzafenat uses "us" to include the suffering of the whole Jewish people. For Jeremiah, the "us" means the people and God, teaching us that God suffers from the violence done to His people.

PASSAGES

Talmud b. Gitten 58a

CONTEXT

This story is one of several that record the horrors around the *churban* (the destruction of Jerusalem by the Romans) and detail the violence perpetrated against individual Jews, including sexual violence.

The stories function on three levels:

- To teach us that God suffers from the violence done to His people
- To keep the memories alive and to continue to bear witness to the atrocity
- To impress on future generations that, despite terrible catastrophe, the ongoing relationship between God and the Jewish people remains a source of comfort

This set of stories features victims who are women and children, who would have been more vulnerable to the deprivations and violence of men at war. They symbolize the Jewish people at their most vulnerable: open to attack and without protection. In addition, this character, Tzafenat, is the daughter of a High Priest who had performed some of the holiest tasks – she symbolizes the Jewish people as the very children of God. Yet the father of this vulnerable woman is absent from the story, unable to protect her – so, too, is God. Finally, there is a link with the biblical book of Eichah, which laments the destruction of Jerusalem, and in which the city is personified as a bereft woman.

AGGADAH

I am Tzafenat, named for my beloved father's favorite Torah hero, Joseph:[4] the beautiful man, who retained his sexual honor even when coerced, though it nearly cost him his life. How bitter that tastes now. My father Peniel,[5] the High Priest, who inspired everyone with

---

4. Joseph is given an Egyptian name, Tzafenat Paneach, when he takes office (Genesis 41:45). Earlier in his story he is described as being *yefeh-to'ar vi'yfeh mar'eh*, well-built and beautiful to look at, and as a slave to Potiphar, he refuses the advances of Potiphar's wife. Enraged, she accuses him and he is imprisoned.
5. Meaning, face of God.

his devotion to God, my mother Immi[6], you strong and pious woman, I grieve for you yet I thank God you did not live to see what they did to your daughter.

I am Tzafenat, famed for my own beauty though I cared little for that. Watched[7] wherever I went, seen, gossiped about, apparently cared about. Famed for my parents' lineage of which I was proud, I'll admit. I tried to live a life of dignity, beyond reproach[8].

I am Tzafenat, abducted, abused, raped as Jerusalem was besieged. Outwardly silent through-out his attack, inwardly frozen. Numb, I felt nothing, I said nothing. Not one cry, my mind blank. I shut myself down in order to survive[9].

I am Tzafenat, staying silent as he layered me with covers and pushed me out the door. Who watched me now, as I was dragged along the busy street to the slave market? I felt utterly alone as people failed to notice what was before their eyes: a young woman debased and being sold into slavery. Did they not see me as a human being?

I am Tzafenat, unrobed and degraded in public, tearing at my innermost layer myself in my grief[10] as I fell into the ashes.[11] As I did so I heard my voice, silent no longer, crying out to God from the depths of my soul: "*Lamah* – WHY?[12] Why, God, do You allow such things which are an affront to humanity, which degrade the sanctity of life and which demean Your very name to happen?" It was a cry, but I also felt it was a challenge to God.

---

6. Meaning, my mother (Jewish texts rarely give women's real names). I have given her a name.
7. The Hebrew root צפה, the root of her name, means "watch." There is a theme in her story of watching, seeing, being seen, and appearance.
8. This modern aggadah seeks to redress a balance, where some Talmudic commentators suggest immodesty and that Tzafenat invited the attention – by not covering up her beauty. This is the "she asked for it" argument, which is unconscionable.
9. It is common for survivors of sexual violence to recall being frozen or paralyzed during the attack, it is one type of automatic response to fear. See more here: https://rapecrisis.org.uk/get-help/looking-for-tools-to-help-you-cope/feelings/fight-or-flight-response.
10. Tearing one's clothes, *keria*, is to this day a Jewish bereavement custom.
11. Covering in ashes is an act of grief in Torah in many places including Esther 4:3, Jonah 3:6, Isaiah 58:5.
12. For me, this echoes the trope in the book of Eichah (Lamentations), the word *eichah* itself means "how" or "why."

I am Tzafenat, and this is my challenge to you who can make a just society safer for women:

> Cry out against violence against women, abuse and trafficking;
> Cry out against rape as a weapon of war;
> Cry out against those who close their eyes and hearts to people torn from their families in conflict, who do not see their dehumanization;
> All this is an affront to God, an affront to sanctity in the world: cry out, do not stay silent.

PROMPTS

- What do you make of the fact that the rabbis of the Gemara connect Tzafenat's individual traumatic experience of sexual violence to the general suffering of the Jews?
- To what extent is Tzafenat's challenge to God the Talmudic equivalent of "Where was God at Auschwitz?"
- As members of a society where sexual violence occurs, we have a dual responsibility: to listen to and truly hear survivors' stories, and to act to end sexual violence. What forms might these actions take: in response to victims and perpetrators, in our personal behavior, in required legislative change, in the lessons and norms we teach children, and in cultural expression?

Rabbi Lee Wax *is a rabbi and educator based in London. She also works part time for Jewish Women's Aid, against violence against women.*

MEDICINAL MAGNESIUM JELLO

A preliminary note:

There is no food which can remedy sexual violence. There are many things that rape survivors urgently need including medical treatment, psychological and emotional support, and sensitive and safe support from the criminal justice and legal systems.

Following traumatic experiences, many people find it difficult to eat. Nevertheless, nourishment and comfort is important. For this reason, I want to offer Tzafenat bat Peniel an easy, magnesium-rich jello.

Agar agar is a plant-based gelatin replacement. You can make this jello with most liquids, including fruit juices (not citrus or high-acid fruits), tea, and plant-based milks.

This jello recipe provides a large dose of magnesium, a calming mineral that helps relax muscles and regulate the nervous system. Magnesium citrate powder can be found in unflavored or flavored varieties, and both will work for this recipe.

This recipe is perfect for anyone feeling:

- *Frazzled: showing the effects of exhaustion or strain*
- *Verklempt: overcome with emotion*

Prep Time: 10 minutes +
overnight chilling time
Cook Time: 10 minutes
Yield: 4–6 servings

Tools:

- 6 individual glass jars or ramekins
- Measuring cups and spoons
- Saucepan

Ingredients:

- 1¼ cups (300ml) cloudy organic apple juice
- 1 cup (240ml) water
- 4g agar agar powder
- 20g magnesium citrate powder
- Canola oil for oiling the ramekins

Optional creamy element:

- 2 tbsp coconut milk

Optional add-ins:

- Fresh fruit pieces: bananas or berries

Instructions:

1. Lightly oil the glass jars / ramekins and, if using, place fresh fruit pieces in the bottom of each ramekin.
2. Combine the apple juice, water, magnesium citrate powder, and agar agar in a saucepan. Add coconut milk if desired.
3. Bring to a rolling boil and then simmer, stirring all the time, for 5 minutes.
4. Remove from the heat.
5. Pour the jello liquid into the ramekins and place into the refrigerator to set for at least 3 hours, or preferably overnight.
6. Garnish with a squeeze of fresh lemon juice, or a small handful of fresh berries.
7. Serve chilled.

From the Jewish Food Hero Kitchen

STORY

Our story starts with Abba Hilkiya, a humble laborer who is also revered as a saintly figure in the Babylonian Talmud. Abba Hilkiya was known as a man who could intercede on the people's behalf and ask God to bring the seasonal winter rains when they were late. In an agricultural community such as that of ancient Israel, the ability to influence the weather, to convince God to bring the appropriate precipitation in its correct time, had resounding effects on the health of the community.

One such year that the winter rains were late in the month of Marcheshvan, three Sages were dispatched to find Abba Hilkiya and ask him to pray for rain. Abba Hilkiya ignored and evaded the Sages while he was working, saying it would be dishonest to interrupt his labor, for which he was paid hourly. The Sages followed Abba Hilkiya throughout the day and were repeatedly perplexed by his strange and evasive behavior. The Sages trailed Abba Hilkiya all the way home to the city, where a woman came out to meet her husband. This was the wife of Abba Hilkiya.

He was in his rags, she was in her finest clothes and jewelry; the couple knew why the Sages had come. They ascended to the roof of their home, where they began praying for the arrival of the winter rains.

The couple stood on opposite ends of the roof, and in a dramatic display of the power of prayer, rain clouds accumulated first over Abba Hilkiya's wife's side of the roof, and only afterwards over her husband's. When the couple descended from the roof, Abba Hilkiya tended to the many questions from the Sages, including the reason for his wife's ability to appeal to God to send rain down from the heavens.

Why, they wanted to know, did God heed his wife's prayers before his own? Abba Hilkiya mused that his wife often fed hungry people from her kitchen – instantly sating their hunger. He, on the other hand, made charitable contributions with money from his pocket, which takes much longer to translate into relief and nourishment for those in need. Abba Hilkiya also mused that on one occasion, he cursed troublemakers in the neighborhood while his wife prayed that they should repent and change their ways. Here, musing over his wife's virtues, the story ends.

PASSAGES

Talmud b. Taanit 23b

CONTEXT

The Talmud tells us that Abba Hilkiya was the grandson of *Choni Ha'Maegel*, Choni the Circle Maker, perhaps the most famous of saintly rainmakers in the Talmud. This creative historiography connects Abba Hilkiya to a powerful lineage and enough raindrops to fill an ocean.[1]

Seasonal prayers for ample rain at the appropriate time are still part of our liturgy today. Beginning with Sh'mini Atzeret and all the way through Pesach, we insert words of praise thanking God for the gift of rain: "the One Who makes the wind blow, and makes the rain descend" – into the Amidah. This connection to the seasons and the mechanisms of the weather still occupy a central role in our liturgy and the way we pattern time.

We learn a few details about Abba Hilkiya's wife from the male perspective in the Gemara. The first is that when we encounter her, she is made up in eye-catching finery. The Gemara tells us she takes care with her appearance so that her husband will not be tempted by other women on his way home. From this passage, we might infer a broader societal expectation for women to use clothing and cosmetics to enhance their appearance.[2]

Through Abba Hilkiya's wife's power to conjure rain with more expediency than her husband, the Talmud asks us to think about different modes of charitable giving and how they affect and aid those in need.

---

1. Wald, Stephen, *Encyclopedia Judaica*, (Macmillan Reference USA, 2006) Second Edition, Volume 1, Page 228.
2. Labovitz, Gail. "'Even Your Mother and Your Mother's Mother': Rabbinic Literature on Women's Usage of Cosmetics." *Nashim: A Journal of Jewish Women's Studies & Gender Issues*, no. 23, 2012, pp. 12–34. *JSTOR*, www.jstor.org/stable/10.2979/nashim.23.12. Accessed 8 Dec. 2020.

In this story, it seems that there is a correlation between the mode of giving and God's response. Abba Hilkaya's wife's gifts of food result in the immediate relief of hunger, which is mirrored in how quickly God answers her prayers for rain.

AGGADAH

From the vantage point of her kitchen's hearth, with her door open to the street, Abba Hilkiya's wife understood intimately how the timing of the rain impacted her own pantry and the health of the community. Late rains led to a poor harvest and hunger. Hunger meant more hungry people at her door in search of nourishment.

Standing here, between an empty pantry and an imminently hungry community, Abba Hilkiya's wife was able to summon the right words to earnestly ask God to send winter rains to fall across the parched land.

Here, Abba Hilkiya's wife offers a glimpse into the heart of God. Her story reminds us that though we are not released from the obligation of giving to charity as Abba Hilkya did, we are also bound in our obligation to provide immediate relief to sustain life.

Abba Hilkiya's wife did not distance herself from the community. Rather, she looked into the eyes of those most in need. Her food provided nourishment for hungry people in the community, and her prayers, hope for *teshuva* for the troublemakers of the neighbourhood. As a witness to their suffering and their humanity, she convinced God to hear her plea.

In the spirit of Abba Hilkiya's wife, this wise but unnamed woman, mentioned only in passing in the Talmud, may we see our kitchens as places meant to feed and nourish and as gathering places open to all. With our actions and prayers, let us bring about a kinder and more generous world, and a world worthy of God's blessing.

PROMPTS

- *Tzedakah* is justice translated into action through charity and good deeds. How does Abba Hilkiya's wife's approach to community care incorporate all of these meanings?
- Does this story privilege one kind of *tzedakah* over another, and if so, what lessons might we translate into our own giving?
- Abba Hilkiya's wife is a woman of impressive strength and depth of character, who also values her appearance. In modern times, do we make space for these aspects (intellectual and emotional depth / materialism and beauty) of female identity to coexist?
- What power does the kitchen hold in this story and how does it resonate with your own life?

Sarah Rockford *is a first-year rabbinical student (2021) in New York and a proud member of the Maine Jewish community.*

ALMOND-CAROB BREAD PUDDING

This healthy and plant-based recipe for bread pudding honors Abba Hilkiya's wife's mode of giving; she provided direct aid to her community in the form of bread, which helped bring the vital rains.

This easy-to-make recipe combines the flavors of carob (in a nod to Honi the Circle-Maker, a relative of hers) and almond, a crop that needs a lot of water.

This Almond-Carob Bread Pudding is delicious for dessert or for breakfast.

Prep Time: 10–15 minutes
Cook Time: Approximately 45 minutes
Yield: 4–6 servings

Tools:

- Baking pan
- Cutting board
- Large mixing bowl
- Sharp knife (optional, depending on your bread selection)
- Spoon or whisk for mixing
- Measuring cups and spoons

Ingredients:

- 4 cups (1 small loaf) of cubed bread (feel free to use the vegan bread of your choice – and slightly stale bread is a great choice that helps reduce waste)
- 2 cups (500ml) unsweetened almond milk
- ½ cup (120ml) maple syrup (or date syrup)
- 3 tbsp (45ml) carob powder
- 1 tsp (5ml) vanilla

Optional:

- raisins and/or chopped almonds for garnish

Instructions:

1. Preheat oven to 350°F (180° C).
2. Cube bread (the size of the cube is up to you – the smaller the cubes, the greater the surface area, which means a better soak-through of the liquids).
3. Place bread in a baking pan.
4. Thoroughly mix almond milk, maple syrup, carob powder, and vanilla in a large mixing bowl.
5. Pour almond milk mixture over the bread and toss to coat well.
6. Bake at 350° F (180° C) for approximately 45 minutes (depending on the size of your cubes and type of your bread, you may need to adjust slightly – finished dish should be spongy but not wet).
7. Garnish with raisins and chopped almonds.

Melanie Weiss is a Jewish educator and an enthusiastic home cook. She lives in beautiful central Maine with her wife and daughters.

THE WIFE OF RABBI HANINA BEN DOSA / ביתהו דרבי חנינא בן דוסא

STORY

The wife of Rabbi Hanina ben Dosa's piety and virtuosity – alongside that of her husband – is extolled on the pages of the Talmud. The stories that feature her show her grappling with poverty in different ways.

Each Friday, embarrassed that she could not afford staples and provisions to cook food for Shabbat, the wife of Rabbi Hanina ben Dosa would heat up her oven and place something inside to generate a large amount of smoke. This gave the appearance that she was baking even though there was no bread in her house.

A particular neighbor, whom the Talmud describes as evil, knew that they had nothing to eat and wondered where all the smoke was coming from. One Friday, she knocked on the door to see what was in the oven, at which point the wife of Rabbi Hanina ben Dosa retreated to an inner room to escape embarrassment. However, upon entering, the neighbor saw that in fact the oven was full of challot and the kneading basin was filled with dough. She called to Rabbi Hanina's wife and told her to "come with a shovel, or else the loaves will be burnt." Rabbi Hanina's wife replied that in fact she had entered the house for that very reason.

PASSAGES[1]

Talmud b. Taanit 24b–25a

CONTEXT

This story falls within a sequence of stories which show Rabbi Hanina ben Dosa and his family grappling with poverty and faith.

Rabbi Hanina ben Dosa was a first-century Jewish scholar of the Galilee who was highly praised for his prayers being answered with miracles. He and his family were poor and

---

1. See also, Talmud.b.Berakhot. 34b; Talmud.b.Taanit.24b; Talmud.b.Bava Batra 74b.

had little to eat. He lived on next to nothing and experienced many miracles on behalf of himself and his family.

Immediately after the story of the miracle of the oven filled with bread, the Gemara tells us that Rabbi Hanina's wife asked him: "Until when will we continue to suffer this poverty?" He replies with a question, "What can we do?" To which his wife responds with a demonstration of her faith, "Pray for mercy that something will be given to you from Heaven."

AGGADAH

The narrative juxtaposes the public life of Rabbi Hanina ben Dosa – the miracles performed on his behalf for so many others – with the private life of his own family. The wife of Rabbi Hanina ben Dosa is praised for being virtuous and pious, and for protecting her husband's image and reputation despite the deep poverty in which they lived. The irony is not lost on the reader: on account of her husband, the world was sustained, but as a family they could not afford to feed themselves.

The wife of Rabbi Hanina ben Dosa goes to great lengths to preserve a sense of dignity and to keep up appearances. Her partner was a scholar, a man of great renown, well-respected in the community, and also poor. This poverty impacted his wife and daughter. In addition to the pain of poverty, perhaps being married to a poor man and living a life of poverty did not meet the expectations that she had for her life, and perhaps she felt social pressure to project a certain image.

That her neighbor is described by the Talmud as "evil" points to the fact that the wife of Rabbi Hanina ben Dosa was under observation, and not from a sympathetic ally. We can all relate to feeling judged rather than supported, and watched by eyes that seem to take voyeuristic pleasure in our hardship. And so the wife of Rabbi Hanina ben Dosa gets into a habit of putting her energy into creating the illusion of having enough. Instead of asking for communal support for money or food, she creates a haze of smoke to conceal their poverty. Meanwhile, it is likely that she went to bed hungry many nights.

Perhaps the social pressures of the day mounted in ways that forced an otherwise pious woman to put her energy into deception. I'd suggest that this miracle is more about providing

protection from shame than physical sustenance. The Divine miracle may be a way of telling us that it is okay to let go and allow forces that are beyond our control to take over.

PROMPTS

- In what ways do you put across an image which conceals something – whether to disguise your true feelings, out of humility or shame, etc.?
- How does this narrative resonate in an age of curated and stylized images that abound? How do other people's standards influence us? Are there any advantages to be won by portraying an outwardly "together" image?
- What might prompt us to come forward publicly with our vulnerabilities and needs?

Shira Hecht-Koller is a teacher, educational entrepreneur, attorney, and collector of images and experiences. She lives in NYC with her creative clan.

ABUNDANT WATER CHALLAH ROLLS

These mini water challah rolls honor Rabbi Hanina ben Dosa's wife's purity of heart and mind as she pretended to bake bread in her oven.

The dough is given a short pre-ferment, where a small portion of the flour, water, and yeast is combined and left to rest, swell, and slightly bubble. This simple step builds a foundation for the overall dough, allowing better integration of the remaining ingredients and resulting in easier kneading, shaping, and braiding.

The braided rolls are each made with a single strand, twisted to create the look and texture of a multi-strand braid. After their final rise, they are gently brushed with a simple maple syrup glaze and topped with seeds.

Prep Time: 1 hour 15 minutes +
2 hours 45 minutes proving time
Cook Time: 20 minutes
Yield: 10 single-strand mini challot

Tools:

- Kitchen scale; it is recommended to weigh the flour so the measurements are only given in grams
- Large mixing bowl
- Mixing spoon (I use my hands)
- 2 half-sheet baking pans
- Parchment paper
- Pastry brush
- Smaller bowl for maple syrup glaze

Ingredients:

For the pre-ferment:

- 1¾ tsp (5g) yeast
- 250g bread flour
- 1¾ cups (410ml) warm water

For the dough:

- 2½ tsp (15g) salt
- 1 tbsp + 1 tsp (15g) sugar (or up to 50g for a sweeter challah)
- ½ cup (120ml) vegetable oil
- 500g bread flour

For the glaze:

- ¼ cup (75g) maple syrup
- Dash of water
- ¼ cup (35g) seeds of choice: sesame, poppy, nigella, sunflower, pumpkin, chia

Instructions:

1. Mix the pre-ferment ingredients and rest for 20 minutes, until puffy and slightly bubbly.
2. Add all the dough ingredients to the pre-ferment, and mix until well integrated.
3. Knead the dough for 5–10 minutes until smooth and extensible.
4. Place the dough in a lightly oiled bowl and cover. Let rise for 1–1½ hours, until well expanded and aerated.
5. Gently deflate the dough and scale into 10 pieces, approximately 125g each.
6. Press the air out and form into cylinders or pre-strands by squaring. Rest the pre-strands for 30 minutes.
7. Roll into strands, each about 14 inches (35m) long.
8. Shape a single-strand braided mini-challot.
9. Repeat with the remaining 9 strands.
10. Place mini-challot on two parchment-lined baking sheets, five per sheet, with plenty of room around each for expansion.
11. Proof for 45 minutes, covered with a large, food-safe plastic bag (or oil-sprayed plastic wrap). It is ready when the dough barely fills an indentation gently made with a damp finger.
12. Preheat oven to 400° F.
13. Generously brush the unbaked mini-challot with the maple glaze and sprinkle generously with seeds of choice.
14. Bake for 20–22 minutes until golden. Remove from the oven and cool on a rack.

Cheryl Holbert is an award-winning bread baker and owner of Nomad Bakery in New Hampshire. She shares her work on her Instagram page, Nomad Bakery.

THE WOMAN FROM DROKART /
ההיא איתתא דמחממא תנורא

STORY

The Woman from Drokart is mentioned once in Tractate Taanit[1] when the rabbis are discussing various incidents of great tragedy that befell towns and cities where great Babylonian rabbis lived.

It is recounted that a great fire occured in Drokart, where Rav Huna lived. Miraculously, the fire spared his neighborhood, which people assumed happened on account of his great merit.

However, in a subsequent dream, it was revealed to the community that Rav Huna's merit had not played a role and that it was rather on account of the Woman from Drokart – whom the Gemara does not name – that the people were spared because she always kept her oven heated and allowed her neighbors to use it.

PASSAGES

Talmud b. Taanit 21b

CONTEXT

This story is one of two stories in this section about natural disasters and disease ravaging communities, while other geographic locations are spared. The Gemara mentions the assumption that protection from disaster is afforded on the merit of the local Rabbi. The Gemara states in both instances that the Rabbi's merit does not play a role.

Both stories in this section of the Talmud show the quotidian kindness and generosity of ordinary individuals who share their tools with their community. In the first, a man lends his shovel to allow the community to prepare burial sites for the dead. These actions of sharing are of such merit that whole towns are rewarded with protection from natural disaster and disease.

Though the Woman from Drokart is unnamed, her keeping her oven hot and making it available to her neighbors saves her neighborhood from a terrible fire. She is therefore a meritorious figure and a symbol of morally upright conduct.

---

1. A section of Talmud that is chiefly concerned with declaring fast days.

375

AGGADAH

Our rabbis leave the Woman from Drokart unnamed, unidentified save for her graciousness. They do not follow the usual custom of naming her according to her relation to male family members.

The Woman from Drokart was known in her neighborhood, and remembered in the Talmud, as the woman who shared her oven. This was not a simple thing. Keeping one's oven heated and ready for use was a tremendous – and expensive – undertaking. It implies but leaves unstated that the Woman from Drokart was stringent about proper observance of kashrut, given that the neighborhood trusted her oven as a kosher vessel within which they could cook.

Though we may no longer ascribe miraculous occurrences to the merit of others, we surely remember and recall the simple kindnesses shown to us by our neighbors and community members. These easily overlooked deeds of everyday folks quietly and seamlessly ensure that communities thrive.

They may never be in the spotlight, their stories may never be known outside of their localities. Yet, those touched by their acts of kindness and love benefit.

PROMPTS

- We can ask ourselves if we display simple generosity, small actions to help others with no expectation of a return favor.
- Do you recognize and appreciate the simple kindnesses you benefit from? Take a moment to reflect on them.
- High-profile people's large-scale generous actions get a lot of attention in the media and in our own minds. How can you pay more attention to people in your own life that do small things that have huge significance to you?

Rabbi Lauren Tuchman is a Jewish educator. She is passionate about Jewish spiritual practice and amplifying the voices of women and other marginalized communities.

KAHK BISCUITS

This recipe originates from the community of Aleppo in Syria, where the Jews shared communal ovens with their neighbors. To me, this resonates powerfully with the story of the Woman from Drokart, who kept her oven alight for the use of others.

This recipe came from my grandmother: Djamile Hakim. She was a wonderful cook who came to the UK from Aleppo at the start of the twentieth century. This recipe is one of my childhood favorites, and I have now passed it on to my daughter.

They are traditionally eaten after the Yom Kippur fast and are deliciously crisp and savory. The flavour of kahk comes from the aniseed – do not substitute anything else! Otherwise, the ingredients are all very simple to find.

The rolling and twisting takes practice, and it can be tricky to get the cookies crisp enough. These cookies will improve with each time you make them – and believe me, you will not make them only once!

Prep Time: 2 hours, including time to rise
Cook Time: 30 minutes + cooling time in the oven
Yield: 40 pieces

Tools:

- Baking trays
- Cling film/wrap to cover
- Large mixing bowl
- Kitchen scale
- Parchment paper
- Surface to roll out the dough
- Wooden spoon

Ingredients:

- ½ cup (125ml) olive oil
- 4 cups (1 lb/450g) plain white flour
- 1 tsp salt
- ½ tsp sugar (if using fresh yeast)
- 1½ cups (375ml) lukewarm water
- 1 oz (25g) fresh yeast or ½ oz (12.5g) active dry yeast or 7g/1 sachet instant dry yeast
- 1 oz (25g) aniseed
- Sesame seeds to sprinkle
- Soy or other plant-based milk for topping

Instructions:

1. If using fresh yeast, mix with the sugar and a little warm water and leave to bubble for 10 minutes.
2. Put flour into a large mixing bowl.
3. If using dried or instant yeast, mix straight into the flour along with the salt, aniseed, oil, and water.
4. Knead on a dry board for about 15 minutes until you have a soft, pliable dough. You may need to add more water or more flour as flour tends to vary from place to place.
5. Place in an oiled bowl, cover with cling film, and leave to rise for about an hour in a warm place, until doubled in size.
6. Punch down. Take a walnut-sized piece of dough and roll out into a sausage shape as thinly as you can.
7. Double back on itself and twist loosely, then join up into a bracelet.
8. Place onto the baking sheet and repeat with the remaining dough.
9. Let rise for about 20 minutes (if the process is taking a long time, put a tray in the fridge to slow down the rising process while you make the rest).
10. Paint with soy or other plant milk and sprinkle with sesame seeds.
11. Bake in a preheated oven at 340° F/170° C/gas 4 for about 30 minutes, then reduce the heat to 225° F/100° C/gas 1 for a further 15–20 minutes.
12. Turn off the oven and leave there to cool completely.
13. If they are still soft in the center, you will need to bake a bit longer – you will get used to trial and error. The thicker the bracelets the longer it will take to bake. They should be crisp and completely dry.

Sally Halon *lives in Manchester, UK. Retired Jewish community professional, now an active volunteer as well as doting grandma. She loves to cook and bake bread.*

WOMAN WHO ASKS ABOUT TAKING CHALLAH / הדא איתא

STORY

An unnamed woman asked Rabbi Mana if her dough ought to have challah taken from it.

Specifically, she had prepared *"itri"* dough which she planned to shape into vermicelli, a thin and brittle pasta.[1] She wondered if the dough would share the same legal status as a standard bread dough.

She asked Rabbi Mana, "Must I take *challah* from this dough?" He replied, "Why not?"

Rabbi Mana then asks his father whether *challah* should be taken from *itri*. His father explained that, yes, *challah* should be taken, lest she change her mind and make bread out of the dough.

As quickly as she came, she went. She had a question; it was answered.

PASSAGES

Talmud.y.Challah.8a

CONTEXT

Challah is the biblical term for ritual bread. There are two challah-bread commandments in the Bible. Leviticus 24:5 records the commandment for the Israelites to have 12 challah loaves of showbread in the Tabernacle, representing the 12 tribes of Israel. In Numbers 15:18–21, we are commanded to set aside a *challah* portion of dough for the priest.

Since the destruction of the Temple in Jerusalem, neither form of challah can be done in their originally intended way. Like many other commandments that once centered around Temple service, we have found ways to meaningfully echo the past into our present Jewish

---

1. Dr. Judith Hauptman and Dr. Michael Sokoloff in "A Dictionary of Jewish Babylonian Aramaic of the Talmudic and Geonic Periods" translate *"Itri"* as "vermicelli," a thin and brittle pasta.

ritual life. On Shabbat we treat our modern challah breads like the Showbreads in the Temple. This is why it is customary to sprinkle salt on the challah, just like the priests would do to animal sacrifices. Instead of providing *challah* to the Priests in the temple, we do this: if we make a dough with approximately 5 pounds of flour (according to most rabbinic authorities), we symbolically remove one ounce of it, bless it, and burn it. We call this ceremony "*hafrashat challah*," meaning "taking *challah*."

The Mishnah in Tractate Challah details which doughs must have challah taken from them. In the Mishnah Chapter 1, mishnah 5 it begins with the simple case: doughs which are made with the intention of becoming bread must have *challah* taken, while doughs which were always intended to be *sufganin*[2] do not.

The woman in our story was unsure which class her *itri* dough fell into. Could it be like *sufganin,* because it is a grain-based food that is prepared through boiling, and therefore no challah need be taken? Or maybe the *itri* could hypothetically become bread dough, in which case *challah* must be taken.

Rabbi Mana's father corroborated his son's teaching, explaining that someone might make bread out of the pasta dough. To account for this concern, one should take *challah* from *itri* dough as well.

---

2. *Sufganin* being a sponge cake boiled in honey. Notice the linguistic similarity of *Sufganin* to *Sufganiyot,* the modern Israeli jelly doughnuts enjoyed on Chanukah.

AGGADAH

The Sabbath Queen,

so fancy and grand,

asked me to join her party

So I adorn my table

with candles, wine, and bread.

The delicacies delight me,

and the tongue savors the taste

while the heart savors the pride:

I made it with my bare hands

Yesterday,

my hands buried

the soft, sticky dough

back forth, back forth

up down, up down

pounding and smoothing

let it rise.

How did I pass the time?

I learned the Torah for when to take *challah*.

after all, if I'm baking, shouldn't I know how?

Then, I read this mishnah.

I wonder:

Do I need to take *challah* if this dough becomes pasta?

Yes, it is dough, but no, it won't become bread:

A question.

I ask the rabbi what he thinks.

I barely get a shrug from him.

"Why not?" is all he musters.

I wonder why he has such a hard crust.

I come home, informed, though a little hurt.

A round, strands, a braided bread.

While it bakes

I feel a tap on my shoulder

It's the Sabbath Queen!

"You asked a good question!" she said,

"The rabbi went to ask his father, too!"

I just wish I could have been there to hear it myself.

PROMPTS

- The rabbi heard a question and gave a blunt answer. When have you brushed someone off, and then later realized they asked a good question?

- The woman in our story thought of a halakhic question while baking. When do you ask halakhic questions? When *don't* you ask halakhic questions?

- In what circumstances do you do your most reflective and curious thinking? Is it while you are cooking, like the woman in the story, doing another activity, or only when you have total free time? What do you think about?

Sarah Robinson *teaches Talmud to middle school girls at Manhattan Day School and is Community Scholar in Beth Jacob in Oakland, CA.*

VEGAN CHALLAH CLOUDS

This simple vegan challah recipe honors the unnamed woman who asked Rav Mana about taking challah. For me, making bread is a reminder that God provides sustenance.

This recipe meets the requirements for hafrashat challah, *since the traditionally established amount is dough containing 5 pounds of flour. The large number of loaves made by the quantity in this recipe makes it ideal for sharing, for when you have a lot of people to feed, or batch baking and storing in the freezer.*

If you want to make less challah, the recipe ingredients for 2½ pounds of flour are listed below.

Prep Time: 30 minute make and 2½ hours rising time
Cook Time: 30 minutes
Yield: 4 large loaves or 6–8 medium loaves

Tools:

- Large mixing bowl
- Kitchen towel
- Whisk (hand or standing mixer)
- Kitchen scale (optional)
- Dough cutter

Ingredients for 5 pounds:

- 3 tbsp or 4 packets (28g) of active dry yeast
- 1⅓ cups (310g) cane sugar
- 5 cups (1,182ml) warm water
- 14 cups (2,310g) all-purpose flour
- 1⅓ cups (316ml) refined coconut oil
- 4 tsp vanilla paste/extract
- 4 tsp Himalayan salt

Ingredients for 2 large or 3–4 medium loaves:

(In case you want to make a smaller batch. Adjust the instructions accordingly.)

- 7 cups (1,155g) all-purpose flour
- 1½ tbsp (14g) instant yeast
- 2½ cups (591ml) water
- ⅔ cup (155g) sugar
- ⅔ cup (158ml) oil
- 2 tsp vanilla paste/extract
- 2 tsp salt

Instructions:

1. In a large bowl (or the mixing bowl of a stand mixer), combine yeast, 1 tablespoon of cane sugar, and 2 cups of warm water. Cover and allow yeast to activate for 10 minutes.

2. Add 6 cups (990g) of flour, remaining cane sugar, the remaining 3 cups of warm water, coconut oil, and vanilla extract to the yeast mixture and mix to form a wet spongy dough.

3. Add 7 cups (1,155g) flour and the Himalayan salt and mix until fully incorporated.

4. Slowly add in the last cup of flour (165g) a little at a time until you have a workable dough. Then, knead the dough for 10 to 15 minutes, either by hand or with the dough hook of a stand mixer.

5. While kneading, use a little water or flour to adjust the consistency of the dough as needed.

6. When the dough is soft, pliable, elastic, and slightly tacky, shape it into a smooth round ball, coat in oil, and place it in a large bowl. Cover tightly inside the oven at room temperature. Allow to rest until double in size (1 to 2 hours).

7. Perform the Hafrashat Challah. Take a small piece of dough, roughly the size of a Ping-Pong ball, and recite the Bracha. Place the piece of challah into some foil to either be discarded immediately or discarded after burning it in the oven, depending on your tradition.

8. Transfer the remaining dough onto a lightly floured surface and knead for a few seconds to release any excess air.

9. Divide dough into 4 to 8 portions, depending on how many challot you want to make and what size.

10. Further divide each portion evenly, according to the number of strands you want your challah to be. Roll into strands: for a more fluffy look, leave the middle slightly thicker and taper the strands at the ends. Now, braid challah in any way you like!

11. Gently transfer braided challahs to a lined baking sheet. Lightly brush each challah with water to prevent the dough from drying and forming a crust. Allow to rest and rise in the oven at room temperature until it has almost doubled in size (about 30 minutes to 1 hour).

12. Remove the challah from the cold oven. Then, preheat the oven to 350° F/ 180° C. Meanwhile, brush each challah with water. With a sifter, sprinkle flour over each challah, creating a light and powdery cloud layer that will create a tender and delicate crust.

13. Bake for 25 to 40 minutes, or until golden brown all around, checking from around the 25-minute mark. When tapping the challah on the top and bottom, it should have a nice hollow sound.

14. Remove from the oven and allow to cool for at least 30 to 45 minutes to allow challah to set and finish "baking" inside.

Doxia Trinidad *has a BA in Biology and an MA in Nutrition. She is currently a food blogger, sharing challah tips via social media.*

THE WOMAN WITH MISTAKEN ARTICULATION / ההיא איתתא דבעיא למימר

STORY

There was a Galilean woman who wanted to say to her friend, "My neighbor, come and I will feed you milk." Instead, because she was imprecise in the articulation of her words, she said to her, "My neighbor, may a lioness eat you."

PASSAGES

Talmud b. Eruvin 53b

CONTEXT

This brief episode is meant to emphasize the importance of choosing our words carefully and speaking those words clearly.

The story is recounted amidst a broader discussion about precision with language. Several examples are given in an attempt to draw distinctions between the sophistication and erudition of the Judeans and the supposed ignorance of the Galileans. The Gemara contrasts the people of Judea – said to use refined language and precise speech in their Torah study – with the people of Galilee, whose dialect was perceived as coarse.

The woman with mistaken articulation's gender is seemingly less consequential than her Galilean provenance. Hers is but one of several anecdotes – some of men and some of women – that recount the supposed inferiority of the Galilean dialect.

AGGADAH

It is difficult to know whether our woman of mistaken articulation is thwarted by a thick accent, a careless choice of words, a misstep in her elocution, or by a speech impediment. We only know that the impact of her actions (accidentally cursing her friend) is at odds with her initial intent to extend a kind gesture by offering milk. And we can only imagine what happens next – is their relationship severed forever? Is it a fleeting faux pas? Does

our woman of mistaken articulation shrink with shame? Apologize? Double down on her error in order to preserve her pride?

In addition to demonstrating the importance of caution in speech, this story unfortunately also showcases the contempt in which we hold those who speak differently than us. Certainly we see this kind of disdain in modern societies, where regional accents are mocked as evidence of provinciality or small-mindedness. We see it, too, in the condescension and scorn that is faced by speakers of culturally specific dialects such as African-American Vernacular English (AAVE) or Cajun Vernacular English, who have in too many instances faced prejudice in the classroom, the courtroom, and the public arena. In addition, immigrants and visitors who speak a local language as a second (or third, or fourth, etc.) language are criticized for imperfect pronunciation, grammatical errors, or having a "foreign" accent. And, of course, those who speak differently due to speech impediments are often derided.

Communication suffers in any interaction in which one party wants to use language, dialect, and/or pronunciation to assert superiority over the other. Thus we must hold both lessons of this story with equal reverence. We must think before we speak, choose our words with care, and make a great effort to ensure that we are understood, lest we offend or even curse a friend. At the same time, we must stop ridiculing people who speak differently than we do and instead focus on listening to and hearing what people are communicating. We might imagine a world in which our dear woman of mistaken articulation is asked to clarify her intent. A world in which her friend assumes the best, laughs together with her over the miscommunication, and sits down with her to enjoy that glass of milk.

PROMPTS

- When in your life have you struggled to be understood?
- When you hear people who speak differently than you, how do you respond?
- What values do you hold dear related to precise speech, and what has shaped those values? What kinds of words, names, phrases, or ideas are the most important to you to express carefully and with precision?

Erica Frankel is a coach, mama, modern dancer, Jewish educator, spiritual leader, and devoted Harlem dweller.

CREAMY VEGAN NOODLE KUGEL

This creamy vegan kugel would have been perfect for the Woman with Mistaken Articulation to offer her neighbor. She could have said, "My neighbor, come and I will feed you delicious creamy vegan noodle kugel."

This vegan remake of a classic Ashkenazi Jewish baked casserole has passed the taste test of even the toughest family members to please.

This recipe is classic and simple, but you can add pineapple, cornflakes, or even raisins.

Prep Time: 30 minutes

Cook Time: 1 hour

Yield: 12 servings (side dish)

Tools:

- Baking dish 9″×13″
- Blender/food processor
- Kitchen scale
- Measuring cups and spoons
- Mixing bowls
- Soup pot

Ingredients:

- 10 oz (280g) eggless pasta, fusilli or any curly/twist shape
- ½ cup (110g) vegan butter
- 1¼ cups (300g) vegan sour cream
- 1¼ cups (225g) sugar
- ¼ tsp cinnamon (and extra to sprinkle on top at the end)
- 1 cup (200g) Just Egg (or another liquid egg replacer)

For the vegan cottage cheese use ¾ cup of the finished mixture below

- 1 cup (200g) soft or silken tofu
- ¾ tbsp nutritional yeast
- ¾ tbsp apple cider vinegar
- ¾ tbsp lemon juice
- ⅓ tsp salt
- 1 cup (150g) firm tofu, crumbled

Instructions:

1. Preheat the oven to 350° F (180° C) and grease a 9″×13″ dish.
2. Cook noodles according to package instructions. Drain and transfer to a large bowl.
3. Add butter and let it melt over the warm noodles. Mix to ensure butter is evenly distributed.
4. Make cottage cheese: to a blender or food processor, add the silken tofu, nutritional yeast, apple cider vinegar, lemon juice, and salt. Mix until blended.
5. Crumble the firm tofu on top and fold to combine.
6. Measure out 1¾ cups of the cottage cheese mixture into a medium bowl.
7. Add sour cream, sugar, cinnamon, and Just Egg to the cottage cheese bowl.
8. Add wet ingredients into the large bowl of noodles; fold.
9. Pour mixture evenly into a greased 9″×13″ dish. Sprinkle cinnamon on top.
10. Bake for 1 hour or until the top noodles crisp to brown.
11. Allow to cool for 5 minutes, then serve.

Laura Williams is the Director of Cultural Resources at Temple Beth El in Bloomfield Hills, MI. She loves to transform her favorite recipes into vegan-friendly alternatives.

YALTA / ילתא

STORY

Yalta is the fierce, sharp-tongued wife of Rabbi Nachman. She appears in different passages in the Talmud at just the right moments. Her cunning boldness reminds rabbis and readers alike that conversations about her cannot happen without her.

Yalta's most powerful encounter can be found in Tractate Berakhot. The *sugya* opens with a teaching from Rabbi Yochanan: "Anyone who recites a blessing over a full cup, they give him boundless inheritance." The scene hones in on a table set for three, a cup of wine, and righteous anger. Rabbi Nachman and Yalta host Ulla for a meal, and at its conclusion, Rabbi Nachman asks Ulla to send over the cup of wine to his wife for the *Birkat Hamazon*. Ulla responds assertively, citing a verse from the Torah to assure his friend that Yalta need not hold the cup of wine; his reciting of *Birkat Hamazon* on her behalf was sufficient. The verse he cites from Deuteronomy,[1] "God will bless the fruit of your body," implies that there was only one body capable of receiving God's blessings for fertility and future generations, and that body belonged to Yalta's husband exclusively. What Ulla did not seem to realize was that Yalta was still sitting at that table. Upon hearing this conversation, she rose from her seat "בזיהרא," or in an angered rage. She entered their wine cellar and proceeded to smash four hundred barrels of wine.

Ulla and Rabbi Nachman remain at the table; the text does not mention any kind of reaction from them as their now embittered hostess is in the cellar smashing barrels of wine in place of glass ceilings. The *sugya* simply continues with Yalta sitting back at the table with Ulla and Rabbi Nachman. This time, Ulla sent her the cup of wine and she sent back a sharp response: "ממהדורי – מילי, ומסמרטוטי – כלמי," or "from peddlers come meaningless words, and from rags come lice."

This is Yalta. Outspoken and blunt. Angry and confident. Cunning and righteous. She is willing to overturn barrels and tables to receive the blessings she deserves.

---

1. Deuteronomy 7:13.

PASSAGES

Talmud.b.Berakhot 51a-b

CONTEXT

This story both challenges and affirms the status quo of women as vessels of fertility. Yalta's rage was in response to her not being considered for a blessing for future children. While it was unorthodox and unexpected, her rage enforced her own desire to be included in the process of bringing forth children.

The rabbis see Yalta as an almost mythical phenomenon and a literary device to explore the depths of women's anger. So few women in rabbinic literature erupt in a fiery and holy rage, and the rabbis take great but cautious fascination with the idea of women acting outside of their expected roles in the home. Yalta's womanhood is fundamental to the story: that it is inherently valid for a woman to request her own cup of wine, to say her own blessings, for her own fertility.

AGGADAH

Famous commentators like Rashi and the Tosafists provide no interpretation of Yalta's rage-driven act. The white perimeter on the *daf* of Tractate Berakhot carries equal weight to the inked words printed onto the page. In the white void surrounding the Yalta story, I will imagine some of the physical and spiritual embodiments of her fervor and rage.

There is no mention of the presence of children for Rabbi Nachman and Yalta, so at this point they could have been anywhere on their journey toward parenthood. Let's imagine that Ulla and Rabbi Nachman did not notice the cramps and waves of nausea that were overcoming Yalta's tired body. They saw her presence at the table, but not the tears stained on her face and in her siddur that she left in the cellar beside the barrels of wine. They heard the shattering of the wine, but perhaps not the shattering of Yalta's hope as each of her fertility cycles ended with menstruation.

Rabbi Yochanan's teaching – "נותנין לו נחלה בלי מצרים", that anyone who recites a blessing over a full cup, is given boundless inheritance – stings Yalta, whose womb is not as limitless as an overflowing cup of wine. Perhaps Ulla and Rabbi Nachman had forgotten that Yalta herself was the vessel for the blessings promised in Rabbi Nachman's cup: a man's boundless fertility is nothing without a woman.

Her patience wore thin as these two men at the other side of what seemed like a longer and longer table discussed whose body God had intended to bless. Like wine without its barrel, the blessings of future children cannot be delivered without Yalta.

Perhaps Ulla and Rabbi Nachman did not see Yalta's wine-soaked clothing as she reapproached the table. They did not hear the drops of fermented alcohol falling onto the table and floor as she snapped back to them after their second attempt at passing her a cup.

Rabbi Maya Zinkow interprets this striking image as a fulfillment of Rabbi Yochanan's original teaching. By breaking four hundred barrels of wine, Yalta became her own vessel to contain and share infinite blessings. Her actions teach us that conversations about giving and receiving blessings, especially about fertility, cannot happen without women, the co-creators of all vessels in whom God's blessings flow. Without women like Yalta at the table and all of their fervor, passion, and even anger that they bring, blessings will not be discussed or negotiated, but rather will become *hefker* (ownerless), which are as worthless as spilled wine.

Yalta spilled four hundred barrels of wine. Yalta need not worry about who holds the cup for this wine, for she is drenched in its overflowing blessings. It seeps from her sleeves and drips from her hair, landing on the chair as she resumes her rightful place at the table.

Yalta's story serves as a reminder that women must be included in conversations and religious rituals that involve their bodies, lest they go shattering wine.

PROMPTS

- How much anger is too much? When is anger constructive and when is it self-destructive? Whose anger moves the needle and whose anger maintains the status quo?
- What is your method for resistance? How do you assert yourself when things feel outside your control?
- Yalta is unique in rabbinic literature as an outspoken woman. Who are our modern-day Yaltas? Are you one of them?

Emily Goldberg Winer *is a student at Yeshivat Maharat in New York. Emily loves sharing Torah with people from all walks of life and generations.*

BABYLONIAN SOUR

Yalta's story illustrates the enduring truth that conversations about women should not happen without them.

Here I offer recipes for Yalta's cocktail, the Babylonian Sour, and its nonalcoholic little sister, the Babylonian Highball.

This recipe is inspired by the New York Sour. The ingredients include gin, bitters, pomegranate, pineapple, and lemon juice, topped off with just a blessing of red wine.

The flavors evoke Yalta's emotions and thoughts that day: of womanhood, fertility, inclusion, balance, bitterness, beauty, and of blessings.

Prep Time: 15 minutes
Yield: one cocktail

Tools:

- Citrus peeler
- Cutting board
- Fine mesh strainer
- Jigger or measuring cup
- Knife
- Hand juicer
- Measuring cup
- Shaker tins
- Spoon

- Wine key (corkscrew)
- Glass: chilled double rocks or wine glass

Ingredients:

- 1 squirt 1821 Tart Cherry Saffron Bitters (or Strongwater Golden Bitters, Angostura bitters, or your favorite)
- .5 oz (15ml) fresh lemon juice
- .25 oz (7ml) raw honey or sugar syrup
- .25 oz (7ml) pomegranate juice
- 1 oz (30ml) pineapple juice
- 2 oz (60ml) London Dry Gin
- 1–1.5 oz (30–45ml) dry red wine float (Cabernet or Merlot)

Babylonian Highball:

- 1 squirt 1821 Tart Cherry Saffron Bitters
- .75 oz (15ml) fresh lemon juice
- .5 oz (15ml) raw honey or sugar syrup
- .5 oz (15ml) pomegranate juice
- 2 oz (60ml) pineapple juice
- Top 2 oz (60ml) or to taste cold soda water

Cocktail garnish:

- Star anise seed, lemon peel expressed and inserted

Instructions:

For the Babylonian Sour:

1. Add all ingredients except red wine and garnishes to a tall shaker tin.
2. Seal tins and shake hard without ice to better incorporate honey or sugar syrup.
3. Open tin and fill the small shaker tin with ice.
4. Fill chilled glass with ice and place one star anise seed on top.
5. Seal tins, shake, and strain into glass over the star anise to open up the aroma.
6. To float the red wine on top, pour the wine very gently and slowly over the back of an upturned spoon held just above the surface of the cocktail.
7. Peel lemon, express, then insert peel, white pith side toward the glass.

For the nonalcoholic Babylonian Highball:

1. Repeat steps 1–6, omitting the soda water.
2. Pour over ice in a long glass and top off with cold soda water.
3. Lightly stir to mix soda without losing carbonation.
4. Peel lemon, express, then insert peel, white pith side toward the glass.

Sarah Iolani Rosner *is an accomplished bartender. She curates cocktail events through Swill Merchants Co., where she infuses passion, creativity, and storytelling into cocktail creation.*

STORY

In Tractate Yevamot, the Babylonian Talmud shares a story about Yehudit.[1]

Yehudit's husband, Rabbi Hiyya, was considered the greatest scholar in Rabbi Yehudah Ha-Nasi's Academy and was known for his religious dedication and scholarship. It is recounted that "all of his prayers were answered."[2]

Yehudit was the mother of two sets of twins: twin girls, Pazi and Tavi, followed by twin boys, Yehuda and Hizkiya. The Talmud recounts that one of the two boys was born in the seventh month, and the second one was born in the ninth month of pregnancy. Yehudit suffered from extremely painful births.

Directly following the birth of her fourth child, she changed her clothes to disguise herself and went to her husband. Posing as a stranger approaching him as a Rabbi, she asked him a halachic question: "Is a woman commanded to be fruitful and multiply?" Not knowing he was speaking to his own wife, he replied, "No." Following this exchange, Yehudit drank an infertility potion.

Many years later, when Yehudit and Rabbi Hiyya's four children were fully grown and renowned in their own right as Torah scholars, or as mothers to renowned Torah scholars, the actions that Yehudit took to prevent further pregnancies were revealed. Rabbi Hiyya told her that he wished she had given birth to another set of twins.

PASSAGES

Talmud.b. Yevamot 65b, Talmud.b. Kiddushin 12b:1

---

1. Yehudit is also mentioned in Talmud.b. Kiddushin 12b:1. in a halachic debate about the validity of marriage in a failed engagement of early adolescence.
2. Sefaria, Resources "Rabbi Chiyya."

CONTEXT

Yehudit's story is shared right after a story of another woman who came before Rabbi Ami and requested divorce due to her husband's inability to father children.[3] The Rabbi tells the woman she is not obligated to be fruitful and multiply and therefore has no legal right to demand a divorce. She counters that she wants to have children so that she will have someone to care for her when she is old, to which Rabbi Ami says that in her situation, the rabbis can force the husband to grant her divorce.

This is followed by the story of Yehudit, a married woman with four children who wishes to prevent further pregnancies. The rabbis support *both* women, whether they need intervention in order to reproduce, or to stop. There is a seeming paradox at play: men are obligated to reproduce, and cannot do so without women; meanwhile, women are *not* obligated to have children at all.

Yehudit drinks some sort of root-based medicinal drink. In the Talmud, there are several discussions of this "cup of roots": a form of orally consumed medicinal birth control. On the issue of birth control, the Talmud also shares a key statement that has been called "The *Baraita* of the Three Women" about specific women and the circumstances in which they are permitted to use birth control.[4]

From the position of Yehudit's story in the Talmud, it seems that the Sages are sharing stories about how deeply fertility impacts women (i.e., Yehudit), men (i.e., Rabbi Hiyya), and marriage relationships. Yehudit's story also points to a larger question of when Jewish law allows women (and men) to use birth control. This issue of contraception and Jewish law is an ongoing discussion.

---

3. Talmud.b.Yevamot 65b:17.
4. Talmud. b. Yevemot 12b.

AGGADAH

The status of women in any society is connected to their control over their fertility.

The story of Yehudit demonstrates the tension around female fertility: for women themselves, for their partners, and in religious and civil law.

By including Yehudit's story, the Gemara gives her female experience legitimacy. She faced unexpected health consequences in childbirth, namely extreme pain. This suffering impacted her so deeply that directly following the birth of her fourth child, Yehudit wanted to prevent further pregnancies. She disguised herself as "another woman" before her husband, a religious authority, for a legal ruling on *their* case.[5]

The Gemara points to the tension at play for this couple by also giving space to her husband's experience. Rabbi Hiyya is able to be objective in relaying the law to his wife precisely because the reality of his personal implication is obscured by her disguise. Perhaps lacking confidence in her husband's capacity to support her decision, or knowing he wanted more children, Yehudit took the decision alone. Despite the fact that Yehudit's final choice was legally allowed, her decision-making process excluded her husband. When Rabbi Hiyya finds out that she took a fertility potion, he finally shares his feelings of regret and his wish that he had had more children.

Today, there is still ongoing debate in many countries and religions regarding if and how women may control their own fertility: under which circumstances is it permissible and what methods are allowed.

Yehudit's story shows an enduring truth: it is essential that women have the religious and civil legal right to access safe methods of birth control. These rights can only be secured when women's lived experiences exert a fundamental influence on laws governing their bodies – this requires women to be consulted and to participate as lawmakers.

---

5. Similar to the story of Tamar in the Hebrew Bible, Yehudit disguises herself in order to obtain rightful control over her own fertility. Genesis 38:13–30.

PROMPTS

- The commandment "to be fruitful and multiply" applies to men and not women. What do you think this means today?
- Yehudit was able to make her own decisions because she understood the law. To you, what are the most important issues or aspects of fertility law today?
- What factors affect negotiation and decision making about fertility in relationships today?

Kenden Alfond

NOURISHING WOMB TONIC

This recipe is to heal Yehudit's womb. It is useful for every female who wants to nourish and support their womb with a natural herbal approach.

This simple recipe brews a highly nutritive tea for the reproductive organs. These herbs are safe to drink daily for toning the uterus, promoting blood flow to the pelvic floor, aiding digestion, and calming the nervous system.

The medicinal herbs and plants ease painful menstruation, and support mothers and babies throughout the birth and postpartum.

These medicinal herbs and plants can be purchased online from reputable herb shops. Herbs can be stored in an airtight container out of direct sunlight for up to one year. I recommend buying at least 2–4 oz of each herb to make your own blend.

Prep Time: 8 minutes
Cook Time: 25 minutes
Yield: 32 oz quart jar

Tools:

- Teapot with a strainer or 32 oz glass jar
- Fine sieve

Ingredients:

- 3 parts nettle leaf
- 2 parts red raspberry leaf
- 2 parts tulsi leaf and flowers
- 1 part hawthorn leaf, flower and berry
- 1 part milky oats tops
- ½ part rose
- ½ part cinnamon bark
- 3 tbsp of herb blend

Instructions:

1. Make the herbal tea blend by combining each herb and store in an airtight glass container.
2. Boil 1 quart of water.
3. Add 3 tablespoons of the herbal tea blend to a 10 oz jar or teapot.
4. Pour boiling water over the herbs.
5. Cover and let steep for 25 minutes.
6. Strain into your favorite mug and enjoy.

Enjoy 3–5 cups per day. Safe for daily use. Safe for pregnant and nursing women.

 Hannah Jacobson-Hardy *is a Community Herbalist based in Ashfield, MA, devoted to connecting people with the land through medicine-making projects and workshops.*

STORY

The story of Yirmatia and her mother is recounted in Tractate Arakhin ("valuations"). This tractate discusses the vow-making system to donate to the Temple based on the value of a person. Our mishnah centers on vows to donate the weight of a person, either in silver or gold. Yirmatia's mother vows to make a monetary donation to the Temple equivalent to her daughter's weight, but does not specify a material. Nonetheless, she brings her daughter to Jerusalem, weighs her, and donates her weight in gold.

PASSAGES

Talmud b. Arakhin 19a

CONTEXT

In the Torah (Leviticus 27), vows to donate fixed sums of money are to be based only on age and sex, but Tractate Arakhin introduces additional measures. These include property value, height, worth (determined by one's hypothetical price as a slave at market), and weight. Donors may also choose what to donate, whether gold, silver, pitch, onions, or any other measurable commodity.

The inclusion of Yirmatia's story in the Mishnah was perplexing to the rabbis of the Gemara. They hypothesize that this story is here to teach the reader how to choose what to donate. The normal practice, as stated by the Mishnah, was to vow to donate a particular commodity, but Yirmatia's mother does not say what she will donate. Why does she then donate gold, when silver would have sufficed? The rabbis know that Yirmatia's mother was very wealthy, and surmise that she gave gold due to her wealth. Ultimately, the rabbis conclude that unless the vower specifies what commodity to donate, she must donate in accordance with her economic situation.

Contemporary scholar Dr. Charlotte Elisheva Fonrobert gives another interpretation of why this story is included in the Talmud. She suggests that this story is centered on women in order to exemplify that women and men can both make vows. Then as now, her story gives a practical example of the laws in the Tractate, allowing the reader to understand how such a vow works in real life.

AGGADAH

Why does Yirmatia's mother speak this vow by weight?

Prior to Arakhin 5:1, donations are determined based on either a scale fixed by age and sex, or one's value as a slave at market. These established methods would be denigrating to Yirmatia, reminding her that she is worth less than a male her age, if she were for sale. A number of modern commentators see vows by weight as similarly demeaning, joking that Yirmatia's mother intended to embarrass her daughter, or provoke her to lose weight.[1] Although anachronistic, this mean-spirited reading might resonate with modern experiences of womanhood, and today's overwhelming societal standards for women's bodies.

However, we can read this story differently. Yirmatia's mother equates her daughter with a precious material – gold – and models how to value one's body and self. In contrast to a vow of Yirmatia's fixed value or market value, which would compare her to others and potentially find her wanting, a vow by weight attests to her body's innate capabilities. Yirmatia's body – exactly as it is – enables her to give charitably and generously. And so Yirmatia – exactly as she is – does good for the community.

This is a story of not just one woman, but two, and Yirmatia's unnamed mother propels this narrative. Neither woman is named with respect to male relations, and it is striking that the mother is defined by her relationship to her daughter, not the other way around. This literary choice indicates that Yirmatia's mother is a role model for her daughter. She demonstrates the importance of charitable giving to the extent of her wealth, and, more importantly, she teaches her daughter to recognize the value intrinsic to her whole body. We would do well to follow her example.

---

1.   For example, Joshua Kulp. Mishnah Yomit commentary on M. Arakhin 5:1.

PROMPTS

- What do you value about yourself and your body? How has this changed since you were a child?
- How can we teach the young people in our lives to recognize their innate worth as human beings?

Rebecca Whitman is a doctoral student in mathematics at UC Berkeley. She mentors girls interested in math research, and teaches Hebrew school and art classes.

GOLDEN TURMERIC LEMON CAKE

This Golden Turmeric Lemon Cake recalls the gold that Yirmatia's mother donated to the temple.

This cake is moist, just dense enough, and is the perfect sweetness level. It has a delicate crumb and a subtle lemon flavor with a lovely golden yellow color from the turmeric. It is oil-free and made with whole-grain flours.

It is delicious tasting on its own or served with a dusting of powdered sugar and/or a dollop of raspberry jam.

Prep Time: 10 minutes
Cook Time: 30 minutes
Yield: 8–10 servings

Tools:

- Kitchen scale
- Large mixing bowl
- Measuring cups and spoons
- Round cake pan
- Small mixing bowl
- Wooden spoon or whisk

Ingredients

- 1 cup (240ml) unsweetened soy milk
- 1½ tbsp apple cider vinegar
- ½ cup (100g) caster sugar
- ¼ cup (60g) unsweetened applesauce
- 2 tbsp fresh lemon juice
- 1 tsp lemon zest
- 1 cup (120g) white whole-wheat flour
- ¾ cup (90g) white spelt flour
- 1½ tsp baking powder
- ½ tsp baking soda
- ½ tsp ground turmeric
- ¼ tsp salt

Instructions:

1. Preheat the oven to 350° F / 175° C and grease a round cake pan with a bit of coconut oil or some nonstick baking spray.

2. In a large bowl, add the soy milk and apple cider vinegar. Stir and let the mixture curdle for 3–4 minutes. This is a vegan buttermilk substitute.

3. Once the soy milk thickens up, add the sugar, applesauce, lemon juice, and lemon zest to the bowl. Whisk to combine.

4. In a separate, smaller bowl, mix together wheat flour, spelt flour, baking powder, baking soda, turmeric, and salt.

5. Fold the dry ingredients into the wet, taking care not to overmix the batter.

6. Transfer the cake batter into the prepared baking pan and bake in the preheated oven for 25–30 minutes, or until a toothpick inserted into the center comes out clean.

7. Allow the cake to cool completely before slicing and serving.

From the Jewish Food Hero Kitchen

ACKNOWLEDGMENTS

This project was made possible with the support of the following people:

Each woman and girl who contributed to this book, Turner Publishing, Rachel Mendelson, Tiki Krakowski, Bonny Coombe, Sonja Luzukic, Ora Weinbach, Elizabeth LaCouture, Debbie Zimmerman, my mother and father, Charles and Yaël.

The Jewish Food Hero
by Yaël Alfond-Vincent

CONTRIBUTOR INDEX

A

Abreu, Hannah, 292
Ackermann-Sommer, Myriam, 129
Alfond-Vincent, Yaël, 18, 410
Andron, Mollie, 101
Angerame, Lisa Dawn, 109
Asch, Erica Seager, 195
Ashworth-Steen, Robyn, 160
Austerklein, Elyssa Joy, 62

B

Balkin, Shana, 244
Barnett, Jordana, 50
Baum, Laura, 120
Benitah, Allegra, 208
Bergadine, Martha, 327
Bodian, Dena, 205
Brawer, Dina, 178
Brenner, Pammy, 259

C

Cabot, Esther, 222
Cagan, Penny, 123
Chandler, Sarah, 279
Cohen, Bailey, 287
Corwin, Alexandra, 76

D

Daniels, Esther, 256
Doherty, Megan, 68

E

Eliassian, Shira, 107

F

Farbiarz, Sarah, 247
Fein, Ronnie, 261
Feuchs, Chelsea, 249

Fisher, Natalya, 180
Frankel, Erica, 388
Fruchter, Dasi, 85

G

Gaventa, Hannah, 141
Golomb, Chanita, 156
Gordon, Anne, 340
Green, Amy, 93
Green, Ginna, 336
Greenberg, Hannah, 113
Gribetz, Daniela, 297
Gribetz, Sarit Kattan, 297
Gribetz, Sophie, 297
Grossman, Lauren Monaco, 302
Grushcow, Lisa J., 239, 241

H

Hain, Elana Stein, 135
Halon, Sally, 379
Hartman, Leah, 284
Hecht-Koller, Shira, 372
Hershkovitz, Rachel, 318
Herszberg, Chaya, 190
Holbert, Cheryl, 374

J

Jacobson-Hardy, Hannah, 403
Jedwab, Ellie, 350
Jehassi, Doreet, 312
Judelman, Shayna, 47

K

Kaltmann, Nomi, 184
Kaufman, Rebecca, 290
Kóatz, Binya, 10
Krakowski, Tiki, 272
Kranjec, Danielle, 44
Kupferberg, Jessica Levine, 347

L

LaCouture, Elizabeth, 34

Lang, Zoë, 321

Lev, Chaya, 99

Levin, Talia, 252

Levitan, Judith, 265

Levkovich, Renana, 237

Levy, Hadassah, 333

Lind, Naomi Gurt, 310

London, Eryn, 224

Lowe, Mitten, 192

M

Marvin, Tamar, 232

Morgan, Jazzie, 203

Moscati, Azelma, 132

Moskowitz, Karyn, 150

N

Nakash, Susie, 247

Nissim, Joanna, 59

O

Olshin, Serena, 307

Osband, Yardaena, 91

P

Paster, Emily, 64

Paul, Heather, 57

Petrulis, Denise, 54

Phillips, Denise, 323

Piñer, Hélène Jawhara, 36

Pinto, Sibel, 88

Prada, Fanta, 12

Prell, Tani, 71

Prever, Victoria, 268

Price, Daphne Lazar, 28

R

Ratzon, Nava, 275

Reich, Maddie, 175

Renetzky, Heather, 316

Robinson, Saah, 383

Rockford, Sarah, 367

Rodin, Lara, 166

Rosenthal, Rebecca, 220

Rosner, Sarah Iolani, 397

Ross, Jade Sank, 200

Ross, Nathalie, 213

Roth, Adina, 154

S

Sanae, Dee, 143

Sanford, Sonya, 82

Sarna, Leah, 118

Shulman, Nelly, 96

Singer, Jennifer, 230

Slutsky, Rachel, 211

Smith, Jane, 103

Solomon, Liat, 163

Souriano-Vinikoor, Marlene, 186

Steinbauer, Chasya Uriel, 79

Stillman, Danielle, 235

T

Trinidad, Doxia, 386

Tuchman, Lauren, 376

Tucker, Megan B., 227

Tucker, Olivia Devorah, 354

Turner, Zissy, 173

V

Vidomlanski, Rachel, 305

Viner-Luzzato, Fabienne, 329

W

Walfish, Miriam-Simma, 22

Wax, Lee, 361

Waxman, Sylvie, 197

Weinbach, Ora, 15

Weiss, Melanie, 369

Whitman, Rebecca, 406

Williams, Laura, 390

Winer, Emily Goldberg, 394

Winston, Penelope, 41

Y

Yechezkel, Nicole Cohen, 138

Z

Zik, Maayan, 31

Zimmerman, Debbie, 148

A

Abaye, 7, 77, 79, 104–106, 276, 293, 344

Abba Hilkiya, 364, 365

Abundant Water Challah Rolls, 373–374

acorn squash, 69, 149

adultery, 133, 134, 164, 238, 239, 337, 339

Aggadah, explained, 2

Agrat bat Mahalat, 7–12

agriculture, 111

Aguají (Green Plantains Soup), 291–292

ahavat chinam (baseless love), 37, 39

alcohol

    Babylonian Sour, 395–397

    Calm Your Nervous System Tonic, 137–138

    Tej-Ethiopian Honey Wine, 11–12

alcohol consumption, 20–23, 106, 209, 212

almond butter

    No Bake Vegan Millionaire Squares, 17–18

    Vegan Nutty Chocolate Chip Cookies, 167–169

almonds

    Gluten-free Amaretto Cake, 201–203

    Vegan Lullabye Bread, 260–261

    Wild Red Rice Roasted Vegetable Platter with Pomegranate Molasses and Fresh Herbs, 207–208

Amaretto Cake, Gluten-free, 201–203

Angel of Death (Death), 344, 346

anger, women's, 110, 161, 224, 304, 391–394

animals

    to be sacrificed, 117, 204

    grazing, 110–111

aniseed, in Kahk Biscuits, 377–379

apple(s)

    Apple Sage Muffins, 174–175

    Creamy Coconut, Red Lentil and Apple Soup, 322–323

    Spiced Acorn Squash Breakfast Bake, 149–150

apple juice, 362–363

applesauce

    Fiery Fudgy Brownies, 108–109

    Golden Turmeric Lemon Cake, 407–409

    Gluten-Free Amaretto Cake 201–203

    Grape and Lemon Squares, 243–244

    Rich Chocolate and Red Wine Mini Cakes, 23–24

    Sweet Beet Loaf Cake, 236–237

    Vegan Carrot Cake, 355–357

apprentice, 37–39

articulation, mistaken, 387–388

astrology, 245–246

B

babies. *See* infants

Babylonian Sour, 395–397

Babylonian Talmud (Talmud Balvi), 2, 25, 32, 42, 49, 77, 78, 104, 126, 157, 158, 187, 198, 282, 295, 364, 398

balsam oil, 100–101

bananas

    Magnesium-boosting Smoothie, 217–218

    Medicinal Magnesium Jello, 362–363

baraita

    on women drinking wine, 105

    on women going out at night alone, 7

Bar Kamtza, 38, 39

barley

    Caramelized Leek Barley, 51–54

    Lemon, Saffron and Barley Risotto, 58–59

    Red Wine Braised Mushroom and Barley Stuffed Cabbage Holishkes, 225–227

baseless hatred, 37, 39

baseless love, 37, 39

Bat Abba Surah, 13–18

Bathsheba, 19–22

Bava Kamma 50a, 110–111, 128

Bava Metsia 59b, 126–127

Bavli, 77, 78

beans

    Black-Eyed Pea Soup, 335–336

    Caramelized Leek Barley with White Bean Smash, Spinach, Asparagus, and Beet Potion, 51–52

    Four Bean Salad with Dry Mustard Vinaigrette, 124–125

Sweet Potato and Golden Beet Cholent, 317–318

Vegan Nutty Chocolate Chip Cookies, 167–169

White Bean Kale Stew with Matzo Balls, 179–180

beauty, 84, 107, 147, 152, 264, 358, 360, 367

beetroot powder, 328–329

beets

Beet, Pomegranate and Parsley Salad, 97–99

Caramelized Leek Barley with White Bean Smash, Spinach, Asparagus, and Beet Potion, 51–52

Grandmother's Borscht, 80–82

Sweet Beet Loaf Cake, 236–237

Sweet Potato and Golden Beet Cholent, 317–318

bell pepper, 285–287

Beloreya, 25–28

Bereshit Rabbah 94, 325*n*6

berries

Magnesium-boosting Smoothie, 217–218

Medicinal Elderberry Syrup, 191–192

Medicinal Magnesium Jello, 362–363

Rich Chocolate and Red Wine Mini Cakes, 23–24

betrothal gifts, 228

beverages

Babylonian Sour, 395–397

Kvass: Fermented Rye Bread and Raisin Beverage, 75–76

Mother's Joy Infusion, 45–47

Nourishing Womb Tonic, 402–403

Tej (Ethiopian Honey Wine), 11–12

birth control, 399–400

bitter water (trial by water), 338

Black and White Cookies, 341–343

black beans, 124–125

Black-Eyed Pea Soup, 335–336

blessings after a meal, 331

bloodstains, 116, 117

Book of Proverbs, 19, 32, 264

borscht, 80–82

Bourbon Cinnamon Pecan Pie, 114–115

Bourekas, Purslane, Pomegranate and Tofu, 267–268

braiding hair, 230

bread(s)

Almond-Carob Bread Pudding, 368–369

Jachnun, 311–312

Kvass: Fermented Rye Bread and Raisin Beverage, 75–80

Seven Herbs and Species Focaccia, 35–37

Vegan Chocolate Babka, 131–132

Vegan Lullabye Bread, 260–261

Bread Pudding, Almond-Carob, 368–369

breaking of bread, 319

breastfeeding, 42–44

broccoli, 306–307

Brownies, Fiery Fudgy, 108–109

Bruriah, 32–36

burial practices, 351–352

burial procession, 214

C

cabbage

Fresh Tangy Cabbage and Radish Spread, 29–31

Grandmother's Borscht, 80–81

Red Wine Braised Mushroom and Barley Stuffed Cabbage Holishkes, 225–227

cakes

Gluten-free Amaretto Cake, 201–203

Golden Turmeric Lemon Cake, 407–409

Rich Chocolate and Red Wine Mini Cakes, 23–24

Sweet Beet Loaf Cake, 236–237

Vegan Carrot Cake, 355–357

Calm Your Nervous System Tonic, 137–138

candied cherry tomatoes, 35–36

candle lighting, 60, 101, 314, 316, 317

cannellini beans, 124–125

capital punishment, 133–134

capsicum, 253, 255, 349, 350

Caramelized Leek Barley with White Bean Smash, Spinach, Asparagus, and Beet Potion, 51–53

carob powder, 368–369

The Carpenter's Wife, 37–39

carrots

Grandmother's Borscht, 80–82

Red Wine Braised Mushroom and Barley Stuffed Cabbage Holishkes, 225–227

Vegan Carrot Cake, 355–357

White Bean Kale Stew with Matzo Balls, 179–180
cashews
  Caramelized Leek Barley with White Bean Smash, Spinach, Asparagus, and Beet Potion, 51–52
  Rich Chocolate and Red Wine Mini Cakes, 23–24
cauliflower, 161–163
Celeriac Purée with Frizzled Leeks, 231–232
A Certain Divorced Woman, 42–44
challah
  asking rabbi about taking, 380–381
  Vegan Challah Clouds, 384–386
Challah Rolls, 373–374
chard, 80–82
charitable giving, 55, 364–365, 405
Charoset Rugelach, 212–213
chickpeas, 124–125
children
  haircuts, 111
  inability to control our, 21–22
  role in parents' relationship, 305, 309–310
  transmission of Jewish knowledge and customs to, 319
chocolate (vegan)
  Fiery Fudgy Brownies, 108–109
  No Bake Vegan Millionaire Squares, 17–18
Chocolate Chip Cookies, 167–169
chocolate chips
  Vegan Chocolate Babka, 131–132
  Vegan Nutty Chocolate Chip Cookies, 167–169
Choni Ha'Maegel, 365
choosing our words carefully, 387–388
churban, 358–359
cilantro, 29, 31, 35, 291, 300
circumcision wound, 77
Clan of Bilgah, 204–205
Cleopatra, 48–50
cocoa powder
  Black and White Cookies, 341–343
  Fiery Fudgy Brownies, 108–109
  Magnesium-boosting Smoothie, 217–218
  Rich Chocolate and Red Wine Mini Cakes, 23–24

Vegan Chocolate Babka, 131–132
coconut milk, 322, 362
compassion, 128–129, 210, 262–264
conflict, 126–129
contraception, 399
converting to Judaism, 26–27, 233
cookies
  Black and White Cookies, 341–343
  Kahk Biscuits, 377–379
  Turkish Sand Cookies, 185–186
  Vegan Nutty Chocolate Chip Cookies, 167–169
Corn Latkes with Mango Salsa, 247–249
court, arguing a case in, 170–171
Couscous with Beluga Lentils and Pomegranate, 248–249
cranberries, 207–208
Creamy Celeriac Purée with Frizzled Leeks, 231–232
Creamy Coconut, Red Lentil and Apple Soup, 322–323
cucumber
  Corn Latkes with Mango Salsa, 253–256
  Sephardic Style Chilled Cucumber Soup, 87–88

D
daikon radish, in Fresh Tangy Cabbage and Radish Spread, 29–31
Dandelion-Pumpkin Seed Pesto, 119–120
dates
  Charoset Rugelach, 212–213
  No-Bake Vegan Millionaire Squares, 17–18
  Nut and Beet Stuffed Dates and Prunes, 328–329
  Seven Herbs and Species Focaccia, 35–36
  Spiced Acorn Squash Breakfast Bake, 149–150
Daughter of Nakdimon Ben Gurion, 55–57
The Daughter of Rabbi Hanina Ben Dosa, 60–62
The Daughter of the Emperor, 65–68
daughters, Rabbis', 295–296
dead body, ritual impurity and, 209–211
death
  Miriam Mix-Up and possibility of an untimely, 345–347
  preventing a fated, 246
death penalty, 134–135

decision-making, 250–252

demons and demonology

    Agrat bat Mahalat, 7–9

    Lilith, 157–160

dessert. *see also* cakes; cookies

    Almond-Carob Bread Pudding, 368–369

    Bourbon Cinnamon Pecan Pie, 114–115

    Charoset Rugelach, 212–213

    Fiery Fudgy Brownies, 108–109

    Grape and Lemon Squares, 243–244

    Slow Cooked Caramelized Oranges, 221–222

Deuteronomy 6:8, 199

Deuteronomy 7:13, 391n1

Deuteronomy 10:17, 25n4

Deuteronomy 28:56, 181

dishonesty. *See* honesty/dishonesty

divorce, 37, 223, 395

divorced mother, breastfeeding and, 42–43

domestic workers, 262–265

Donag, 72–74

Dressing, Mustard, Miso and Maple, 280–281

drinks, serving to others in one's home, 73–74

E

Ecclesiastes 7, 308n1

education

    girls asking "why" and "from where is this derived"

      in, 246

    in the home, 77–79

    Jewish law, 90–91

eggplant

    Fesenjoon: Tangy Eggplant and Walnut Stew, 40–41

    Smoky Eggplant Salad with Herbs, Tahini

      and Pomegranate, 285–287

    Wild Red Rice Roasted Vegetable Platter with

      Pomegranate Molasses and Fresh Herbs, 207–208

elderberries, 191–192

Em, 77–79

Erev Yom Kippur, 303–305

Esther 4:3, 360n11

Ethiopian Honey Wine (Tej), 11–12

executions, 133–135

Exodus 13:22, 313

Exodus 22:20, 27n8

Exodus 35:3, 60n1

Exodus from Egypt, 324

F

falling on one's face, 165

family

    leaving home to study the Torah and responsibility

      to, 258, 282, 283, 289

    sibling relationship, 272, 289

fennel, in Roasted Garlic Soup, 196–197

Fermented Lemon Spread, 273–275

Fermented Rye Bread and Raisin Beverage (Kvass), 75–76

fertility

    women controlling their own, 400–401

    Yalta's anger and, 392–393

Fesenjoon: Tangy Eggplant and Walnut Stew, 40–41

Festival pilgrimage, 139, 140

Fiery Fudgy Brownies, 108–109

figs

    death of Marta bat Beitus by, 181–182

    No Bake Vegan Millionaire Squares, 17–18

financial independence, 13

First Temple period, 146

flaxseed

    Bourbon Cinnamon Pecan Pie, 114–115

    Fiery Fudgy Brownies, 108–109

food preparation, 277–295

Four Bean Salad with Dry Mustard Vinaigrette, 124–125

free will, 245–247

G

Galilean dialect, 387

Garden of Eden, 157–160

Garlic Soup, Roasted, 196–197

Gemara

    about, 2

    on candle lighting, 314

    Cleopatra story, 48, 49

on hair covering, 146

Homa story, 104–106

Kimchit and her sons story, 144–146

on mitzah of Festival pilgrimage, 139

on Nakdimon ben Gurion, 55

on Rabbi Elazar, 133–134

story of Homa, 104–105

story of Tzafenat bat Peniel, 358–360

story of Yehudit, 398–399

woman of mistaken articulation story, 387–388

gender boundaries, transgressing, 33

gender roles, 235, 295

generosity, 375, 376. *see also* charitable giving

Genesis 9:20, 20*n*5

Genesis 17:17, 165*n*1

Genesis 38:13–30, 400*n*5

Genesis 38:15, 94

Genesis 46, 17, 324*n*2

Genesis 50:1, 165*n*5

"ger," 26

ghosts, 351–354

ginger, 11, 12, 114, 142, 191, 306, 322

gin, in Babylonian Sour, 395

Gluten-free Amaretto Cake, 201–203

God, railing against, 205

Golden Turmeric Lemon Cake, 407–409

Grace after Meals, 330–333

Grape and Lemon Squares, 243–244

grazing flocks of animals, 110, 111

green chillis, in Corn Latkes with Mango Salsa, 253–256

H

habanero peppers, in Black-Eyed Pea Soup, 335–336

hair and skin remedy, 155–156

hair covering, 146, 147

haircuts, 111

hairdresser, the potential bride and the, 228–230

halachic knowledge

    in Rabbinic households, 294

    Rav Hisda's daughter, 293–296

halachic law, 32, 33. *See also* Jewish law

halachic ruling, use of names and, 223

halachic world, machismo in, 271

Hama bar Tovia, 133–134

HaMotzi blessing, 319

Hanina's Daughter-In-Law, 89–91

Hannah, the Wife of R'Mani, 83–85

Haruta, 94–96

The Hated-Daughter-In-Law, 100–101

Hauptman, Judith, 294

Havdalah candle, 60

hawthorn leaf, flower and berry, 402

hazelnuts, in Vegan Chocolate Babka, 131–132

healing treatments, 179, 188, 191, 196

Hebrew Bible, 19, 26, 94

heimira datah, 204

herbal tea, 45–47, 403

hibiscus, 92

historiographical misogyny, 188

Homa, 104–106

home. *see also* household(s)

    building a, 121–122

    education and religious ritual in the, 77–79

    serving drinks in the, 73–74

honesty/dishonesty, 308–310

honey, 11–12, 191, 260, 311, 395

hospitality toward guests, 73–74

household(s)

    decision-making in the, 250

    domestic workers in, 262–265

    halachic knowledge in Rabbinic, 294

    power issues, 229

Hova, 110–113

husbands, leaving their family to study the Torah, 258, 283, 303–305

I

Ifra Hurmiz, 116–118

Ikku, 121–123

Immarta bat Talei, 133–135

Imma Shalom, 126–129

impurity, of Nazirite status and, 203

independence, financial, 13

infants

breastfeeding, 42–44

    Lilith and, 158

infidelity. *See* adultery

inherited wealth, 14

intermarriage, 198

Isaiah 31:32, 34:14, 158*n*8

Isaiah 34, 14, 157*n*2

Isaiah 58:5, 360*n*11

J

Jachnun, 311–312

jam, 23–24

Jannaeus, Alexander, 330

Japanese yams, in Vegan Yakitori, 142–143

Jello, Medicinal Magnesium, 362–363

Jeremiah 269, 270, 308*n*2, 358*n*3

Jerusalem

    Festival Pilgrimage, 139, 140

    Roman siege of, 182

Jerusalem (Palestinian) Talmud, 2, 158, 187, 188, 198

Jewish law. *see also* mitzvah/mitzvot

    on contraception, 399

    on haircuts, 111

    lighting candles, 313–316

    mother caring for her son within the confines of, 219

    responsibility of keeping, 111

    taught by mothers, 320–321

Jewish learning

    conversion and, 25–27

    female Torah knowledge, 33–34

    role of women in the home and, 219

"Jewish mother" stereotype, 220

Jonah 3:6, 360*n*11

Jonah's Wife, 139, 140, 141

Joseph, 165*n*5, 324–326, 359, 359*n*4

K

Kahk Biscuits, 377–379

kale

    Grandmother's Borscht, 80–81

    Magnesium-boosting Smoothie, 217–218

    White Bean Kale Stew with Matzo Balls, 179–180

Kamtza, 38, 39

ketubah, 13, 37, 55, 56

kidney beans, 124–125

Kimchit, 144–148

kindness, 55, 154, 263–265, 375–376

King David, 19

King Lemuel, 19

King Saul, 198

King Shapur II, 116

King Solomon, 19–20

King Yannai, 182, 330–331

"konam to me," 151, 152

Kurabiyes (Turkish Sand Cookies), 185–186

Kvass: Fermented Rye Bread and Raisin Beverage, 75–80

L

language(s), 387–388

Latkes, Corn, 253–256

learning. *See* education; Jewish learning; Torah study

leeks

    Caramelized Leek Barley with White Bean Smash, Spinach, Asparagus, and Beet Potion, 51–54

    Creamy Celeriac Purée with Frizzled Leeks, 231–232

    Roasted Garlic Soup, 196–197

Lemon, Saffron and Barley Risotto, 58–59

Lemon Spread, Fermented, 273–275

lentils

    Creamy Coconut, Red Lentil and Apple Soup, 322–323

    Saffron Couscous with Beluga Lentils and Pomegranate, 248–249

Leviticus 16:10, 158*n*8

Leviticus 19:27, 110

Leviticus 21:1, 215*n*1, 215

Leviticus 24:5, 380

Leviticus 27, 404

lighting candles, 60, 61, 62, 313, 314, 315, 316

Likhlukhit, 151–154

Lilith, 157–160

liliths, 157

local customs and cultures, 72

London Dry Gin, 395

lust, 38

M

machismo, 271

machtzelet shel kanim, 352

magnesium, 217, 362–363

Magnesium-boosting Smoothie, 217–218

The Maiden Who Prays Constantly, 164–166

maidservant, 228, 229, 231, 262–265

main dishes

    Creamy Vegan Noodle Kugel, 389–391

    Fesenjoon: Tangy Eggplant and Walnut Stew, 40–41

    Red Wine Braised Mushroom and Barley Stuffed
        Cabbage Holishkes, 225–227

    Saffron Couscous with Beluga Lentils
        and Pomegranate, 248–249

    Sweet Potato and Golden Beet Cholent, 317–318

    White Bean Kale Stew with Matzo Balls, 179–180

    Wild Red Rice Roasted Vegetable Platter with
        Pomegranate Molasses and Fresh Herbs, 207–208

Mango Salsa, Corn Latkes with, 253–256

maple syrup, 17, 23, 24, 114–115, 131–132, 260, 280, 299,
    306, 368, 373

Mar bar Ravina, Mother of, 219–220

marriage/marital relationships, 106, 151–154, 224, 283,
    309, 399. *see also* household(s)

Mar Shmuel's Daughters, 170–172

Marta bat Beitus, 181–184

Mar Ukva's Wife, 176–178

materialism, 183, 367

mat of reeds, 351–352

Matron Healer from Tiberias, 187–190

Matun, 193–195

Matzo Balls, White Bean Kale Stew with, 179–180

meat consumption, 293–294

Medicinal Eldberberry Syrup, 191–192

Medicinal Magnesium Jello, 362–363

men

    doubting women's knowledge, 49–50

    female Talmud knowledge and, 33–34

    greeting women, 72–73

    leaving their family to study the Torah, 258, 282–283, 289

men's haircuts, 111

menstruation, 116, 118, 392, 402

Michal bat Kushi, 198–200

Midrash

    Eichah Rabbah 1, 83

    Lilith's origin story, 157

    on marriage and love, 153

Midrash.Leviticus.Rabbah.12.5, 19n4

Midrash on the Book of Proverbs, 32

Midrash Tanhuma, 337–338

Midrash Tanhuma, Naso 6.1, 337

Millet Coriander Croquettes with Pumpkin Truffle
    Cream Sauce, 161–163

mimetic tradition, 78–79

mince "meat," in Curried Nettle Vegan
    Sausage Rolls, 102–103

Mini Fire Roasted Stuffed Peppers, 349–350

miracles/miracle workers, 60–62, 67, 83–85, 121–122,
    250, 309, 371–372

Miriam ("Miriam, the Childminder"), 344–346

Miriam bat Bilgah, 204–205

Miriam Magdala ("Miriam, the Braider"), 344

The Miriam Mix-Up, 345–347

Miriam of Tarmod, 209–211

miscarriage, 89

Miscarriage Recovery Tea, 92–93

The Mishnah

    about, 2

    on doughs for challah, 380–381

    on Queen Helena of Adiabene, 239

    on *sereifa*, 133–135

    on vows to donate, 404

Mishnah Bava Metzia 4:10, 27n8

Mishnah Nazir 3:6, 238

Mishnah Yevamot 6:4, 182n2

Mishnah Yoma 3:10, 238

misogyny, 118, 188–190

miso, in Mustard, Miso and Maple Dressing, 280–281

mitzvah/mitzvot. *see also* Jewish law; Torah study

    on Festival pilgrimage, 139

    lighting candles, 61

    Sotah ritual, 339

    time-bound, 140

    of wearing *tzitzit*, 233–235

modesty, 145–148

monsoon rains, 330, 332

Moses, 324–326

The Mother from Tzippori, 214–216

mother-in-laws, 100–101

The Mother of Mar bar Ravina, 219–220

Mother's Joy Infusion, 45–47

mothers/motherhood, 14, 20, 21, 42, 44, 144, 215, 219, 158

Muffins, Apple Sage, 174–175

mushrooms

Caramelized Leek Barley with White Bean Smash, Spinach, Asparagus, and Beet Potion, 51–52

Mini Fire Roasted Stuffed Peppers, 349–350

Red Wine Braised Mushroom and Barley Stuffed Cabbage Holishkes, 225–227

Red Wine Mushroom Soup, Baked in Acorn Squash, 69–71

Mustard, Miso and Maple Dressing, 280–281

mustard preparation, 276–278

Mustard Vinaigrette, Four Bean Salad with Dry, 124–125

N

Nakdimon ben Gurion, 55, 57

names, 84, 122, 223, 345, 346, 360

natural disasters, 375

Nazirite vows, 209, 211, 238, 240

Nefata, 223–224

nettles/nettle leaf

Curried Nettle Vegan Sausage Rolls, 102–103

Miscarriage Recovery Tea, 92–93

Nourishing Womb Tonic, 402

night demon (Lilith), 157

nighttime, women going out at, 7–9

No Bake Vegan Millionaire Squares, 17–18

non-Jewish women, 116–118, 193–195, 234

Numbers 1:15, 231

Numbers 5:20, 337, 339n2

Numbers 6:1–8, 238

Numbers 6:26, 25n5

Numbers 15:18–21, 380

Numbers 16:4, 165n4

Numbers 26, 46, 324n3

nursing, 42, 45, 403

Nut and Beet Stuffed Dates and Prunes, 328–329

nuts. see also walnuts

Bourbon Cinnamon Pecan Pie, 114–115

Caramelized Leek Barley with White Bean Smash, Spinach, Asparagus, and Beet Potion, 51–52

Gluten-free Amaretto Cake, 201–203

Rich Chocolate and Red Wine Mini Cakes, 23–24

Spiced Acorn Squash Breakfast Bake, 149–150

Vegan Chocolate Babka, 131–132

Vegan Lullabye Bread, 260–261

O

oats

Grape and Lemon Squares, 243–244

No-Bake Vegan Millionaire Squares, 17–18

olives, in Seven Herbs and Species Focaccia, 35–36

Oral Torah, 1, 77, 78, 79

oranges/orange juice

Slow Cooked Caramelized Oranges, 221–222

Vegan Carrot Cake, 355–357

Wild Red Rice Roasted Vegetable Platter, 207–208

other perspectives, value in exploring other, 49–50

outspoken, being, 204, 391, 394

oven, sharing one's, 375

P

parenthood, 23–24. see also mothers/motherhood

pargod, 351

parsley, 35, 80–82, 97–99, 207, 253–256, 285–287

pasta, 380–381

patriarchy, 4, 9, 14, 159

peanut butter

No Bake Vegan Millionaire Squares, 17–18

Salty Peanut Spaghetti Squash, 306–307

Turkish Sand Cookies, 185–186

pecans, in Bourbon Cinnamon Pecan Pie, 114–115

period shaming, 118

Pesikta de-rav Kahana 11:13, 325n7

Pesto, Dandelion-Pumpkin Seed, 119–120

Pharisees, 331

philanthropy, 57

physical appearance, 104, 144, 147, 152, 153, 251

piety

    excessive, 95, 165

    forced onto others, 194

pineapple, 355

pineapple juice, 395

pistachios, 212–213, 328–329

plantains, 291–292

pomegranate

    Beet, Pomegranate and Parsley Salad, 97–99

    Saffron Couscous with Beluga Lentils

        and Pomegranate, 248–249

    Smoky Eggplant Salad with Herbs, Tahini

        and Pomegranate, 285–287

    story of Haruta, 94, 95

pomegranate juice, 395–397

pomegranate molasses, 40–41, 207–208, 267–268

potatoes

    Grandmother's Borscht, 80–83

    Sweet Potato and Golden Beet Cholent, 317–318

The Potential Bride and the Hairdresser, 228–230

poverty, 57, 60, 283, 370–371

power issues, 229

prayer

    causing harm to others, 126, 127

    "falling-on-your-face" kind of, 164–166

    miracles and, 121

    for rain, 364

predetermination, 344

prostitute, 96, 233–235

The Prostitute from a City Overseas, 233–235

Proverbs 4:3, 264

Proverbs 13:23, 345*n*1

Proverbs 31:1–4, 19, 19*n*3

Proverbs 31:10, 35*n*3

Proverbs 31:30, 84

prunes, 328–329

puff pastry (vegan), 102, 267

pumpkin, 161–163

pumpkin seeds, in Dandelion-Pumpkin Seed Pesto, 119–120

purslane, 264, 267

Purslane, Pomegranate and Tofu Bourekas, 267–268

Q

Queen Helena of Adiabene, 238–241

Quince, Quick Pickled, 63–64

R

Rabban Gamliel, 25, 65, 89, 90, 126–128, 250

Rabbi Akiva, 245, 246, 247, 250, 282

Rabbi Akiva's Daughter, 245–247

Rabbi Chiya, 308–310

Rabbi Elazar ben Azaryah's Wife, 250–252

Rabbi Eliezer ben Hurkanos, 126

Rabbi Hama Bar Bisa's Wife, 257–259

Rabbi Hanina ben Dosa, 60–62, 121, 122, 370–372

Rabbi Mani, 83–85

Rabbi Nachman, 391–393

Rabbi Oshaya, 257

Rabbi Yehoshua, 65, 89, 90, 91, 250

Rabbi Yehuda Hanasi's Maidservant, 262–265

Rabbi Yishmael, 49, 151, 152, 154

Rabbi Yitzchak Ben Elyashiv, 83, 184

Rabbi Yochanan, 56, 187, 188, 338, 391

Rabbi Yohanan's Sister, 269–272

Rabbi Ze'eira's Wife, 276–279

Rachel, the Wife of Rabbi Akiva, 282–284

radishes, 29–31

rains, prayer for, 364, 366

raisins

    Kvass: Fermented Rye Bread and Raisin

        Beverage, 75–76

    Vegan Carrot Cake, 355–357

    Vegan Lullabye Bread, 260–261

rape, 13, 14, 215, 217, 361, 362

Rav Adda bar Mattana's Wife, 288–290

Rav Beivai, 313, 344

Rav Hanina, 170–172

Rav Hisda's Daughter, 293–297

Ravina's Mother, 319–321

Rav Nachman, 72–74

Rav Rehumi's Wife, 303–305

Rav's Wife, 308–310

Rav Yehuda, 72–73

Rav Yosef, 133–135, 313–315, 345

rebellion, 20

red clover, 92

red raspberry leaf, 92, 402

red wine

Babylonian Sour, 395–397

Red Wine Braised Mushroom and Barley Stuffed Cabbage Holishkes, 225–227

Red Wine Mushroom Soup 69–71

Rich Chocolate and Red Wine Mini Cakes, 23–24

Reish Lakish, 269–271

Reish Lakish's Wife, 269–271

religion, changing one's, 26, 204–205

religious values, forcing others to follow one's, 194

responsibilities, deflection of one's, 113

revenge, 8–9

rice

Mini Fire Roasted Stuffed Peppers, 349–350

Wild Red Rice Roasted Vegetable Platter with Pomegranate Molasses and Fresh Herbs, 207–208

Rich Chocolate and Red Wine Mini Cakes, 23–24

riches-to-rags story, 55–57

righteousness, 19, 21, 95, 211, 330

risotto, Lemon, Saffron and Barley, 58–59

ritual bath, 293, 330

ritual fringes (tzitzit), 233–235

ritual impurity, 210

Roasted Garlic Soup, 196–197

Roasted Sweet Potatoes with Tamarind and Crispy Shallots, 299–301

rolls

Abundant Water Challah Rolls, 373–374

Curried Nettle Vegan Sausage Rolls, 102–103

romaine lettuce, 217

Roman siege on Jerusalem, 182

rose hips, 92

rose petals, 92

Rugelach, Charoset, 212–213

Ruth 1:8–12, 26n7

Ruth 1:16, 26

Ruth 2:10, 165n2

Ruth 4:17–22, 26

Ruth Rabbah 2:16, 26n7

S

sacrifice(s)

of Rachel, wife of Rabbi Akiva, 282–284

ritual impurity and, 210

Saduccees, 331

Saffron Couscous with Beluga Lentils and Pomegranate, 248–249

sage, in Apple Sage Muffins, 174–175

salads

Beet, Pomegranate and Parsley Salad, 97–99

Four Bean Salad with Dry Mustard Vinaigrette, 124–125

Smoky Eggplant Salad with Herbs, Tahini and Pomegranate, 285–287

Salty Peanut Spaghetti Squash, 306–307

sambal oelek, in Roasted Sweet Potatoes with Tamarind and Crispy Shallots, 299–300

Samuel 14:49, 198n2

Samuel 16:15, 23, 158n8

Samuel 18:20–28, 198n2

Samuel 19:11–17, 198n2

Samuel 25:44, 198n2

Samuel 25:23, 165n3

Samuel 25:44, 198n2

Samuel of Nehardea, 170

Scutellaria Latifloria (skullcap), 137

Second Temple period, 145, 146, 209

Serach bat Asher, 324–327

sereifa (burning), 133–134

serving others in the home, 73

sesame seeds, 267, 285, 206, 377–379

Seven Herbs and Species Focaccia, 35–36

sexual intimacy/experiences

conversation by about women's, 14

husbands returning from Torah study for, 303

story of Haruta, 94–96

sexual violence, 357–358. see also rape

Shabbat

food prepared for, 370

healing treatments used on, 188

t'fillin worn on, 139, 198–199

Shabbat candles, 60–62, 313–316

Shabbat lamp, lighting the, 100

shallots, 299

sharing, 375

Shimon ben Shatach, 330–331

shinui, 276, 277, 332

shiny-leaf buckthorn, in Tej (Ethiopian Honey Wine), 11–12

Shlomtzion/Salome Alexandra, 330–333

Sifra.Bekhukotai.1:12, 331

sinat chinam (baseless hatred), 37–39

skin and hair remedy, 155–156

Smoky Eggplant Salad with Herbs, Tahini, 279–281

sotah, 238, 239, 285–287

Sotah ritual, 339–340

The Sotah Woman, 337–340

soups

    Aguají (Green Plantains Soup), 291–292

    Black-Eyed Pea Soup, 335–336

    Creamy Coconut, Red Lentil and Apple Soup, 322–323

    Grandmother's Borscht, 80–81

    Red Wine Mushroom Soup, Baked in Acorn Squash, 69–71

    Roasted Garlic Soup, 196–197

    Sephardic Style Chilled Cucumber Soup, 87–88

sourdough starter, 35–36

soy nuggets, 142–143

Spaghetti Squash, Salty Peanut, 106–107

speech, differences in, 387–388

Spiced Acorn Squash Breakfast Bake, 149–150

spinach

    Caramelized Leek Barley with White Bean Smash, Spinach, Asparagus, and Beet Potion, 51–52

    Magnesium-boosting Smoothie, 217–218

    Purslane, Pomegranate and Tofu Bourekas, 267–268

squash. see also zucchini

    Red Wine Mushroom Soup, Baked in Acorn Squash, 69–71

    Salty Peanut Spaghetti Squash, 306–307

    Spiced Acorn Squash Breakfast Bake, 149–150

Wild Red Rice Roasted Vegetable Platter with Pomegranate Molasses and Fresh Herbs, 207–208

stewing tomatoes, 335–336

strawberry jam, 23–24

sugya(s), 8, 152, 164, 165, 391

suicide, 187, 189

sukkah, 238–239

supernatural, the, 351

Sweet Beet Loaf Cake, 236–237

Sweet Potato and Golden Beet Cholent, 317–319

sweet potatoes

    Roasted Sweet Potatoes with Tamarind and Crispy Shallots, 299–300

    Sweet Potato and Golden Beet Cholent, 317–318

    Vegan Nutty Chocolate Chip Cookies, 167–169

    Vegan Yakitori, 142–143

    Wild Red Rice Roasted Vegetable Platter with Pomegranate Molasses and Fresh Herbs, 207–208

T

tachanun, praying, 126–127

tahini, 114, 115, 273, 280, 285, 287

Talmud, about, 1–2

Talmud.b.Arakhin 19a, 404

Talmud.b.Avodah Zarah 17a, 233

Talmud.b.Avodah Zarah 28a, 187

Talmud.b.Bava Batra.73a-b, 157n.1, 157n6

Talmud.b.Bava Kamma 80a, 110, 111

Talmud.b.Bava Metsia 59b, 126, 127

Talmud.b.Bava Metzia 59b:13, 27n8

Talmud.b.Bava Metzia 84a, 270

Talmud.b.Bava Metziah.85a, 262n5

Talmud.b.Berachot.39b, 319

Talmud.b.Berakhot 20a, 193

Talmud.b.Berakhot.27b-28a, 251

Talmud.b.Berakhot 31b, 60n2

Talmud.b.Berakhot 33a, 121

Talmud.b.Berakhot 51a-b, 392

Talmud.b.Berakhot 18b, 186, 351

Talmud.b.Chagigah 4b-5a, 345

Talmud.b.Chagigah 5a, 293, 294

Talmud.b.Eruvin.18b, 157n1, 157n4

Talmud.b.Eruvin 22a, 288

Talmud b.Eruvin 53b, 262, 263n8

Talmud.b.Eruvin 53b, 386

Talmud.b.Eruvin 53bn2, 32

Talmud.b.Eruvin 63a, 126

Talmud.b.Eruvin.65a, 219

Talmud.b.Eruvin.96a, 198

Talmud.b.Eruvin 96:a, 139

Talmud.b.Eruvin.100b, 157n.1, 158

Talmud.b.Gitten 56a, 38, 182

Talmud.b.Gittin 58a, 37, 358

Talmud.b.Gittin 60a, 238

Talmud.b.Hullin.60a, 66

Talmud.b.Ketubot 23a, 171

Talmud.b.Ketubot.39b, 13

Talmud.b.Ketubot.52b–53a, 13

Talmud.b.Ketubot 60a, 42

Talmud.b.Ketubot 62b, 257, 297

Talmud.b.Ketubot 62b–63a, 283n1

Talmud.b.Ketubot 65a, 104

Talmud.b.Ketubot 66b, 56

Talmud.b.Ketubot 67b, 176

Talmud.b.Ketubot 72a-b, 146

Talmud.b.Ketubot 104a, 263n7

Talmud.b.Kiddushin 31b, 77

Talmud.b.Kiddushin.49a, 228

Talmud.b.Kiddushin 70a, 72

Talmud.b.Megilah.17b, 66

Talmud.b.Megilah.18a, 262n2

Talmud.b.Megillah 15a, 198n1

Talmud.b.Megillah.18a, 262–263

Talmud.b.Menachot 43a, 235

Talmud.b.Menachot 43b, 235

Talmud.b.Menachot.68b, 319

Talmud.b.Moed Katan.17a, 262n6

Talmud.b.Nazir 57b, 110

Talmud.b.Nedarim 50a, 283n1

Talmud.b.Nedarim 66b, 152

Talmud.b.Niddah.20b, 117

Talmud.b.Niddah.24b, 90, 157n1, 157n3

Talmud.b.Niddah.30b, 48

Talmud.b.Pesachim.40a–40b, 219

Talmud.b.Pesachim.111a, 7, 8n3

Talmud.b.Pesachim 112a, 157n1, 157n6, 158

Talmud.b.Pesachim 112b, 7, 121

Talmud.b.Rosh Hashanah 17b, 25

Talmud.b.Sanhedrin.14b, 13

Talmud.b.Sanhedrin 19a, 214

Talmud.b.Sanhedrin 19b, 198n1

Talmud.b.Sanhedrin 21a, 198n1

Talmud.b.Sanhedrin 52a-b, 133

Talmud.b.Sanhedrin 70b, 20

Talmud.b.Sanhedrin.70b, 19n1, 20

Talmud.b.Sanhedrin.90b, 48

Talmud.b.Sanhedrin.91a, 66

Talmud.b.Shabbat.3b–5a, 48

Talmud.b.Shabbat 16b, 331n1

Talmud.b.Shabbat 23b, 313n4, 314

Talmud.b.Shabbat 26a, 100

Talmud.b.Shabbat 59b, 283n1

Talmud.b.Shabbat 129a, 294n1

Talmud.b.Shabbat 134a, 77, 78

Talmud.b.Shabbat 140a, 276

Talmud.b.Shabbat.151b, 157n1, 157n5, 158

Talmud.b.Shabbat 156b, 128n4, 239

Talmud.b.Sotah 2a, 239n3

Talmud.b.Sotah 13a, 324n1, 324n5

Talmud.b.Sotah 13a:14, 325

Talmud.b.Sotah 22a, 164

Talmud.b.Sukkah 2b–3a, 238

Talmud.b.Sukkah 56b, 204

Talmud.b.Sukkot.28a, 158n9

Talmud.b.Taanit 21b, 375

Talmud.b.Taanit 23b, 83, 365

Talmud.b.Taanit 24b–25a, 370

Talmud.b.Taanit 25a, 60, 121

Talmud.b.Taanit.71–7b, 66

Talmud.b.Yevamot 34b, 293, 294n1

Talmud.b.Yevamot 46a, 25n2

Talmud.b.Yevamot 63a, 308

Talmud.b.Yoma 47a, 141n1, 145

Talmud Kiddushin 81a, 313

Talmud.y.Berakhot.14b, 198n1

Talmud.y.Challah.8a, 380

Talmud Yerushalmi, 2

tamarind, 293–295

Tart Cherry Saffron Bitters, 395

tea

    Miscarriage Recovery Tea, 92–93

    Mother's Joy Infusion, 45–46

    Nourishing Womb Tonic, 402–403

teaching Jewish law, 91

tea tree essential oil, 155–156

Tej (Ethiopian Honey Wine), 11–12

t'fillin, 139, 198, 199

time-bound mitzvah, 139, 140, 198

Timtinis of Tiberias, 187–189, 337, 339

Tisha B'Av, 37

tofu

    Creamy Vegan Noodle Kugel, 389–390

    Purslane, Pomegranate and Tofu Bourekas, 267–268

Tofu Nuggets, 142–143

tomatoes

    Black-Eyed Pea Soup, 335–336

    Grandmother's Borscht, 80–81

    Red Wine Mushroom Soup, Baked
      in Acorn Squash, 69–71

Torah knowledge, 32–34, 220, 282

Torah study

    abandoning family for, 258

    family neglect and, 258

    obligation to family and, 258, 289

    Rachel's sacrifice, 282–284

Trotula of Salerno, 188

tum'at met, 209

Turkish Sand Cookies, 185–186

The Two Miriams, 344–347

Two Spirits Speaking with Each Other, 351–353

Tzafenat bat Peniel, 358–361

tzedakah, 57, 176–178, 367

tzitzit, 233–235

V

Valeriana, 137

Vegan Carrot Cake, 355–357

Vegan Chocolate Babka, 131–132

Vegan Lullabye Bread, 260–261

vessels, breaking and rebuilding, 330–331

violence against women, 14, 215–216, 358–361

virginity, loss of, 14

vodka, 137–138

vows

    marriage, 151–154

    Nazarite, 209–211

    by Queen Helena of Adiabene, 238–239

    by weight, 404–405

W

walnuts

    Charoset Rugelach, 212–213

    Fesenjoon: Tangy Eggplant and Walnut Stew, 40–41

    Nut and Beet Stuffed Dates and Prunes, 328–329

    Spiced Acorn Squash Breakfast Bake, 149–150

wealth, 14, 55–57, 72, 83, 182, 184, 282, 283, 404, 405

weight, vows by, 403–404

wet nurses, 42

white beans, 51, 53, 167–169, 179, 180

widows, 153, 270

The Wife of Abba Hilkiya, 364–367

The Wife of Rabbi Hanina ben Dosa, 370–372

Wild Red Rice Roasted Vegetable Platter with
    Pomegranate Molasses and Fresh Herbs, 207–208

wine. see also red wine

    debate over serving women, 104–106

    Queen Helena's vow and, 238–241

    in story of Bathsheba, 20–22

    Tej-Ethiopian Honey Wine, 11–12

    Yalta's anger and, 392–393

wine storage, 67

wisdom, 33, 65–67, 264, 284, 310, 326

witchcraft, 7, 8, 9

The Woman from Drokart, 375–376

Woman Who Asks About Taking Challah, 380–383

The Woman with Mistaken Articulation, 387–388

women, in the first century CE, 3–4

X

xanthan gum, 280

Y

Yalta, 72–74, 391–393

Yehudit, 398–401

Yirmatia and her Mother, 404–405

Yishmael (son of Kimchit), 144, 147

yogurt

    Spiced Acorn Squash Breakfast Bake, 149–150

    Vegan Chocolate Babka, 131

Yom Kippur, eve of, 303, 304

Z

za'atar

    Seven Herbs and Species Focaccia, 35–36

    Vegan Yakitori, 142–143

Zoharit Skin, Hair and Gut Support, 155–156

Zoroastrianism, 116*n*1

zucchini

    Mini Fire Roasted Stuffed Peppers, 349–350

    Wild Red Rice Roasted Vegetable
        Platter with Pomegranate Molasses
        and Fresh Herbs, 207–208